THE ROYAL BAVARIAN CASTLES

Herren-Chiemsee

Neuschwanstein :

Hohenschwangau

Linderhof : Berg.

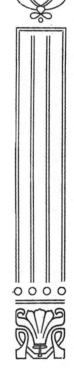

BY **HANS STEINBERGER**

TRANSLATED BY

FRANZ SPEISER IN **PRIEN.**

▽▽▽

MUNICH 1905.

▫▫▫ Printed by FRANZ HUMAR, MUNICH. ▫▫▫

Published by FRANZ SPEISER, PRIEN-on-Chiemsee.

All the plates of the illustrations bearing the remark «United Art Establishments, Munich«, are furnished by the said Company after the originals from the Photographic Studio of the **"Vereinigten Kunstanstalten, Aktien-Gesellschaft"** (United Art Establishments Shareholders Company), ══ Kaulbachstrasse 51 a, **Munich**. ══

─────

The Plates of the illustrations bearing the remark „After an original photograph by Franz Hanfstaengl" are furnished by the **"k. Hof-Kunstanstalt"** (Court Art Studio) **of Franz Hanfstaengl,** ══ Maximilianstrasse 7, **Munich**. ══

THE CHIEMSEE

AND THE ROYAL CASTLE OF

HERREN-CHIEMSEE

601   Photogravure Ver. Kunstanst. A.fr.München

Ludwig II. König von Bayern
(Letzte Aufnahme in Civil)

Nürnberger Königsschlösser Verlag: F.Speiser in Wien.

PREFACE.

In the midst of the Chiemgau there sparkles like a priceless jewel a creation of King Ludwig II of Bavaria, the state Castle of Herrenchiemsee, furnished with fairy like magnificence and built in the best Rococo Style. Here where the grandeur and beauty of Alpine scenery unite in enchanting harmony with the romantic past of a thousand years, there rose at the beck of the unhappy monarch a structure which, after its completion in its kingly splendour, was meant to excel all the works of men's hands in the brilliancy and richness of its ornamentation. But even in its uncompleted state the Castle of Herrenchiemsee works a charm on every beholder. It offers for Art and still more for works of Art, in richest fullness a mine of thousand fold motifs and suggestions; but what enhances still more the charm of this gigantic and lonely situated structure is the wonderful situation it enjoys on the large wooded island Herrenwörth, surrounded as it is by the deep blue expansive waters of the lake and topped by the sublime majesty of the range of Alps. Situated as it is in close proximity to the great railway line running between Paris and Vienna from which it is reached by the local railway and the steamboat, the Royal Castle is easily accessible. From Munich the journey by rail takes only about two hours. If, after viewing all the rich and splendid objects collected within its walls, the mind and eye of the visitor grow wearied he has only to take a trip to the lovely island of Frauen-wörth in the midst of the Chiemsee. Here will be seen the old church of King Thassilo, and the huts of the fisher folk with their gardens of many coloured flowers. There too will be heard the whispering of lime trees which seem to tell the visitor about the savage inroads of the Huns, who once swept over this little island, and also of the peace of God which to-day, even as a thousand years ago, reigns in this quiet isle. If time allows, a trip round the lake should also be made to explore its far-stretching eastern side. The sacrifice of time entailed (1¹/₂ hours) is richly rewarded, nor is the view one that can ever fade from the mind's eye. Yon have the panorama of hills stretching far away in ever changing beauty before the astonished eye — thus contributing to make for the traveller a day spent on the Chiemsee one of the most beautiful and the most profitable amongst his reminiscences. The chief object of this little work is to give a detailed description of the charm and grandeur — both too little appreciated – of the Chiemsee, and of the Royal Castle with its pomp and magnificence. It will also give in a reverent manner a brief account of the Royal Builder of Herrenchiemsee, without entering into too many details. The aim of the builder may appear at first sight puzzling, but on wandering through the state rooms, one is filled with a consciousness of the wonderful work that under the king's patronage Art and artistic industry have vied in creating. All that enchants in Herrenchiemsee need not fear a comparison with the high towering and kingly Castle in Schwangau which, based on German legend and tradition testifies to the many-sidedness, the artistic intellect and the refined taste of this unhappy sovereign. Like the other Royal Castles, Herrenchiemsee has helped to increase largely the tourist traffic every summer in this beautiful Alpine world; for the fame of King Ludwig's structures has travelled far beyond the confines of Bavaria and even of Germany. None of the other Castles are more easily and comfortably accessible. This is because of its proximity to the capital of the country—Munich. Its situation in the midst of wonderful lake and mountain scenery will always draw to it an ever-increasing number of visitors who, enchanted by all they see, will have for the Bavarian Highlands a warm corner in their hearts.

The King.

In the 19th century King Louis II of Bavaria, the most ideal of princely figures, stands conspicuously out of the troubled times which comprise his reign.

Unlike most of the contemporary German sovereigns, who by their heroic feats assured themselves an eternal glory in the annals of war, King Louis was drawn to peace. His aspirations, before he was enveloped by the shades of his tragic destiny, consisted in taking care of the welfare of his people, in favouring the improvement of Art in all its branches; and — with a view to preserving Bavaria's traditional loyalty, — he came forward as the Champion of Germany's greatness and Bavaria's honour.

He was born on the 25th of August 1845 at Nymphenburg, the Royal pleasure seat near Munich, on the name's day of his grand-father King Louis I, from whom he inherited a love for the Arts that this great king possessed.

A careful, strict education was given to the Prince by his father, King Maximilian II, whom Bavarians will never forget, and his amiable wife the Queen Mary, a daughter of the Hohenzollern House. It was in the sublime beauty of the Schwangau that the young Prince's love of sylvan and mountain solitude was early formed. The Tusculum, which King Maximilian II, when Crown Prince, had created in Hohenschwangau and dedicated to German legend and history, was the merry play-ground of both the princes, Louis and Otto, during their occasional hours of recreation.

On the 10th of March 1864, in the 19th year of his age, he was called to the throne upon the sudden death of his beloved father. Louis II, freed from all restraints, found himself his own master and the head of the State in troublous times.

To none of its princes has the Bavarian nation ever looked forward with more confidence than to this young king, whose manly beauty captivated every heart from the very first.

In political matters he followed at first the inclinations of his father; he sided at first with Austria and won the confidence of everyone by his warm-hearted intervention for Schleswig Holstein; with a heavy heart he entered upon the unhappy Civil War of 1866, and when, after the war was over, the king passed through the Frankish provinces which had suffered the most under the scourge of war, great was the reception accorded to their young king by the inhabitants.

Ever memorable will be his fidelity as an ally towards the Pan-German States. And when, after the great war of 1870/71 a plan was set on foot to give the imperial Crown to the old King William, it was Louis II who first suggested the idea. He was received in Munich on the 16th of July 1871 at the head of the Bavarian troops, side by side with their victorious leader, the Crown Prince Frederic William of Prussia, the future Emperor Frederic, amid a scene of the greatest enthusiasm. To the king, meanwhile, bitter deceptions were not spared. His sensitive nature suffered much through the unhappy result of a love romance, and as jealousy and intrigues conduced to hinder his dearest project which was to prepare a worthy home in the Capital for the great composer Richard Wagner, his well-justified exasperation made him retire more and more into the beloved solitude of the mountains and forests among the enrapturing magnificence of nature; and the world of romance round Hohenschwangau grew daily upon him. There it was that his tragic destiny was gradually evolved.

In spite of all this he was able with a firm hand to direct the affairs of state; full of majesty, he knew how to preserve the right of the Crown amidst the agitation of party strife. The 700th jubilee of the dynasty in 1880 gave him an occasion to display his noble generosity in a princely gift of money, although he avoided all celebrations on this memorable day. The flights of his fancy led him further and further into the realm of the insane. A stranger to the warm-throbbing life of his time, the epoch of the great king of

France, Louis XIV, whose glory shone over princes and nations, who was celebrated in songs by a whole world of poets, seemed to him more and more enviable and ideal. By a zealous study of the literature of that glorious age, he created for himself a true and faithful picture of the Court life of the "King of the Sun". Several journeys to Versailles confirmed still further his impressions. Can one wonder if this king, living only in the spirit of that time, modelled his buildings after those of Versailles and astonished everybody by the astounding lucidity of his orders regarding architectural affairs, as well as by his artistic understanding, which was far above the ordinary? On the other hand it is true, life's misfortunes came as a threatening reminder to knock at the doors of the royal castle. — When in 1885, the financial crisis of the Cabinet made itself felt, the alarming state of the king's health predicted a serious catastrophe. On the 10th of June 1886, his Majesty, Prince Luitpold of Bavaria was called to the Regency in place of the king, who had fallen seriously ill. The news of this event had the effect of lightning from the clear sky on the faithful Bavarian people. When on Whitsuntide (the 13th of June) 1886 the king buried his sorrows in the waves of the lake of Starnberg, the whole of Bavaria was filled with a great and deep sorrow.

The Royal Builder at Herrenchiemsee.

A remote and much agitated past, similar to that surrounding the Schwangau, lies over Herrenwörth in the midst of a country where culture had early found a home.

About the hoary rocks, where the bright Pöllat-Fall glistens in the sun, glorified by legends and poetry, a truly German atmosphere seems to hover about everything. Here at Herrenwörth, where in ancient times has been the holy oak-grove of the Bajuvars, rose at Duke Thassilo's command a monastery whose reputation was world-wide for the scholarship of its inmates. When, at last, it succumbed to the devastating storm which broke out in Hungary and swept all over the German lands, creeping plants began to grow round the ruins of the sacred precincts and more than two hundred years passed away until it awoke once more to a new life.

In 1231 Herrenwörth became the seat of the episcopal diocese of Chiemsee and the ecclesiastical potentates took up their residence here. Once again the monastery was filled

with joyous life and restored to a state more flourishing and
prosperous than before. Good were the results that crowned
the efforts of the holy Fathers to promote the welfare of
their flock.

The vast structure stands as a lasting witness of their
artistic tastes. It rises to view on the highest point of the
island, and looks majestically over the waving tops of trees,
down upon the azure surface of the lake. But more tragic
was the destiny of Herrenwörth, when the wave of secularisation
penetrated into these peaceful haunts. The splendid cathedral,
the interior of which was copied from the Church of Saint
Michael in Munich, was transformed into a brewery, the crypt
of the monastery being ransacked by greedy hands and
changed into beer-cellars. The high towering spires were
pulled down; the soul-stirring chimes no more resounded over
the lake in their magic and enchanting sweetness. The bells
were sold; one proprietor came after another, but none of
them enjoyed possession for long. The blessing had departed
from this formerly so peaceful island, and the hour seemed
to have come for its complete destruction.

In spring 1873, a syndicate of timber merchants from
Wurtemberg acquired the island from Count Hunolstein for
300,000 florins. Renewed maladministration began with the
cutting down of the extensive timber forests on the southern
half of the island; but fortunately this was checked by a speedy
acquisition of Herrenwörth with all its annexes. The Court
Secretary von Düflipp purchased this jewel of the Chiemgau
for the king for 350,000 florins. The vendors reserved to
themselves the right of retaining 200 of the most beautiful
trunks, but these also were finally included in the king's new
possession by cash payment of the value to the speculative
merchants.

In anxious suspense, the whole country-side round Chiemgau had looked on at the doings of the Wurtembergists.
For was it not the intention of these men to deform for once
and always the most beautiful ornament of the lake? It was
consequently with enthusiastic and inspiring words that all
the parishes of the district and societies therein thanked their
much loved king for this generous action in an address which
— as it is only known to very few persons — we think
proper to add here: "Since many a century the political and
economic life in the Chiemgau has fallen into a state of
unproductive slumber. Ruins of noblemen's estates, as well
as the venerable abode where culture has reigned for a
thousand years, give testimony to this. Amongst the people,

confidence in their own strength had gradually died away. Feeble had been their efforts to free themselves from the bonds of servitude. Since many years the meadow lands had lain deserted and waste.

"The mountain streams began to run dry, and the banks of the lake were strewn with mounds of sand. Only in these latter days had a ray of hope and consolation come to lighten their darkness. All branches of art began to be revived, but lack of money and a cruel usury restrained the ardour of the workers in their task. At this moment it pleased Your Royal Majesty to form with fatherly care the magnanimous resolution to rescue by a speedy purchase from the grasps of Vandalism and speculation the island of Herrenwörth — an island, gay with the lotus flowers of poetry, ressembling the basket of reed in which the good fairy once caused smilingly to awake the little child that one calls Civilisation. Indescribable joy unites with a genuine feeling of thanks for the recovery of this fine historic jewel of nature, which Your most gracious Majesty has caused to bring about."

There is Pindar's poetic fire in these eloquent words of thanks for the generous act. They alone would have secured for King Louis II an ever grateful remembrance by posterity, even if his fairy castle had never been built.

In purchasing the island the king at first had in view the preservation of the magnificent forest and consequently the beauty of the landscape, but after the completion of Castle Linderhof, the resolution grew stronger in him to erect in a larger and grander scale a similar structure upon the island, fanned by the breezes of lake and wood, whose solitary situation was in harmony with his natural disposition; — in short an "Island Versailles" faithfully copied from the French Royal Castle, but surpassing and putting into shade the original model by its pomp and splendour. He wanted to consecrate it to the period in which the great French king lived — a period which charmed so much the eye of the king by its glory and transcendent power. Before commencing to build, several years were passed in study of the plans. The king himself in company with his architect, von Dollmann, the Royal Superintendent of Works, several times visited Paris and Versailles where in his honour the fountains were playing. By the perplexing and bewildering magnificence of everything, as well as by the great historic remembrances connected with these places, the king was enchanted. The impressions made by these journeys frequently manifested themselves in the comprehensive changes that were subsequently made. In particular the exquisite artistic taste of the highly gifted Monarch made itself felt in many of these details which deviated from the original.

In 1878 the first cut with the spade was made at Herren-wörth, where soon many hundreds of diligent workmen were engaged at high wages. Many a mighty trunk fell before the axe to make room for the gigantic structure; with great labour and at immense cost the foundation ground was levelled and filled up. At last on the 21st of May 1878, the foundation stone was laid. Upon the lake will never again be seen such active life and animation as during the period of the con-struction of the castle; the conveying to the spot of the building materials could, considering the natural situation, only be effected by boats; a small steamer transported the heavy-laden tugs to the island, where their contents were emptied into the transport train, ready to receive them. The continual unloading and reloading naturally made the price of the transport expenses rise immensely. The circle in which those, who came to pay a visit to the Herreninsel, could move, grew smaller and smaller until at last it was limited to the old castle. Under the continual and stimulating insti-gation of the Royal architect, the construction was speedily urged forward, and already in 1879 a part of the main front was roofed in and the interior ornamentation begun, whilst with the same haste, at the same time, the construction of the backward wings was commenced. Contrary to the original plan, the construction was then given over to the well known builder and subsequent government surveyor Brandl. The supreme directions remained in the trustworthy hands of the Royal superintendent of Works von Dollmann, and later passed over to the Royal councillor Hofmann. With the con-struction began at the same time the laying out of the extensive gardens and water works under the direction of the Royal superintendent of horticultural works von Effner.

After 1881 his Majesty came every year for a few days to the Herreninsel to make a survey of the advancing state of the works, especially of the interior ornamentation; and occasionally his great expertness in matters of art found vent in drastic criticisms. At the beginning, the king took his lodging in the so-called state rooms of the Prelacy wing, whence he could follow the creation of the lofty structure, his own Versailles. During the years 1884 and 1885 the king was able to occupy the sumptuous apartments of the new castle; then at night the fairy-like saloons and galleries glittered in a thousandfold splendour with their magic lights.

The gigantic structure must have appeared to its royal builder like a fairy castle of nothing but light and fire, when the waterworks were in action and fine dazzling rain came down like powder mixed with the fragrance of flowers; and the surrounding woods and lake and mountains glittered in magic moonlight. According to the king's habit, his arrival took place always at night. Usually on one of the last days of September, the Royal train stopped about midnight between Prien and Endorf at a lonely situated stopping-place erected for the purpose in the midst of the woods near Rimsting. The king and his attendants, consisting only of a few persons, mounted the Court carriages awaiting them, and on they went at full speed. The courrier rode ahead with torches shining far into the distance, passing along the silent woody creeks, through peaceful sleeping villages, to the far projecting neck of land at the end of which lies Urfahrn, where the Royal boat awaited the king ready to cross over to the neighbouring Herreninsel. The lake glimmered like liquid silver in the wonderful autumn night. In a sublime wonderment the mountain tops sent down their greeting, and from the Lady's Isle, with its minster standing out in bold relief from the silver-gleaming waves, the midnight hour sounded across the lake in long-swelling tones. There was something like gratitude in this greeting, with the lake unfolding its charms at the approach of its Royal protector.

The few days of his Majesty's sojourn upon Herren-wörth passed away rapidly in close investigation of what had recently been done. He met with many things in an un-completed state, as the time intervening between the giving of the orders and their achievement was measured out too shortly. The board of directors, instead of frankly reporting the impossibility of their execution, resorted to "manoeuvres de force", to satisfy the impatience of the monarch, though, it is true, rarely with the desired success. In like manner, they had, in order to give the king an entire picture of the avenues of the garden, to have recourse to provisory under-takings, to interweave the high trellis work with foliage and fagots, and many a waggon load of hot-house plants arrived, to conceal the slow growth of the ornamental pleasure grounds.

Many a hasty judgement was passed, after the death of the king, with regard to the choice of Herreninsel for the construction of this state castle. But a glance back into the 17th and 18th centuries shows that King Louis II had infinitely better taste than the princely builders of those days.

Bavaria has in the castle of Schleissheim an example of that aesthetic tendency, which made their castles to be created in regions the least favoured by nature. And yet, in our days, the lustre of the interior in its French style, and the splendour of the ornamental grounds, has still its effect, whilst King Louis II moreover gave to his castle a situation in the midst of magnificent Alpine and lake scenery.

Menell writes in his "Fantasies of the King": "In any case, the Herreninsel appeared to the king to be a site better adapted to the construction of a fairy castle than any other island in the vicinity of his mountains. At the foot of the Säuling in a castle like that of Neuschwanstein, it could well be thought proper to sing and imitate in lofty song the brilliancy of German chivalry; Castle Linderhof could hide itself, and remain concealed in the midst of the peace and solitude of the forests like some "Belle" tired of the world and the joys of life. Castle Herrenchiemsee however requires, according to its whole nature, a far extending space, where it could rise in all its magnificence and glory."

Whosoever has seen Herrenchiemsee and its wonderful mountain and lake scenery, surely will agree with this wise judgment. It is the tragic fate of Herrenchiemsee that its unfinished state will ever give testimony to the sudden and dreadful destiny of its Royal Builder. Like an eruption of lava upon a peaceful town, that buries all life and prosperous enterprise, was the effect of the financial crisis in 1885.

The stirring activity of hundreds of diligent workmen ceased for ever. Everywhere, within the brick works and round the castles, half finished works and workmen's tools were strewn about awaiting in dumb sorrow the commencement of a new activity.

On the 11th of October 1885, King Ludwig II parted for ever from the gigantic Tusculum similar to those created during the flourishing age of France by her mightiest kings. But all that he left finished at his departure, meant the highest triumph of industry which prospered under his patronage, in his Bavarian capital. And this fact, whose consequences have so much contributed to establish the world-wide fame of Munich's artistic skill, will serve to reconcile the German visitor with regard to the general tendency of the structure.

In Herrenchiemsee, art and industry created an artistic fashion of a decorative sort which far excelled that of the original at Versailles, and with regard to its particularities will hand down to posterity rich sources and subjects for suggestion to coming generations. Herrenchiemsee has undergone many a change since the death of the king, the most remarkable being the discontinuance of the fountains; although their maintenance would have demanded considerable expenses and thus, to let them play, from an economical point of view could not be approved of, on the other hand the Royal Castle has thus been robbed of one of its greatest charms. Castle Linderhof — equipped with the same gorgeous and pompous luxury as Herrenchiemsee — assumes from the jets of sparkling water and from the gurgling of its fountains in cascades a homely, comfortable impression. But here the effect is more chilling and disenchanting. A death-like silence reigns in the immense gardens where we miss the animating murmur of the fountains and something akin to melancholy overcomes the visitor in this grand solitude. The figures of the fountains, whose tanks are filled in with earth, looking beautiful in their floral garb have lost their former charm. The statue of the Latona in particular, a master work of sculpture, makes a rather comic impression upon the spectator by reason of its base. Here frogs and tortoises are to be seen sitting on dry ground between rose-bushes.

After the death of the king an end was put to the constraint, with which he knew how to protect his work from frivolous curiosity and malicious criticism. Thousands traverse every year the long flights of stairs and extensive grounds; but whilst many, overhasty in their judgment of the individuality of the king, in sight of all the splendour before them, turn away with a shrug of the shoulders and hasten after other pleasures of life, there are again others who, full of sympathy with the tragic destiny of the king and mourning his loss, come here respectfully and stand in admiration and amaze in these rooms.

It seems as if the restless disposition of the king had left its melancholy trace, despite the intentional want of allusion on the part of the guides to the sorrows of the king. Yet tender memories of the much regretted monarch force themselves upon us, as we go through this temple of royal splendour. One seems to see his angry shade again take shape and drive away the intruder from the threshold, vainly endeavouring to restore to the sumptuous rooms their loved and cherished solitude. The castle of Herrenchiemsee, grown over and covered with creeping plants will, like some sleeping Beauty, speak of its king and his love of splendour.

The Chiemsee.

(See title-picture).

There is no other lake in Bavaria, where the change from the high Alps to the lower Alps and to the plain is so wonderfully and enchantingly arranged as in the far stretching basin of the Chiemsee; there one cannot find the gloomy majesty of the mountain lakes encircled by precipitous rocks. Its peculiarly captivating charm lies in the enormous expanse of water which reflects the sky in its many changing colours; in the idyllic isles — of which the largest shelters the Torso of the king's Castle in its mournful seclusion; the creeks hemmed round with wood; the many heights on its Northern and Eastern banks; and in the many pointed Alpine ranges which rise up on the southern shore and form a magnificent panorama.

Distance is so deceptive that the mountains seem to approach us and rise from the shores of the lake. The deep blue haze which mantles them and hides them from the plain has disappeared, and the eye beholds their light green Alpine meadow lands, the deep green woods covering the lower heights and the grotesque formations of the rocks, all silver grey and weather-worn.

Equally captivating and attractive is the wide-extending picture of the vast waters stretching far away and bounding in the far distance a ridge of low hills. The stern grandeur of the mountain world and the serene and sunny loveliness of the lower Alpine land vie with each other in the possession of this lovely and at the same time priceless jewel of the Old Bavarian country.

The distance, extending for several miles from the East to the Western bank and from the Southern to the Northern shore, makes the slopes on the other side appear diminutive and narrow; and one guide book after the other thoughtlessly quotes the familiar words: "The banks of the Chiemsee are flat and without charm".

And yet from these heights one enjoys distant views of surprising beauty which satisfy the highest expectations. The north-westerly shore is rich in such lofty situated points of view, which reward abundantly a short excursion to them. Most enjoyable of all will be found an excursion round the lake on its Eastern part. It can be broken several times at different places. The following description will not fail to allude to those little excursions and points of view, all well worth a visit.

He who approaches the Chiemsee from Rosenheim may even feel disappointment on his first view of the lake. A large inhabited creek, the Aitbacher Winkel, surrounded by moorland and dusky woods and other promontory land covered with underwood and alderbushes, and lastly the wide extending Herreninsel, hide from our view the large surface of the lake. But although our first impression of the lake will not be a good one, in the background there towers up the mountain chain in all its picturesque beauty, thus outweighing the first and feebler impression. But gradually the visitor is conquered by the spell of its many charms. He is tempted to leave the shore, to go out on its isles and afterwards across the lake where the shores ever seem to recede and where only the Alpine circle forms in its glittering and hazy splendour a fitting frame for this wonderful landscape painting.

The large expanse of waters covers 82 square kilometres into which flow, together with smaller brooks, two rivers that rush down from the mountains, the Kitzbüheler Ache and the Prien. The river Traun belonging to the lake territory gathers its waters in the lonely valleys of the high Alps, and runs into the brown Alz near its junction with the lake.

The valleys through which these three rivers wind their way divide the mountain chain, surrounding the lake in the South, into mighty groups reflecting their peaks, high walls and sharp edges in the blue glittering waves and create enchanting vistas upon the giant of the Berchtesgaden-Salzburger and Tyrolese Alps. From the Höllengebirge in Salzkammergut on to the mountains of the Isar Valley stretches in ever changing formations and positions the Alpine Panorama. On a clear morning, especially after rainy days, one can see in the course of a tour round the lake, close to Chieming, the Gross Venedig Peak with its perpetual snow, towering up in rosy and glowing splendour.

Between the lake and the mountains there stretch out extensive and desolate moorlands that give testimony to the fact that in early times the dimensions of the lake were much greater. The heights of East and West Buchberg can be distinguished. Churches and farms seem to send a welcome greeting from the fir groves. Far behind, the high mountains look down in all their majesty making a most effective picture in the midst of the monotony of the moorlands. In the East and West above the smaller hills which enframe the lake, two mountains famous for the view to be obtained from them are visible. These are the Hochberg near Traunstein and the Ratzingerhöhe near Prien. From the Hochberg the view comprises the greater part of the lake which glistens in the morning sun like liquid fire; from the Ratzinger Height a wonderful panorama extends before the enchanted eye; it is most charming during the evening hours: Over the undulating table land, through the woody promontories, the blue waters are gleaming round the proud castle. Herrenchiemsee shines in scintillating beauty through the dark forest, and behind stretches the clear bosom of the lake glowing like purple in the evening sun and in the midst of it — a picture of quiet and repose — lies the Lady's Isle. The whole forms a gladsome and delightful picture.

The most beautiful time to pay a visit to the Chiemsee is in the spring when all around the hills and meadow lands are resplendent in their fresh green garb and the blossoming trees and flowers of May-time are everywhere visible. As a striking contrast to the lovely picture, beyond the mountain valleys the snowy jagged ridges of the Wildkaiser, the Loferer Stone Mountains, the High Göll, Hochkalter and Watzmann peep through.

The chief point of attraction for every tourist lies in the islands Herren- and Frauenchiemsee. They claim the interest of every one who lands on their banks, both because of the charm of their situation and by reason of their romantic past of a 1000 years.

It is to be regretted that the greatest part of the travelling world only visits Herrenchiemsee for the purpose of seeing the Royal Castle. Small is the number of those who, taking the advice of their guide books, also pay a visit to the Lady's Isle. But to make a trip round is impossible for the majority, because of their mania to see as much as possible in one day and to get over the greatest possible amount of ground. To have been on the Chiemsee and to have devoted only one hasty hour to visit the royal castle, is to rob one of the most beautiful of travelling reminiscences. The ideal of the most faithful and enthusiastic lovers of the Chiemsee, the ideal of every artist, is a summer evening upon one of the islands, with its manifold charms, enchanting by its ever changing light effects upon the lake and on the mountains. This has till now been the exclusive property of artists and others of an equally sensitive and artistic temperament. The chief centre for a visit to the Chiemsee, the lovely market town of Prien, is reached from Munich by express train in 1½ hours and in 3 hours by a slow train; from Salzburg and Reichenhall in 1 and 2 hours respectively. In summer a great animation at the railway station in Prien can be witnessed

BIRD'S EYE VIEW OF PRIEN.

BY O. BLASCHKE, PRIEN.

with its lively local and international traffic. The same bustle and anxiety take place when a train comes in at Prien, as was the case some time ago when the traveller had almost to fight for a seat in one of the coaches that stood waiting to receive him. Now there is a local railway with comfortable I and II cl. carriages which leads us in a few minutes to the port. Leaving the railway station, we enter at once the little market town, a well known and much frequented summer resort, beautifully situated in proximity to the Chiemsee and the mountains, in the midst of a mountainous landscape covered with pine forests. There are elegantly furnished hotels close to the railway station and a great number of villas strewn around the town, offering cheap and comfortable accommodation. The principal charm of the much frequented surroundings of Prien, with the exception of the lake and the mountains, are the different villages, all beautifully situated on the tops of the hills and commanding glorious views. The valley of the river Prien (valley of the oaks) affords shady walks; from the road high up, stretching along the edge of the valley, lovely outlooks can be enjoyed down into the plain animated by the rattling of mill wheels, and over pastures to the jagged mountain peak of the Kampenwand. From the Höhenberg, with its delightful walks through the woods, extends an immense panorama of lake and mountains in ever changing beauty, that invite us to stop or to come again for a longer stay. The Parish church of Prien possesses a peculiar ceiling piece, the representation of the naval battle of Lepanto. The old little church of Saint Salvador looks down from its elevated position; the legend tells us of the dwarfs of the Untersberg who used once to hold a service in the middle of the night. Churches glistening in the sun, farms and villas greet us from the hills on our short trip to the lake, and beautiful beyond words is the distant view on to the Kampenwand and Hochriss Groups and to the steep precipitous incline of the Kaisergebirge, appearing between them.

Further on in the blue summer's heat the mountains of the Inn valley glitter, overtopped by the Pyramid of the Wendelstein and the huge rocky square of the Breitenstein. After a short trip, we see the blue waters of the lake glistening in the sunshine. The railway, cutting through the much frequented watering place of Stock, stops directly at the pier where the steamers start. During the summer the landing place and the port present a scene of continual bustle and animation; the summer guests of Prien come down to

amuse themselves with boating and sailing; the passing to
and fro of the steamboats and the local railway still animate the
charming country. Two bathing establishments invite one
to a refreshing bath in the warm waters and a beautiful
promenade runs along the lake, past lovely situated villas
into the magnificent natural park of the Ernsdorf forest.
A trip to the Herreninsel gives one an idea of the great
beauty of the larger part of the lake. Broad and extensive

STOCK.

CHIEMSEE RAILWAY TERMINUS AND STARTING POINT FOR THE STEAMERS

lies before us towards the east, almost obstructing the view,
the wooded Herrenwörth. From the dark of the forest the
light coloured front of the royal castle stands ont distinct.
The figures of the fountains shine brightly in the midday
sun; the great staircase and the many windowed front, increase still further one's high wrought expectations. A look
towards the west discovers the lovely grouping of the mountains
far away to the Wendelstein, where the Kampenwand is
reflected in the vibrating and glittering waves. Far in the
back ground one sees the mountains belonging to the Ziller-
thal group. On the left opens out a lonesome wood-embosomed
creek at the farther end of which lie the cheerful looking

homesteads of Holzen and Uhrfahrn. One is still attracted by the beautifully-outlined mountains of the Inn valley that slowly fades away in the distance, when on rounding the north point of the Herreninsel a new and enchanting landscape is unfolded to our eyes. Amid the deepest steel blue, the wide lake extends to the distant eastern shore and to the imposing back ground of the mountains whose base seems to be lapped by the waters. In the midst of this grand and yet so lovely picture lies the idyll of the Chiemsee, the Lady's Isle with the old, grey and weather-worn tower, the extensive monastic buildings and the low homely fisherhuts, half hidden by huge limetrees.

Plying along the east banks of the Herreninsel the steamboat reaches the halting place. Most impressive is the appearance of the spacious and noble pile of the prelates — now called the Old Castle, that looks down over mighty trees upon the lake.

The way up to the Hotel leads past the wooden hut where the entrance tickets for the royal castle are to be had.

The Castle of Herrenchiemsee is opened daily from May the 15th to October the 15th (with the exception of June the 13th; the day of the king's death). The hours of admittance are from 9 a. m. till 5 p. m. Admission is in groups of not more than 25 persons. The entrance fee per person is 3 Marks on week days, 1.50 Marks on Sundays and holy days. On Sundays there are issued besides return-tickets at considerably reduced fares, from the railway offices of Munich, Salzburg and Reichenhall, which include state and local railway, steamboat and admission to the castle.

Wonderful old trees cast their shadows on the easy ascent to the old castle. An exuberant vegetation envelopes the hill, which carries on its top the scattered structures of the former monastery; the northern part of the island consists of extensive meadow lands where Spring lavishly strews her rich floral decorations. Lofty larches surround the little church — formerly the chapel of the burial place of the monastery — in which, since the suspension of the cathedral, service is held for the small insular community.

The large edifice next to the chapel, out of which now comes the aromatic odour of the two chief ingredients of the Bavarian national beverage which is brewed here in excellent quality, is the former cathedral of the island, which the march of human progress in the 19th century has so rudely altered; annexed in a square form is the so-called Convent Prince's and Prelacy Wing, the former being now used as official premises and lodgings of the royal administration, whilst the other wings have been suitably furnished for the Hotel.

With befitting reverence the apartments formerly occupied by King Louis II have been kept in their state of unpretentious equipment. This is a proof that luxury was not the king's personal want, but simply requisite for him in his capacity as king. From the windows a wonderful outlook can be enjoyed upon the fresh green fields and woods of the island and the splendours of the Alpine world.

The old library on the ground floor shows on the vaulted ceiling representations from the life of St. Thomas, and above the hall entrance one reads the rather strange inscription for a library contained in the Bible words "faciendi plures libros nullus est finis": of the making of books there is no end.

On the first floor amongst the king's apartments the dining room is especially remarkable. The simple and plain furniture helps to set off the rich wainscotting on the walls and the ceiling; three pier glass tables carry chandeliers of bronze; upon another stands a Rococo clock of bronze representing a galloping horse to the back of which a man is tied. On the wall hangs a huge painting representing Castle Hohenschwangau with the two lakes, which on a more minute inspection proves to be a fine masterpiece of cork carving.

Both of the gentlemen's rooms equally show the simplest taste in furniture, with flowered tapestry and white curtains and, as the only decoration, beautiful paintings: The lake of Starnberg, the Königssee, and, upon a bracket, a marble statuette of Albrecht Dürer are most worthy of note.

A winding staircase leads to the second floor, to the apartments, which the king himself occupied. The first room we enter is the studio of the king.

Upon the exceedingly simple writing table are standing candlesticks and an ink-stand. A pier-table is adorned with girandoles and a clock representing Galileo; a tremendous telescope, turned towards the mountains on the Eastern shore, charms by reason of the distinctness and precision with which the surrounding objects can be seen. The stoves are made out of white Dutch tiles, and simple white curtains cover the windows. The adjoining toilet room with blue tapestry hangings, contains upon the toilet table a green porcelain service with vases upon the pier-glass table near the mullion, and again paintings: Hohenschwangau and lake of Starnberg. The bedroom, lined with blue tapestry, contains the king's bed covered in with a blue canopy. It is a simple bedstead without any decoration; and a bust of the Queen Marie

Antoinette, as well as a Saloon clock with the figure of the astronomer Galileo are in the apartment.

The other two rooms, whose purpose cannot any more be recognised, are only remarkable for oil-paintings:

In the first, representations from the life of Venus and lovely Cupids; in the second a draught of fish near Heligoland and a "Dance" of the Dervishes in a mosque.

The Audience chamber is hung with red, rather discoloured tapestry. Two big pier-glass-tables with high mirrors carry girandoles and China vases with paintings of Garmisch, cloister Tegernsee, Benediktbeuern, Ohlstatt and a marble statuette of King Maximilian II of Bavaria. A glass lustre is suspended in the midst of the room. There is also a beautiful oil painting "View of Herreninsel" from the Northern banks; in the fore-ground boats are loaded with reed. — This painting is remarkable on account of its happily chosen colouring.

The Reception Room, which comes next still remains as a creation of the clerical lords of Herrenchiemsee. Executed wholly in the style of the 18th century, the clever design and perspective are spoiled by the gaudy colours, which are in their amateurish execution quite out of keeping with the taste of the subject. The painting on the walls shows Roman emperors — and a garden laid out in the style of the Renaissance — whereas the ceiling decoration shows the "Washing of the feet by the penitent Magdalene". Only the wonderful woodcarving at the doors is worthy of praise. Its execution far excels the pictorial ornamentation of this room.

On the West of the Prelacy are the farm buildings of the estate Herrenchiemsee, well known as a model farm to all the agriculturalists about the country-side.

On the South of the old castle, where the foot path leads down to the royal castle, the magnificent Park opens out, pleasantly setting off by its richness and variety of trees and its exuberant vegetation the formal arrangement of the ornamental grounds of the king's castle.

Amongst the dark-leaves of the red-beeches and the weeping beeches with their branches touching the ground proudly stands the gigantic trunk of a broad-branched Weymouth pine. The walls of the Prelacy buildings are covered with the green of fruit trees trained on trellis work, and towards the West stretches out the nursery garden with thousands of young fruit trees. In this spot the transition between artificiality and the openness of nature is most conspicuous.

The corner-pillar. of the so-called Prince's Wing is clad with ivy round which the path leads along sweetly smelling flower beds to the shady restaurant terrace. He, who has once sat here under the broad-branched trees, must have felt his eyes and heart open at the sight of the wonderful Panorama which presents itself to his gaze. With delight we look upon the deep blue surface of the lake animated by many little boats, — over to the charmingly situated Lady's Isle and out into the lake stretching far beyond it, to the Eastern shore, whence churches and castles send us their greeting. From the Gaisberg near Salzburg to the Hochgern it is possible to overlook the many-shaped mountain panorama; the king's castle looks over the tops of the fir trees with the Hochgern for its background.

The lake ,well known on account of its splendid colouring, makes the wide panorama assume a still more effective and varying aspect in the iridescent rays of the sun. In the morning the lake glitters like a hazy veil; at noon its waters are of the deepest, most enchanting blue, and reflect in the evening in purple, golden and violet hues the last brilliancy of colour of the parting day.

Not rarely, the melancholy charm of the past which envelopes Herrenwörth mixes itself up with the charm of this wonderful panorama. Here, upon the Herreninsel, wild enthusiasm at the dawn of a new epoch, and cool-headed statecraft laid in ruins with its rude grip the thousand-years'-old monastery's dignity.

One cannot help always thinking of the tragic destiny of the unhappy monarch whose marvellous structure down there towers high above the forest. When the moonlight shines and glitters in its numberless windows, the lonely spectator may think that a brilliant and magic illumination was being prepared to meet the king coming down from his mountain castle; one seems to hear the gurgling of the fountains in the midst of the silence of the mild summer's night, filled with brilliant moonlight. — Yet silence always reigns; the delusive glitter of the moon disappears from the windows, cold and once more silent the noble structure rises gloomily in the night. He who once has felt the enchanting impression of a moonlight night on the Chiemsee or has admired the

THE HERRENINSEL AND THE OLD CASTLE

IN THE BACKGROUND THE KAMPENWAND — BY O. BLASCHKE, PRIEN.

sunrise in the early morning here upon Herrenwörth, will cherish these remembrances of the most ravishing scenes of his whole life, and will turn from a dispassionate visitor into a faithful and devoted friend of the Chiemsee and its charming islands.

> The restaurant of the old castle of Herrenchiemsee and the hotel connected with it enjoy far around an excellent reputation with regard to cookery and cellar. The management is capital. We recommend it warmly as a pension.

ROYAL HOTEL OF THE CASTLE ON THE HERRENINSEL.

On beautiful summer Sundays Herrenchiemsee is, with its huge, shady garden, the gathering place of the country folk, especially at Whitsuntide, when, according to an old tradition, the country fair of the island is celebrated. To the soft and yearning sounds of the zither the vigorous lads and buxom maidens, smartly dressed in their mountain costumes, dance and sing. Lusty cheers announce to the visitors assembled from all the corners of the world the beginning of the usual, universally practised "Schuhplattler". Many an old rustic with his eternal cutty in his toothless mouth looks on at the cheerful scene. He calls back to mind the days, when he came himself as youngster to hold the country fair, dancing with his "Miadei" who long since was laid beneath the green turf; but the remembrance won't make him too sad to-day, for the stone-ware jug surely will drive his care away.

The principal charm of Herrenchiemsee lies in the large natural park, a magnificent forest with gigantic trees, traversed by shady and well-kept paths. It stretches ont from the castle to the southern shore, descending sharply to the lake.

Very few visitors to the castle, after a fatiguing inspection of it all, give themselves the pleasure of this wonderful walk, in the course of which so many charming views of the lake and mountains are to be had. A direct road leads from the landing stage of Herreninsel along the east bank with superb outlooks to the Lady's Isle, the vast lake, the mountains and the forest.

A surprising picture is presented by the sudden aspect of the east front of the king's castle and the vast, long-extending lawn hemmed round by ranges of young, thriving limes and beeches.

The thick boughs protect the path to the Paulsruhe from the burning rays of the sun. Outside, the lake lies immoveable in dazzling brightness and not the slightest breeze bends the stems of the thicket of reeds stretching out far into the lake. Herds of deer can be seen making their way to the water to quench their thirst.

A wonderful view is to be had at the very end of the island, under the shade of a single huge fir tree. Gently the waves wash against the shore which, during stormy weather, they overflood with raging fury.

It is difficult to describe the beauty of the panorama which presents· itself here to the eye. It is an observation point full of magic fascination. As far as the eye reaches, the glittering, silver-gleaming surface of the lake lies before our eye; yonder on the Eastern shore stands, scarcely discernible, the church of Chieming; over the translucent waters pass hay-laden boats steering towards the Lady's Isle. Towards the south the Alpine panorama, here unsurpassed in extent and of scintillating beauty fills the very soul with a wondrous ecstasy; we see also an imposing row of peaks amongst which the Kampenwand group especially attracts the eye. Stern and silent its wild rocky brow is bathed in the azure of the heavens. A sublime majesty is spread over it, standing as it were as a guardian at the portal of the high Alpine world, which unrolls itself at the top as by the stroke of a magic wand.

The whispering of the forest unites itself with the faint murmur of the waves; no steamer, no boats with noisy people are plowing this part of the lake.

The most beautiful spectacle however is reserved for the calm evening. The shadows of the mountains are already hovering in the valleys. Yonder the dusky forest frowns. Drearily the stony ramparts loom up into the clouds. Upwards we look at the Alpine glow! The countenance of the virgin mountain radiates in luminous purple as it receives the goodnight kiss of the Sun God. All nature is glorified — every where silence reigns supreme; man however is overwhelmed; a faint perception of the grandeur and majesty of nature fills his inmost soul. He must confess to having witnessed a phenomenon of transcending beauty. Whosoever parts from here, will feel conscious that the Chiemsee has captivated him with its magic spell.

The rustling of the wood accompanies us on the path which leads to the north of the island and gives us the sudden view of the gorgeous edifice of the king's castle, the waterworks and the flowery garden terrace. In the evening sunshine, the gigantic front of the castle glares out into the lake, hiding its dreary solitude with bright animating splendour. A large carriage road leads from here in scarce ten minutes to the old castle. A ramble round the southern half of the island requires a little over an hour; but at its conclusion it will be richly rewarded by the peerless Alpine panorama, framing the Chiemsee in the west and which opens itself with surprising beauty on our backward journey from Herreninsel to Stock.

Lovely indeed is the Lady's Isle, abounding in picturesque charms, the idyll of the Chiemsee, whereto the steamboat brings us in a quarter of an hour. Imposing is the aspect from the boat of the monastery Herrenwörth, which, as if shooting up from the lofty tree tops, sends down its greeting and seems to tell us how the masters of the Crozier were happy in the choice of their residence. The royal castle too captivates the eye, peeping out from its sylvan solitude, with the jagged Kampenwand as its background.

More extensive and wider becomes the view towards the North, the woody and hilly shore receding gradually; and the lake opens out in its whole enormous extension down to the end at Seebruck.

Neat farms, half hidden in the midst of orchard groves, greet us from the heights; nice villas frame the shore down

to the halting place of Gstadt, with its quaint little church
and pointed spire, situated above the village and looking far
out into the lake.

The height near Gstadt, at the red cross, presents one
of the most charming views of the Chiemsee; a picture full
of sweetness and harmony is here unrolled.

It is above all the lovely Lady's Isle emerging from the
sparkling surface of the lake which charms the eye. Like

MEETING-PLACE OF THE ARTISTS ON THE LADY'S ISLE.

a green leaf, upon which childish hands put a church, houses
and trees and left to be a sport for the waves, the little
island swims upon the blue waters, adorned with the spell of
ancient myths of a thousand years past and filled with an
elevating peace. The gentle south wind, which at the approach
of the evening fans the waves, reflects in the translucent
surface of the lake the quivering image of the island; the well
known picture of the Lady's Isle with the high towering
cupolas of the Hochfelln and Hochgern behind it, can be
viewed from here.

A most beautiful walk leads from the village of Gstadt,
which enjoys as a summer resort a great popularity on account

of its wonderful situation, through the Aigelsbuch Park, close
along the shore up and down the hills to the heights
above the lake where is situated the solitary village of
Gollenhausen.

The landscape unrolling itself beyond the low walls of
the cemetery is of transcendant beauty and undoubtedly the
grandest of the whole Chiemsee; for here can be viewed the
whole extent of the lake and the Alpine panorama. Nowhere

VIEW OF THE LADY'S ISLE FROM HERRENINSEL.
BY O. BLASCHKE, PRIEN.

can the peculiarity of the immense Chiemsee basin be enjoyed
better; towards East and North the picture of an extensive
lake in a plain country, toward the South the picture of an
Alpine lake. Before our eyes, far in the distance, like a
picture of fancy, the Lady's Isle; the mountains throw their
shades far into the lake, whose silver gleaming waves sparkle
like liquid fire. Especially magnificent and indelibly impressed
on the memory becomes the aspect of this panorama in the
evening hours, when the lake and mountains display their rich
variegation of colours. But if the mountains in the West
put on the skull cap and a furious stormwind sweeps over the
surface of the lake, this picture turns into one of wild beauty

and there is nothing any more to indicate the inland lake. The mountains on the Southern bank have disappeared with the hills at the East, and the roaring and foaming waves remind one of the wide and boundless sea.

On the passage from Gstadt to the Lady's Isle, the mountains advance gradually in all their magnificence, glimmering with

PART OF THE LADY'S ISLE.
BY O. BLASCHKE, PRIEN.

the splendour of the golden sunlight. The Lady's Isle, with the glittering waves flowing round it in thousand fold succession of colours, appears swimming towards us.

Behold! What a peerless and lovely picture! Fisherhuts crowded closely together, covered as it were, with a roof by the gigantic limetrees half hidden between orchard trees, the characteristic tower of the Minster and the grey walls of the extensive monastic buildings!

The small island, easily wandered through in a quarter of an hour, offers an abundance of picturesque charms which are not even to be found on the extensive Herreninsel.

The peace of God surrounds the little isle, encircled by the roaring waves; by the waves of time even it seems to have remained untouched. A small path leads from the pier along the margin of the lake round the southern point to the Minster.

Broad branching trees cast their shadow on it; their

PART OF THE LADY'S ISLE.

BY O BLASCHKE, PRIEN.

long arms, hanging down to the ground, are bathed by the up rushing waves; a high wall encircles the monastery buildings, as a shelter at the same time to the wild assaulting waters during stormy weather. A pretty view is offered by the aspect of the Krautinsel — the kitchen garden of the inhabitants of the Lady's Isle — by the beautiful Alpine panorama, the Herreninsel and the white, shining pyramid of the Wendelstein.

The solitary tower of the church, is, like its portal, one of the most antique constructions of the Chiemgau.

The porch shows in its clumsy and awkward execution the beginning of the Roman style. Upon the heads of animals, almost indiscernible, are standing pillars: the tympanum, instead

3

of being adorned with figures, is decorated with a flower
ornamentation. Over the grave-stones with their long effaced
epitaphs, the way leads down to the church. The high-
vaulted interior, supported by hoary columns, is bathed in
solemn twilight; along the walls the artistically chiselled
marble tombstones are remarkable. Beneath the choir rises
the simple flower-adorned sarcophagus of the first abbess
Irmengard who was descended from the royal family of the
Carlovingians. A thousand years ago she ruled with clemency
upon the solitary isle.

AVE MARIA

AFTER A PAINTING FROM RUBEN. — BY O. BLASCHKE, PRIEN.

The ranges of tombs in the church yard are richly
adorned with flowers; two statuettes of angels, grey with age,
carry the fonts filled with holy water, which the passer-by
sprinkles reverently over the resting place of those lying
beneath. A huge block of stone with a medallion portrait
watches over the tomb of the talented Ruben, the creator of
the famous picture "Ave Maria". A slim pillar keeps in
memory the tragic fate of two faithful summer guests, who
found their death in the lake during a wild tempest and whose
bodies were never recovered from the deceitful waves, which
now sparkle brightly round this place of rest.

FRAUENINSEL IM CHIEMSEE.

LADY'S ISLE.

Druck von Franz Hanfstaengl, G. m. b. H., München.

Gigantic lime trees cast their shade upon the garden of the inn, in whose small and low-roofed interior reigns all the romantic poetry which is inter-twined with the name of the Lady's Isle. Since the time, when Munich artists brought upon the island their joyous and merry humour, long before the Chiemsee could boast of any influx of visitors, scarcely another beautiful spot has been so much celebrated in songs and paintings as Frauenwörth. To the creative artist the change of sweet harmonious pictures representing every day

GSTADT.
BY O. BLASCHKE, PRIEN.

life and natural scenery offers plenty occasion to imitate in ever different variations this wonderful and powerfully framed picture of this happy isle, this lake and its mountains, more particularly as the life of the fishermen supplies a pleasing transition.

Whosoever has once been inside the inn, with its manifold and odd decorations, which serves as the common rendezvous of the artists; and has admired and laughed over the pearls of humour and wit stored up in chronicles consisting now of three big volumes, will not remember to have seen a more miscellaneous mixture of merriment and gravity,

3*

which famous artists have adorned with their multi-coloured brush, and renowned poets (such as Scheffel, Stieler) have created with their poetry.

The quiet fisher village cheerfully greets us with its modest huts, peeping out through their rich floral decoration and covered with creeping plants, which create a very cozy and homely impression. In front of the houses the little gardens in rich floral garb stretch down to the lake, where the banks are crowded with fishing boats and others containing produce of the fields. Elegant sailing boats with merry holiday makers are ploughing through the smooth surface, and far beyond a wreath of smoke announces the saloon steamer coming back from its trip round the lake.

The same animation as on the Herreninsel can be observed here in the much frequented garden restaurant on beautiful summer days. At the same time, when the summer guests and visitors to the royal castle enjoy from the terrace the commanding view over lake and mountains and do full justice to the dainties furnished by the kitchen (which has in the Chiemgau a wide spread reputation for excellency), fishermen of the Lady's Isle are closely sitting inside the low and smoky parlour; and the stalwart, weather worn figures, at the vesper hour, talk over the manifold dangers overcome at their last fishing in stormy weather; of their hopes, of the newly stocked fish fry; whilst in the kitchen the produce of their last fishing is roasting, confirming and anew strengthening to the tourist the reputation of the Chiemsee fish.

The magnificent beauty of the panorama which the terrace of the Restaurant affords with its manifold variations, according to the hour of the day, captivates and retains the visitor for hours and even for days. When mountains and lake radiate in the splendour of the setting sun, the wide azure surface changes into liquid gold and the mountains are dipped in a hazy purple and glowing red. The sun sinks slowly to rest behind the hills of the western shore and throws its streaks of light through the foliage of the gigantic limetrees. The soft-golden hue of the surface gradually changes into blueish green, higher and higher the shadows climb the precipitous sides and tops of the mountains until they are plunged into the pale grey of the dusky twilight. The high Göll, kissed by the burning rays of the setting sun, raises its proud head amid the evening peace.

Scarcely has the sunset-glow passed away, when upon the mountain-tops lights shine forth. The mountain fires announce, as they did a thousand years ago, the festival of the solstice. A low, mysterious whispering of long by-gone days passes through the old lime-trees; a little bell within the monastery summons to the chants of prayers, and the sound of gentle splashing waves mixes itself with the choral singing that breaks forth from the church. In the east the moon rises in silvery brightness, spreading its magic lustre over lake and mountains. At noon the mountains appear to us in a hazy veil far in the distance; the scintillating waves are rolling to and fro; through them now the steamer rushes up to receive the passengers, who intend making the trip round the lake.

After a short time the Lady's Isle remains far behind us; the wide extent of the lake opens itself out now, when the heights upon the north-western shore sink together and become dark lines on the horizon. On the other hand the eastern shore never seems to come nearer. The Alpine panorama changes continually during the passage; the mountains seem to separate themselves from one another and form with their grotesque forms ever new and attractive pictures. The wide opening of the Achen valley on the western shore of the Chiemsee gives one an imposing view of the snowy Loferer Stone Mountains. On approaching the eastern bank, the wild jagged edges of the Wildkaiser spring up, forming a background to the Chiemsee such as no other Bavarian lake in the vicinity of the Alps can boast of.

Beginning from the east only, the principal names of this magnificent and extensive picture may here be mentioned.

Above the broad, wooded back of the Teissenberg rise, in glimmering splendour between the Stauffen near Reichenhall and the beautifully-shaped cupola of the Hochfelln, the giants of the Berchtesgaden district, the Untersberg, the high Göll, the Watzmann and the Hochkalter; also, joined in characteristic formation, the Rauschenberg, the Kienberg, the Sonntag'shorn, the Hochfelln, — upon whose top the little chapel and the house for the refuge of travellers can well be distinguished with the naked eye; some of the Loferer Stone-mountains, the Hochgern, Lerchenkopf (from whose woody slope the Schnappen chapel looks far out into the country from the background of the wide valley of the Achen); next to the Fellhorn and Kitzbühelerhorn, the long stretching and jagged edge of the Kaisergebirge, in its wild ruggedness and fantastic formation, looks grand with the pale grey of its rocks and the snowy threads in the dreary ravines harmonising effectively with the smiling lands on every side.

To the right of the Achen Valley rises the beautifully-formed cupola of the Hochplatte, a long ridge picturesquely shaped by the sharp inclining mass of rocks of the Gedererwand leading across to the jagged crown of the Kampenwand; beyond the edge, the Geigelstein, the Rigi of the Chiemgau, peeps over for a few moments. The Kampenwand group descends in rocky precipices to the valley of the Prien, but down below its spurs are pasture lands in which neat farms look far out into the country. The Zellhorn, Riesenkopf and

CHIEMING

BY O. BLASCHKE, PRIEN.

Hochriss form the connecting link with the mountains of the Inn valley. With their sharp outlines the three rocky needles of the Heuberge stand out from the Wendelstein Group that rises up behind in its manifold formation, its highest peak of the same name towering up like a haughty ruler over the confusion of mountain tops and ridges. The Breitenstein and the Brecherspitze complete the frame of this wide picture, which, on a clear day, becomes still more extensive.

To him, who makes an excursion round the lake in the early morning hours (see time table) of a clear summer's day, the panorama will appear, with its surprisingly beautiful effects of light upon lake and mountains, far grander than during the sultry noonday hours.

We have now speedily approached the eastern shore, and the steamer, taking a sharp turn, touches the pier of the landing place at Chieming.

Here the banks are barren and deserted; a light breeze is of itself sufficient to cause the waves here to wash the shore with impetuosity and rage; but when lead-coloured clouds rise from behind the Kampenwand and, chasing over the lake, break up in a heavy storm, it becomes impossible for the steamer to land at Chieming; for the waves are roaring with rage and fury towards the shore and in a wide circle the steamer avoids the deceitful rocky cliffs covered with the foaming waters.

Only since the last few years has this charmingly-situated Chieming been frequented by summer guests; grand is the view from the pier over the immense surface of the lake, that glitters in the warm sunshine, on to the many peaked Kampenwand group; only those with a good knowledge of the place will be able to recognise far in the distance, in the dazzingly bright surface of the lake, the Lady's Isle; and, in the long white streak, the royal castle of Herrenchiemsee.

The scenery along the beach north of Chieming remains still monotonous; only at a greater distance from the lake ranges of hills again raise their proud heads, and, skirting the shores of the lake westwards, give to the scenery here a lovely character.

The story goes, that far out in the midst of the lake lies, sunk down into the bottom, an engulfed town. The gleaming marble splendour of its palaces and temples, the sun's glare upon its spires, and the sounds of bells penetrate out of the depth of the waters.

Above the fine old timber-forests that come close to the beach, rises in pinnacle after pinnacle, the high-towering castle of Ising, in the midst of well-cultivated gardens and a park. It offers indeed a lovely picture. At the landing place of Seebruck, it appears that all the landscape beauty of the Chiemsee and its magnificent Alpine panorama is massed here into an enormous and enchanting picture. Far away stretch in their wide expanse the glittering waters to the southern shore; the mountains seem to rise immediately out of the waves, which at our feet wash the beach, just as if they were bringing a greeting from that fairy-like Alpine world, which is reflected in its smooth surface. It is a wonderful moving spectacle. He who once has seen this picture, whether in the morning shimmer, or in the purple evening glow or when all is bathed in sparkling moonlight, feels himself again drawn towards the quiet village of Seebruck to rejoice in peaceful, quiet contemplation, sure of finding a good place for recreation, far from the noise and bustle of men and traffic. Here the Alz leaves the lake, a broad river with but an insignificant descent. All the wildness and impetuosity with which, on the opposite side, the brooks and rivers dart

SEEBRUCK
BY O BLASCHKE. PRIEN.

forth into the lake is wholly strange to these waters, that, leaving the basin of the Chiemsee, wind slowly through lovely woodlands and pastures.

From Seebruck the keel of the steamer turns southwards; again the Minster of the Lady's Isle emerges from the waves; on the beautiful wooded bank to the right stands the little church of Gollenshausen. The mountains rise in sharper outlines now in the already advanced hour of the afternoon and wonderful light reflections are created by the setting sun upon the wide surface. Far behind, over the infinitely-stretching waters, Seebruck, Ising and Chieming send their farewell; the islands are slowly passing by, and one takes a last glance upon the lake and mountain peaks, displaying their full magic splendour in the evening light.

The saloon-steamer makes, three times a day, the trip round the lake (morning, midday and afternoon, see time table); this can comfortably be combined with the visit to the Royal Castle and the Lady's Isle.

A beautiful and shady foot-path leads in 15 minutes from the landing place to the Castle of Herrenchiemsee. Enchanting views are to be had of the azure gleaming lake and the idyll of the Chiemsee, the lovely Lady's Isle.

With a gentle ascent, the path winds up to the immense water terrace; and — in its entire and captivating magnificence of the Renaissance period — the King's Castle presents itself to the eye as an emblem of kingly might.

The principal front, looking towards the broad terrace, (352 ft. long) is copied exactly from that of the Castle of Versailles and reminds one of the genius of the French architect Mansard; also at the very outset it gives an imposing and majestic appearance to the Castle of Herrenchiemsee.

It is true, the long stretching and monotonous wing, joining the front on the right, at first sight makes a rather disenchanting impression; but this momentary uncomfortable feeling soon passes away when we behold the lofty structure of the main front with its noble architecture, the gigantic windows of the Mirror-Gallery shining down upon the extensive terrace, and three enormous golden gates attracting us to enter into the fairy-like apartments.

In the Castle of Herrenchiemsee, King Louis II re-created an eminent and lasting memorial of the French Rococo Style. The majesty of the structure was obtained by the enormous length of the front, and would have been enhanced still further by the two immense side wings, the pavilions and the castle dome. The etiquette of the French court forbade the many-storied buildings, like the Italian state palaces in the Modern or Later Renaissance Style. For this reason, it would have displayed a lack of aesthetic feeling to expect the king to ascend several flights of stairs. It was moreover felt necessary to avoid the construction of apartments above those of the king.

The castle comprises, with the exception of the ground-floor, apparently two stories, but the uppermost is filled by the vaults of the first floor.

The middle structure contains 23 high bay windows, out of which 17 give their rich light to the great Mirror-Gallery. This structure is divided into three projections and richly adorned with pillars and pilasters. Equally richly decorated is the attic story with trophies, emblems and medallions, whilst the flat roof is crowned by allegorical statuettes. Both of the wings joining the back of the principal structure

THE FRONT OF THE CASTLE.

contain the well of the stairs, which lead up through all the flats, affording, by their vastness, an imposing effect. These wings at the back encircle the court, 136 ft long, which is inlaid in chess-board fashion with white and black marble.

The back part of the principal structure is likewise richly ornamented with stucco ornaments, helmets and emblems, and crowned by a huge clock with winged genii and symbolical figures.

From the marble court five stairs lead down to the long extensive lawn or parterre, which, as on the western side of the castle, is framed with limetrees and hedges, and stretches down gradually, in a gentle incline, to the lake, which opens out here.

An enchanting view over lake and hills to the distant mountain peaks of the Salzkammergut is to be had.

The enterior of the principal structure is not completely finished. The sudden contrast, which is so sensibly felt by the visitor, whenever he passes from the gorgeous state rooms to the brick work, compels one to recollect that everything will for ever remain in its unfinished state. All that we see however speaks more eloquently than words of what was begun in the same unfinished state and was shaped later into such wonderful perfection.

Plan

of the first Floor.

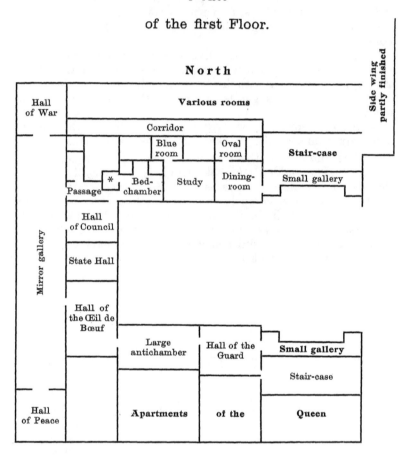

*) Toilet room.

The black letters indicate that these rooms &c. are not completely finished.

Druck von Franz Hanfstaengl, G. m. b. H. in München.

Aus Steinberger's Königsschlösser

KÖNIGL. SCHLOSS HERRENCHIEMSEE

Verlag von F. Speiser in Prien am Chiemsee.

The Interior of the Castle.

The decoration of the splendid apartments of the Royal Castle of Herrenchiemsee is by no means confined to the style of Louis XIV. It varies from the distinctive style of Le Pautre to that of Jean Berain, as well as from that of the Regency to Louis XVth; but all these different styles unite in that of Le Pautre which seems to be the base of it all. In fact one can without hesitation assert that this style was meant to have a preponderating place in the construction of the whole. The attempt at the suggestion of vast spaces by all manner of perspective devices is arrived at by the abundant use of pilasters, columns and mirrors which play a conspicuous part in the interior decoration of the castle. Everywhere the profusion of gold testifies to the influence of Le Pautre. In the salons is reflected the great period of French art that flourished in the reign of the "Sun King". The splendour of the decorative arts which are found united therein is still further enhanced by the richness of the motifs which, side by side with Baroc, Rococo and Rocailles, has emphasised in so brilliant a manner the wonderful choice and variation of colouring. If all this magnificence appears splendid, sublime, and unique of its kind to the strangers who behold it, it ought to be much more so to the eyes of the German visitor, for the artists, responsible for the work under the patronage of King Louis II, belong to Munich. They knew better than any one else, how to execute the difficult orders given them by their sovereign, and strove to surpass all the grandeur and all the marvels which at Versailles have made the honour and glory of the French people in the time of Louis XIV.

There are and will always, of a truth, be persons of bad taste who, after a casual inspection of the castle, will find occasion to run down and decry the prodigality of gold expended in its decoration.

The "Chambre de Parade", against which these unfriendly criticisms are most often directed, gives the best example of the artistic taste with which the gold is used in keeping with the ground-colouring of the apartment.

By the richness of the golden embroidery displayed on the walls, the purple takes on a most splendid aspect; the fine effect of the white marble fireplaces is set off by the magnificent gilding.

The fact that the full effect of this splendour can only be arrived at by the use of artistic illumination ought once and for all to suffice in silencing those people who are ready, notwithstanding, to decry the splendours they behold. It is difficult, very difficult, to describe, in passing from one room to another, the gradual increase of splendour. Despite frequent study and numerous visits, the pen can give but a feeble impression of every thing presented to our eyes. By the help of technical science only a few works have in our days arrived at such a pitch of perfection that they succeed to some extent in a reproduction of the reality in all its details.

The division of the rooms is similar to that at Versailles; however there are to be found in it some arrangements copied from other royal French Castles (for instance Fontainebleau). It is easy to recognise the efforts that have been made to surpass the original in the lavish magnificence and spacial extension. It is true, the question arises how this could have been effected if the castle with its wings and pavilions had reached its completion. Before entering in detail into a description of each room, I venture to make the following remark in conclusion:

Each room by the original and predominant colour of the decoration has its characteristic physiognomy, which gives it an incomparable charm, which is not found again in the variation of all the other rooms and galleries; the graceful form of everything entrances us but chiefly in the rooms, decorated in the Rococo Style.

The Vestibule.

Three barred gates, lavishly gilded, admit the visitor, on the garden side, to the sumptuous interior. The King used always to enter the castle by the marble court from which a broad avenue leads down to the lake. The porch and vestibule afford some idea to the traveller, by reason of their noble architecture, of the surpassing grandeur of the vast interior apartments. The white columns of Tyrolean marble give to this vestibule a majestic appearance. The decorative ornamentation of the walls and ceiling, with their pictures and designs in gold, would have, if the original plan had

been carried out, itself given to the vestibule a princely
appearance; but, as it is, the very simplicity of this hall forms
an effective background for the much admired centre-piece,
— a group of pea-cocks standing on a pedestal.

This masterpiece of French industrial art rises to a height
of nearly ten feet. On the pedestal of many-coloured marble

THE PEACOCK.

is a huge vase of Italian marble; the block in the middle is
made of Belgian granite.

A gigantic pea-cock is perched in a majestic pose upon
the vase. Its head and neck are of silver, whilst the body
is cast in bronze; the eyes of its long trailing tail are enamelled
in gold. The female is seated on the pedestal, and completes
by its pose a group full of nature and life. This interesting
masterpiece of Parisian art was produced by the firm of
Thierry and Breul in Munich.

One cannot fail to observe in each feather the exact imitation of nature, and at the same time the charm of the long, waving tail with its magnificent colours, that stand out in bold relief against the dazzling whiteness of the hall. One is bound to admit that this great work is well chosen with a view to preparing us for all the splendours that will entrance us in the other rooms.

From the Vestibule one crosses a marble court and arrives, through large barred doors, at the

Marble Staircase

116 feet long and 43 feet broad.

A look of astonishment is visible on every face when the beauty of colours and light here displayed first bursts upon one's gaze. Every visitor, on entering this vast apartment, goes into ecstasies over its pictures with their sparkling colours, over its many coloured marbles and over the rays of light intensifying the splendour of the whole.

"The eye revels in the splendour of the colours; and this staircase, the out, come of the colossal fantasy of an artist, tells us that the beauty of the fairy castles of which one reads in old stories has been fully realised in the present structure".

But despite all its magnificence, the marble staircase, in which the gods of antiquity seem to live and breath, give one so far no idea of the richness and grandeur of the rooms that come next. All the sculpture, paintings and industrial art in this apartment, breathe an air of tranquillity and repose.

White and gold are the principal colours of this hall. Two crystal chandeliers, with 125 candles in each, hang from the ceiling.

The white marble steps divide, after ascending for a short distance, into two parts, that lead right and left to the gallery. The steps leading to the incompleted and inaccessible apartments of the Queen are covered with a carpet of red velvet.

On the landing, in a niche of the wall, stands the large basin of a fountain in Belgian marble, surmounted by a group of sculpture — Diana entering her Bath admired by two Nymphs. The lifelike formation of this group, which is of great artistic value, makes one wish that it had been executed in marble. Similar to this group are the statues to be found in the niches of the 1st floor separated from each other by a rich variation of pilasters and columns. These statues represent

Apollo, Flora, Minerva and Ceres. The magnificent fresco paintings in the niches along the two walls (creations of

THE MARBLE STAIRCASE.

Francis Widnmann of Munich) represent beautiful female figures and Cupids in the act of throwing flowers who extend a friendly welcome to the visitor. Four other radiant tableaux,

4

(the work of Louis Lesker of Munich) on the wall facing the
entrance, represent the four estates:

On the right, the Military Estate; on the left, Juris-
prudence and Science;

On the wall at the back: Commerce and Industry, on the
right; and on the left, Agriculture.

In the frieze surmounting the principal moulding are the
following figures in plaster: the 5 Divisions of the Earth, the
four Seasons of the Year, the four Elements, War and Peace.

One can scarcely believe that all these marble groups
on the walls, these balustrades, columns and pilasters are
(with the exception of the staircase and the parapets) imitations:
truly an astounding witness to the zeal in industrial art on
the part of the firm of Detoma in Vienna. It was the chief
Superintendent of Works, von Dollmann, who planned this grand
stair-case; groups and figures were modelled by the sculptor
Perron whose many-sided and artistic creations delight at every
turn the visitor's eye.

A look cast behind from the gallery of the staircase
upon all this magnificence and light is well repaid. Only
from that point can one properly see the noble distinction
with which the Gods of Antiquity and the allegorical representations of the life of Man form an artistic whole most perfect
in every respect.

In this spacious hall, radiant with its thousand charming
colours one point which, in the majority of the other rooms,
does not have an advantageous influence on the visitor, has
been happily avoided: the manner in which the fairy-like
beauty of the artificial light is not altogether in keeping with
the general splendour and magnificence. The harmonions blen-
ding of light and colour that the Court of Honour offers to
the ravished eye would not have been so marked in candle-
light, especially as dark colours have been altogether avoided,
whilst one finds quite the contrary in the other apartments.

A short corridor, whose high folding-doors are ornamented with sculptures of gilded wood leads into the first salon,

The Guard Room of the King.

On emerging from the principal staircase, the visitor to
Herrenchiemsee finds himself, after some steps, in the midst
of the Castle of Versailles. The mythological representations
are found in this room as in the others, and are all directed
to the same end. The mural decoration, the panelling of

the doors and fire-places of this room, whose ruling tint is
gray mingled with gold, are all of gray stucco with red marble
for the panels. The walls are richly ornamented with emblems
and reliefs symbolical of royalty. The decorations above the
doors and in the corners are of bronzed plaster. The four
busts in Carrara marble standing on pedestals of Bordiglio

THE GUARD ROOM.

marble (all copies of Professor Perron) represent the generals
of the Sun-King Louis XIV — Condé, Turenne, Vauban and
Villars, whose glory, inseparable from that of their master,
shines resplendent in the history of France. The great picture
on the ceiling a creation of Dr. Widnmann of Munich, has
for its motive the "Triumph of Mars". "Mars in a war chariot
driven by Bellona accompanied by the Furies — Anger, Terror,
Fear and Hate stet. Eris (Strife) swings in the fore ground. At the
foot is a victorious general making his triumphal entrance into a

4*

conquered town." In its effect and general execution the savage picture is exactly in keeping with the epoch which this room represents. One would think it formed an apotheosis for the generals whose busts adorn the spacious apartment. The pictures on the walls are in greater part copies of those at Versailles and have for their subject war scenes from the life of Louis XIV. The entrance of the King into Arras by Rögge, the entrance into Derais, the battle of Neerwinden by Langenmantel; as well as the six small pictures by Professor Widnmann:

The Capture of Orsoy, the battle of Leus, the Bombardment of Oudenarde, the Entrance into Dunkirk, the Capture of Limburg, the Capture of Salins, all illustrating the victories of the Sun-King in his different campaigns. Four medallions on the frieze treat, in allegorical fashion, of the life of Mars:

"Education of Mars", "Mars fighting with the Giants", "Mars and Venus", "Mars and Minerva". This collection of paintings and sculpture gives to the room a warlike appearance.

The 20 halberts with blue velvet handles, attached to the walls by frames, testify to the fact that this room was meant, like the one at Versailles, to be used by members of the Royal Lifeguards. The entire furniture consists of three benches covered with gilded leather; a crystal chandelier with 85 lights; several brackets on the walls and over the fireplaces. Small wall-tables, on which stand Sèvres vases and time-pieces, complete this charming picture which, in spite of all its splendour, gives one only a faint idea of all the splendour that awaits us further on. The next room (which is richer) is the

First Antechamber.

As in the preceding rooms, columns and pilasters have been avoided here, and variety has been brought in by the arrangement of large spaces for mirrors, wall paintings and fireplaces and by the round heads of the windows opposite them.

Enormous mirrors on the pillars and wall, richly gilded trophies, reliefs and ornaments, give a gorgeous appearance to the saloon of which the principal colour is lilac with gold. The curtains at the windows and before the doors (of lilac-damask) as well as the upholstered furniture display luxurious fittings in rich golden embroidery. Upon the fire-place, made

of stucco and framed with Griotte marble, a gilt Bronze-watch
and girandoles (by Schweizer, Munich) make a fine show;
the wonderful brackets in front of the mirrors consist likewise of Griotte marble. The wainscottings of white stucco
are richly inlaid with gold. The highly artistic embroideries upon
the curtains and benches and the Bourbon lilies, representing

FIRST ANTECHAMBER.

the royal initials, are of gold; the enormous crystalline chandelier with ornamentation is of great beauty.

The magnificent ceiling-painting (original composition of
the painter Hauschild at Munich) treats of the myth, of the
entrance of Bacchus and Ceres, a most ingenious representation and very rich in figures. The huge, magnificent wall-
paintings, copies of those at Versailles, represent the most
brilliant period of the French dynasty; especially remarkable
is "the Reception of the great Condé". This picture repre-

sents in a lively conception the truly pompous display of
French royal power and is worthy of the greatest attention.

THE CABINET.

The huge wall painting opposite shows the Capture of
Lille. Both are by Professor Jules Jury.

"The Capture of Valenciennes" by Schultheiss, "the Famous Carroussel", "a Visit of the King to the Gobelin Manufactory" by J. Munsch, "the Alliance with the Swiss" (by Schultheiss) have again, as their subject, scenes from the eventful life of the Sun-King.

Charming in its beauty is — when seen through a telescope — the perspective in the other paintings. "View from Marly" and "the View of Versailles" both by Watter; a historic aspect is given to the latter by the animated picture of court-life in the fore-ground.

Already powerful in this room is the impression of the immense industrial activity which meets the eye; not only in the charming stucco-works which can be admired throughout the castle and which give it its peculiar gorgeous stamp, but also in the highly artistic embroideries in gold upon curtains and upholstered furniture, which show the initials of the king beautifully worked in gold, a standard work by the Munich firm Jörres. Perfect artistic skill is manifested in the magnificent cabinet standing along-side the wall, created in accordance with orders given by the king himself during several years of work in the cabinet factory of Grünig and Ton at Munich. It testifies, even in its unfinished state, to the highly developed artistic trade of Munich. Standing upon four curved feet, this cabinet has a height of over 12 feet, and is lined inside with blue silk and on the outside richly inlaid with tortoise shell and ornamented with gilt bronze. The panels in the door and on the sides still await the ornamentation of the artist; the panel on the back wall represents Juno with a team of peacocks. Beneath the doors of the shrine the emblems of music find a place, and the royal crown, with the king's initials and surrounded by goddesses, forms the head.

Resplendent in the noblest forms of Rococo (only observe the Cupids on the front in their masterly formation), this cabinet excites the fullest admiration of the beholder. It is unknown for what purpose this piece of furniture was destined; perhaps it was meant to serve as a musical box — the emblems at least indicate such a use — the more so as, according to official sources, the intention was planned, to put it up in the "unfinished" Apollo Saal.

Whilst this magnificent room is resplendent with deep lilac and gold, the following apartment opens itself out to the astonished eye.

The Salle de l'œil de Bœuf

radiates in its rich colours of green and gold in still increasing splendour and the highest artistic perfection but yet fanned with a touch of modest dignity.

Also in this room the memory of the King Louis XIV forces itself on us with renewed vigour; at Versailles during his epoch it was used as a waiting room by the old nobility admitted to the Levée, and was the rendezvous of the courtiers. It was as such almost notorious for the intrigues and courtly jealousy that went on.

The room takes its name from the two oval windows, a strict copy of those at Versailles, where they are designated as "ox eyes". Whilst the one going out into the court gives access to the day-light, the other reflects in its pane of plate glass and oblique position the wonderful ceiling painting of "the Aurora" (by Professor Schwoiser), the enormous size of which affords a surprising effect when passing the threshold of the salon, and symbolises in its subject in a most characteristic manner the purpose of the room as an antechamber to the bed-room.

The picture shows Aurora rising in the east of the ocean and sending the morning salutation to her spouse "Asträos" which causes him to turn pale. Mercury precedes them and shows the way; the four gods of the winds roll up the vault of heaven studded with stars; in the background Hecate is disappearing in her chariot drawn by owls; the aged Saturn shows the time on the sand dial; Venus throws broad-cast the sparkling dew.

The entire representation, so rich in figures, as well as the charm of colouring give this picture the appearance of one of the greatest masterpieces in the castle.

The narrow side-walls are richly divided by pilasters, the doors opposite the high windows, leading to the gallery, are inlaid with glass mirrors; two enormous mirrors on the side-walls (the largest in the castle) and the small ones on the pillars form a rich perspective and give to this magnificent chamber an appearance of infinite size. A fire-place of precious marble from Herculaneum is surmounted by one of these huge mirrors; a pier-glass table opposite of the same material displays a beautiful decorated work by Thierry and Breuil:

The "Pendulum of Aurora" a piece of Parisian workmanship of great artistic value in the Rococo style. The panels between the pillars are decorated with rich emblems, symbolical of Agriculture, Music and the Fine Arts. In this chamber, as in the others, the wall pictures and mural decoration are subjects drawn from the history of Louis XIV.

THE SALLE DE L'ŒIL DE BOEUF.

The four great wall pictures, copied from the originals at Versailles by French artists, have for their subjects: "The Family of Louis XIV" after Jean Nocret; "King Louis XIV in antique costume" after Mignard; "Philip of France" after Mignard; "Louis of Bourbon, Prince of Condé" after Serrure.

Three other pictures are:

"The Anointment of the Dauphin", "The Hotel des Invalides" by Watter; "A Reunion of the Court at Versailles"

by Langenmantel. The first and the third in the arrangement
of their colours give a perfect representation of the splendid
life at the court of Louis XIV. But the object most deser-
ving of admiration in this apartment is a statuette in bronze
standing on a marble pedestal, representing Louis XIV on
horseback. If one looks at this chiselled masterpiece carefully,
one cannot help being struck with the perfection which industrial art in Munich has reached. The same can be said of
the golden embroidery on the curtains and furniture; of the
chandeliers on the fire-place and on the side-tables, of the
girandoles and the three large magnificent crystal lustres,
which set off in a marked degree the charm of this apartment.

As in the other rooms the eye, on taking a farewell look
at this one, admires its solitary beauty, which has only its full
effect when seen by the artificial light of the wax-candles.
One thinks, that all the grandeur and splendour of this marvellous castle have already been seen by this time; however
the door that gives the visitor entrance to the following room,
proves that he has been mistaken.

We enter

The Chambre de Parade (State chamber).

One finds in this apartment the best illustration of the
development of industrial art at Munich under Louis II. One
sees in it marvellous embroidery in gold and silk on the curtains, the panels, the draperies, the Gobelin tapestries, the arm
chairs, the foot-stools and door hangings as well as works in
stucco and metal. One is particularly struck by the marble
groups, all executed in the grandest style.

The purple and gold dazzle the eye to such an extent
in this apartment, that the pen fails to describe all that one
sees therein. The architectural arrangement alone gives it the
appearance of a master-piece, which decorative art has transformed into a truly incomparable splendour. The walls are
divided into equal compartments which assign to the doors,
fire-places and mirrors, their proper place.

The wall opposite the windows is divided into compartments richly ornamented with golden embroidery.

The dividing line between the side walls and that at
the back takes the shape of a semi-circle, thus rendering more

conspicuous the principal ornament of this apartment, the
state bed.

The panels of the doors in white marble are decorated
with gilded ornaments and bronze. Huge hangings of purple
velvet with charming golden embroidery hide the wall where
the windows are. On the parqueted floor are displayed the

STATE ROOM.

royal lilies of France. One observes on the principal ledge
a frieze with groups of figures as follows, "the Fear of God,
Pity, Faith, War, Peace, Science, Music, Poetry, Art, Industry,
Virtue, Perseverance, Justice and Truth".

The allegorical representations in the arches overhead
form a rich background of colour and afford to the eye,
dazzled by the golden splendour, a pleasing point of repose.

The genii standing above the gigantic mirrors are of
great artistic value; on the left this group, holding aloft the

royal crown, displays the kingly monogram, and on the right,
in the same arrangment, the royal arms. The four pictures
above the door are by Professor Jules Benczur, Munich: "The
Baptism of the Duke of Burgundy (1682)," The Marriage of
the Duke of Burgundy, "The Reception of the Siamese Legation",
"The Founding of the Order of Louis". These life-like and
magnificent representations in colour of the splendour of the
Court are most artistically executed. The marble groups by
Perron over the side-tables and fire-places are also highly
interesting:

"Diana of Poitiers", "Love and Psyche", "Ariadne asleep" —
in white Carrara marble. The Apollo clock on the mantle-piece
to the right is a master-piece of the artists Widnmann, Perron
and Harrach.

On a splendidly ornamented pedestal, flanked by trophies
and drapery, stands the case borne by Caryatides; Cupids
support the dial, garlands of flowers ornament the top, on
the flat base of which appears Apollo, the god of the sun,
with a restive team of four horses.

A magnificent chandelier with 108 candles is pendant in
the midst of this splendid room; girandoles on the fire-places
help to enhance still further its magnificence.

The original ceiling painting, by Schwoiser testifies by
the happy choice of its colours to the great imaginative power
of the artist:

It represents the life of the gods of Olympus. At the
head of all is Jupiter whom a procession of Bacchantes with
Silenus and Aphrodite is passing; Hephaistus and Ares, Pluto,
Proserpina and Demeter are gathered in symbolical groups.
A hunting expedition comes up with Diana; Mercury, Posei-
don, Fama and Flora with their emblems surround the carriage of the Sun God "Helios", who rushes along in radiant
splendour; and his features, shining in eternal youth according
to the myth, resemble the traits of the Sun King Louis XIV.

Positively fairy-like is the effect, when the eye falls
upon the back-wall of the chamber. Enclosed by a wood-
carved and gilded balustrade upon a three stepped platform
rises the State Bed, glittering all over with gold and adorned
with magnificent sculptures in relief. The purple velvet carpet upon which it stands, is ornamented with wonderful embroideries, representing radiating suns.

A fascinating brilliancy hangs over this part of the room.
A thorough examination of all the gorgeousness and display
of art accumulated on the bed, the curtains and the backwall
would require hours.

A wonderfully carved dais, with gold-embroidered draperies and vases with snowy white ostrich and heron feathers

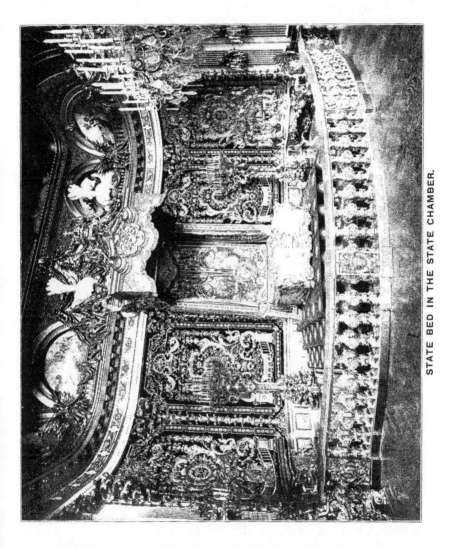

STATE BED IN THE STATE CHAMBER.

at the four corners, the king's crown in front, sparkling with
precions stones, overcanopies the state bed.

In the frieze behind the canopy is placed the group
"Bavaria with the Sceptre and Lion", flanked by the alle-

gorical figures "Prudence and Vigilance". The heavily brocaded counterpane of the immensely broad state bed is richly embroidered with gold and shows, in the midst of other ornamentations, a relief of "Venus" embroidered in gold and silver; and "Venus and Mars" embroidered in silk.

A worked tapestry — a perfect work of art — on the backwall represents "Nymphs cutting the wings of Love".

Beneath is a magnificent piece of gold embroidery on purple velvet "The Sun in radiating Glory".

The dome-shaped interior of the canopy is adorned with the relief picture "Venus leaving the Bath". The water is made of thousands of silver threads; Venus and Love with his bow and arrow are glistening in rich golden embroidery.

This masterpiece of an embroidered picture is surrounded by four gilded busts: "Venus, Jupiter, Mars and Apollo". The hangings of the canopy are richly embroidered with golden ornamentations. The curtains of the state bed give evidence to an equally masterly ability. On their inner side they consist of highly artistic Gobelin tapestry, representing "Jupiter and Ganymede", "The Rape of Ganymede", "The Rule of Venus in Olympus" and "The Activity of Venus upon Earth"; whilst the outside of these enormous draperies shows rich golden embroideries upon purple velvet in plastic formation. The medallion at the end of the bed-stead is ornamented with a lovely painting "Venus and Love". —

The toilet-table, standing at the left of the bed, is of great excellence and holds a wonderful service of richly gilded bronze, of which every part represents a masterpiece of industrial art in its artistic chasing and the extreme richness of allegorical groups in embossed work.

Precious golden embroidery is exhibited upon both of the arm-chairs standing beside the bed. Gold brocaded purple covers the hassock at the right of the state bed, the embroidery of which represents Saint Louis. The lovely image of the Virgin Mary is printed upon copper and together with the kettle, containing consecrated water, adorns the wall above the kneeling stool, where is also a representation "The Annunciation" after Raphael.

The gigantic chandeliers at both sides of the state bed as well as the two posts containing the fumigating candles at the parapet, form in their rich carving work and gorgeous gilding an ensemble, which makes this chamber appear to be a holy sanctuary of the greatest royal splendour.

The whole pomp, so tastefully united in this room, the purple, the gold and the dazzling white marble are all calculated to set off the magic light effect produced by hundreds of candles in the chandeliers, the girandoles and the brackets. Then everything glistened and glittered forth from the walls in fascinating shimmer; the wonderful white of the Carrara, the gold and the deep red of the purple velvet produced a most wonderful effect. The genii along the frieze seemed to be animated with life and to render homage to him, for whom all this unearthly magnificence was consecrated.

But to the lonely king this state room must have offered a delight, which is granted to but a very few mortals, when he stood in contemplation of all this pomp created at his command; and when he allowed its whole spell to work upon him.

The visitor may imagine the fairy-like beauty which this room must have afforded with its magic illumination, when the red silk curtains were drawn together before the bay windows, giving entrance to the daylight.

A wonderful and indescribable charm is produced by this change of illumination. In glowing red tones, a stream of light pours over this golden splendour and sparkles and glitters from the ornaments, embroideries and mirrors and from the crystals of the chandeliers. Entirely different is the effect produced by this glowing illumination of the room upon the ceiling paintings.

From it the world of Gods seems to receive new life. It is above all the brilliancy of the Sun God, which bestows on this sanctuary its indescribable and splendid charm. In the ornamentation of this room, King Louis II has given a task to the artists of Munich; it is altogether unique with regard to grandeur and perfection.

Unanimonsly, all the branches of artistic enterprise have joined hands in order to create this highest combination of Art, pomp and purity of forms in the noblest style, observed by the visitor to-day with an astonished eye.

The designs of the embroideries were originated by an artist (Professor Hauschild) and were brought to their present great perfection by the firms: Jörres, Bornhauser and Alkens at Munich. No other chamber in the castle shows in its magnificence the highest development of art and artistic enterprise in such perfection as this. — — —

With this apartment terminates the almost exclusive and strictly classical character of the decoration, as well as the entire style of the apartments in pure Barock.

Already the next chamber shows the transition to Rococo, to the style of Louis XV, especially in the decorative ornamentation. Yet, let it be pointed out, that, as already observed at the beginning, the interior equipment of the castle does not strictly adhere to a single style. In all those apartments already seen, the eye of the connoisseur notices many a digression from the high standard and yet harmonically adapted to the entire effect. Also hereafter, whilst the eye is indulging in pure Rococo, it will find out slight reminiscences of the classical style, although, without any derangement of the general impression, at the same time ingeniously adapted to the principal motif of the apartment.

After the magnificence of the state bed-room, we are enchanted by the

Salle du Conseil (Council Chamber)

which comes next in order.

This apartment like the preceding delights the eye of the visitor especially in the morning. Its predominent colours are blue and red. The style in which the richness of the ornamental motifs on the walls and the works of stucco on the principal frieze, play a conspicuous part, is altogether charming. Columns and pilasters are conspicuous by their absence in the architecture of the interior. In place of them the walls are divided up into symmetrical panels hy huge swinging doors of glass.

The middle panel on the backwall, surrounded by a magnificently sculptured frame, contains a lifesize portrait of Louis XV, a copy from Jules Jury. It forms an imposing back ground to the Conference Table, which stands on a rich Smyrna carpet, and which is covered with blue velvet, as is also an arm-chair, the back of which is surmounted by the royal crown in gilded sculpture. The arm-chair and the foot-stools are of light blue velvet and embroidered with gold; the magnificent girandoles on the table are a creation by Harrach. Two candlesticks each holding twenty lights stand on either side of the arm-chair. A gigantic chandelier, with 96 candles, hangs from the ceiling. The side-tables, whose tops are of red Spanish marble, display the following gilded groups in bronze:

"Juno on the Peacock", "Jupiter on the Eagle".

The clock over the fire-place to the right is a piece of Parisian workmanship. The fire-place opposite displays once again a group by Harrach: Bacchus, Venus and Ceres.

The masterpiece of the room however is the precious clock standing at the window. It is a copy of one at Versailles, and is called the Louis Clock. Every time it strikes

COUNCIL CHAMBER.

the hour, Louis XIV appears at the door in the middle. In the clouds, which are divided above him, a genius is holding a laurel crown.

The magnificent blue curtains at the windows are adorned with Bourbon lilies embroidered in gold; and the frieze with gilded emblems representing: "Religion, Peace, War and Royal Power".

The magnificently framed pictures above the panels have for their subjects incidents in the eventful life of Louis XIV:

5

"The Reception of the Doge of Genoa 1684", "The King declaring his grand-son Duke Philip of Anjou as King of Spain 1701", "The Apology of the Pope Alexander VII to a Cardinal (1662)", "The King's Visit to the Academy of Science in Paris".

* The picture on the ceiling designed and executed by Schwoiser has a distinguished appearance in this apartment by reason of the brilliant technique of its colours and representation. Its subject is: "The Council of the Gods on Olympus".

Jupiter and Juno are surrounded by the gods in a semi-circle, Mercury brings glad tidings; Fortuna presents her crown, Flora scatters her flowers, and above all is Justice holding a pair of scales and a sword. This picture, despite the number of personages which it contains is full of movement; the descent of Mercury is very happily executed. His shape presents the appearance of a plastic image; every detail connected with those personages all executed in a perfect style gives to this harmonious composition the very expression it ought to possess. One hesitates before leaving this magnificent apartment, for one is still ignorant of the wonders that meet the eye on entering the

Great Gallery of Mirrors.

It is in full daylight, not subdued by heavy curtains, that this gigantic hall radiates in its wonderful colours, excelling far in artistic perfection and space the original at Versailles.

Including the two corner-rooms, the gallery takes up the whole length of the western front.

Walls and pilasters consist also here of artistically worked stucco; the richly ornamented frieze supports with Caryatides the ceiling in the form of a barrel-vault and magnificently adorned with paintings and gilded stucco sculptures, created by Perron after the designs of Lebrun.

This gallery also surpasses that of Versailles with regard to its ornamental equipment. From the wall paintings, side sculptures project; at Versailles the whole decoration is presented in the pictures, whilst here in Herrenchiemsee art and artistic enterprise celebrate their highest triumphs by the plastic and ornamental arrangement of this glimmering splendour. Then it must be added that everything is resplendent in a

garb of freshness, whilst at Versailles the entire magnificence
has faded away and solely affects us by the unction which it

GALLERY OF MIRRORS.

receives from history. Chandeliers glittering and glistening
in golden brilliancy form an endless row on both sides
(44 pieces). They are made of zinc and each of them is a
masterpiece, as well as the chandeliers of which there are

5*

33 hanging from the ceiling. Between the chandeliers there are benches the royal blue velvet of which is tastily embroidered with Bourbon Lilies in gold.

In the window-niches stand vases of gilded zinc destined to receive orange trees; six vases of silver and of the former metal stand out effectively from the glittering abundance of gold. They are adorned with Cupids and winged genii, carrying the Bavarian crest with the king's crown above. The pedestal displays over the gleaming sun Medusa's head — a perfect artistic performance. The abundance of ornamental and plastic motifs gives testimony to the high development of art.

Such considerations may only casually be indulged in, the eye having scarcely leisure to observe closely the principal features of this artistic exuberance, splendour and pomp, during the time allotted to the inspection.

Only a repeated and exhaustive examination gives one the possibility of passing an objective judgment on the whole majestic beauty of this gigantic hall, which will then for ever remain engraved on the mind.

The seventeen high, arched windows are covered with white hangings; the equally high door panels opposite are inlaid with mirrors; their height being 36 feet and divided into three equal parts. The exuberant light entering through the gigantic windows makes the rich colours of the ceiling-paintings, and the golden row of the chandeliers hanging from the ceiling flash out in renewed splendour.

The arch paintings shutting off the gallery from the corner-rooms towards the north and south, above the gigantic pillars flanking the way out, are executed by Professor Widnmann. They represent the beginning and end of the Battle of the Titans, which Germany, Spain and Holland waged with France in the years 1672—1678 and which was brought to a triumphant conclusion by the Sun-King.

Explanation of these paintings as well as of the huge frescoes on the ceiling is given here upon brass-plates. The northern arch painting has for its subject:

"The Alliance of Germany and Spain with Holland 1672". "Holland accepts the Peace and detaches itself from Germany and Spain 1678.

The magnificently coloured frescoes on the ceiling copied by the Munich artists Hauschild, Schwoiser, Graf Courten, Watter and Ferdinand Piloty are divided into seven large historical and eighteen smaller allegorical paintings and have for their subject the history of France from the Peace of the Pyrenees 1659 to the Peace of Nymwegen 1678.

The plates run thus:

"The King as Absolute Ruler (1661)", "The Pomp of the neighbouring Powers of France", "La Franche Comté conquered for the second time (1674)", "The Resolution to declare war against the Dutch (1671)", "The King gives orders to attack at the same time four of the strongest places in Holland (1672)", "The King arming by water and by land (1672)", "The passage over the Rhine in the presence of the enemy (1672)", "The King takes Maastricht in thirteen days (1373)".

Copies of the Gods of Antiquity in marble find their place in the four wall niches, and along the side walls of the gigantic gallery of which the snowy glitter stands out effectively from the miscellaneous colours of the stucco and from the gold of the sculptures: They are: "The Muse Urania", "A Vestal Virgin", "Venus of Kindos" (Praxiteles), "Germanicus", "Venus of Arles", "Bacchus", "A Priestess", "Diana of Ephesus".

Equally charming is the effect of the eight busts of the Roman Emperors in antique marble upon multi-coloured marble pedestals (by Professor Spies, Rome) with which the panels together with the back ground are richly adorned as well as with gilded trophies. The busts are copies after originals in the museums of the Vatican and are of the greatest excellence: Vespasian, Aelius, Verus, Vitelius, Antonius, Pius Hadrian, Commodus, Titus and Julius Caesar.

The impression of this gigantic hall already indescribably beautiful in daylight is especially magnificent during the evening hours. What a brilliancy of light must it have had, when at the King's command the 2188 candles were burning and that unique splendour of gold, glass and marble was resplendent in a sea of light, which by the richness of the golden ornaments was of an orange-coloured tone; when the wood and lake were envelopped in the shades of the silent night, to the outside world the front of the castle appeared to be a miraculous creation emerging from a fairy dream. On the western bank stood hundreds of people, astounded before the abundance of light flowing from the windows, whilst here, surrounded by the radiating glory of this un-earthly splendour the king stepped to and fro, seeing emerge before his gaze the brilliant court-life, which had throbbed in the great Gallery at Versailles under Louis XIV.

On both sides of the great gallery, the two corner-rooms, the Salle de la Guerre (Chamber of War) and the Salle de la Paix (Chamber of Peace) form a harmonious conclusion to the whole. Both in their painting and plastic decoration pay a worthy tribute to the glory of France.

The next room following is the

Salle de la Paix.

Bright sunshine enters the gigantic windows, whence a pleasant view of the green of the woods and the mountains

SALLE DE LA PAIX.

rising up in shimmering splendour behind them, can be enjoyed.

The leading tone of this salon is blue and gold; the door frames consist of green marble.

Appropriate to the signification of the room is the rich ornamental decoration showing festoons, little Cupids and olive branches symbolical of peace.

The fire-place is made of green Spanish marble and the walls again of artistic stucco. The mantel-piece of the fire-place carries a wonderfully executed equestrian statuette of Louis XV in bronze.

Also the decoration on the walls, the paintings in the dome-shaped roof and in the arched vaults as well represent emblems of peace. The middle picture in the ceiling depicts France sitting upon the round earth in a carriage supported by clouds and surrounded by the allegorical figures of Peace, Glory, Plenty, Religion and Innocence.

The paintings in the arches, exhibit female figures: Europe, Germany, Holland and Spain. The principal ornament of this chamber is formed by the panoramic picture of Lemoine, a copy of the Count de Courten:

Louis XIV giving peace to Europe by the presentation of an olive branch.

If this picture has any connection with the Peace of Utrecht (1714) it asks more than is right from the beholder who is versed in history. The paintings in the ceiling and arches are created by the artists Munsch, Frank and Rogge.

In continuation of the Emperors' busts erected in the great gallery, we see here such of the Roman Emperors as Trajan, Domitian, Tiberius and Augustus upon marble pedestals and themselves of antique-coloured marble.

Imposing in its grand beauty, the gigantic hall of the Gallery of Mirrors is visible from the Salle de la Paix. Enrapturing is the sight of this abundance of light and gorgeous perfection of form and indescribably noble splendour.

In the apartment on the north side,

La Salle de la Guerre,

the decorative ornaments consist of victorious trophies. The predominant colour in this room, dedicated to Bellona the Goddess of War, is red mingled with gold. The ceiling is embellished with 5 pictures. That on the dome shows: France surrounded by the Goddesses of Victory. The pictures of the arch represent afresh female forms: France, Germany, Spain and Holland. At the corners of the arch is the proud Motto of Louis XIV "Nec pluribus impar", and the sun in a halo of its rays. Above the fire-place a gigantic relief displays: Louis XIV triumphing on Horseback, by Perron.

One observes underneath this relief, to the right and left,
bronze figures of warriors in chains. On the marble pedestals
are busts of the Emperors Caracala, Marcus Aurelius, Septimius,
Verus and Nero. As in the Salle de la Paix, charming crystal
lustres hang from the ceiling; in the corners shine 4 gilded
candelabra each containing 18 lights, and 2 girandoles over

SALLE DE LA GUERRE.

the fire-places complete with the mirrors in the panels the
splendid and magnificently sparkling decoration of this room.

The sequence of apartments just visited takes one only
as far as the Gallery of Mirrors.

The following rooms are destined exclusively for the
King's own use. That is why their decorative motifs are
not altogether like those at Versailles. The King's many-sided
and cultivaded artistic taste has led him to have recourse to
other creations of the Bourbons, the charm and magnificence

of which had captivated his eye. If up to this point, the
visitor to the castle has been struck by the splendour reigning
in all the rooms, those which come now may be considered
worthy habitations for a monarch; nor will they fail, by
reason of the predominating colours in the interior of each,
as well as by the grace of their decoration in the Rococo-
style to awaken (amongst the ladies most of all) a feeling of
pleasure and curiosity.

From the Gallery of Mirrors a corridor leads into the

Bedroom.

This apartment with its magnificent colours suggests in
miniature the Chambre de Parade, although it differs from
this last in the decorative style of its interior. The royal
blue of the silk stuffs in this room has an enchanting effect.
The same is produced by the gold-embroidered arabesques
and the magnificent statuary.

As in the Chambre de Parade the King's bed is separated from the space in front of it by a gilded balustrade
with sculptures of wood in a grand style. The pillars in the
niche containing the bed are formed by palm-branches carved
and splendidly gilded. The richly decorated leaves stretch
as far as the ornamentation of the Rococo frieze.

On a daïs of three steps covered by a blue velvet carpet
glittering with golden stars stands the richly sculptured bed.

The medallion at the foot represents "The Toilet of
Venus", who is surrounded by the figures "Love and Psyche",
a charming creation by Perron. At the back of the bed the
sun is shining in all its glory and above is the following
picture, wrought in precious silk embroidery: "The Triumph
of Louis XIV over the Vices".

The heavy bed-curtains display inside charming embroideries
in gold or blue velvet, and the same outside on moirée-silk
of a similar blue; the brocaded bed-cover is also composed of
golden embroideries. White ostrich feathers adorn the corners
of the canopy which is surmounted in the middle by a medallion
bearing the king's monogram; and two Cupids playing with
palm branches are seated on both sides of the royal crown.

Instead of a picture on the ceiling there is an ornament
in relief in white and gold at the corners of which are medallions
with the double letter L. Above the bed canopy is Apollo

with the chariot of the sun. One sees further "Venus and Adonis", "Diana and Endymion", "Bacchus and Ariadne", "Love and Psyche"

BEDROOM.

The kneeling stool on the left of the bed is a veritable masterpiece of industrial art. The silk embroidery covering it represents the legend of St. Hubert and the stag. Equally remarkable is the vessel containing the holy water on which is the image of the risen Lord. On the right of the bed stands a charming toilet-table service, a masterpiece in white porcelain richly gilded and beautifully painted in Rococo style. The curtains hanging from the mirror to the table as well as the cover of the table are made of Brussels lace. The subjects of the paintings in this apartment are drawn from events in the life of Louis XV.

Four pictures rich in colouring, framed by charming sculpture in wood, the creations of Rögge, Munsch and Schultheiss have for motifs:

"Louis XV playing in the Grande Gallery", "The Rising on the day of the Coronation", "A Festival in the Chapel at Versailles", "The Coronation at Rheims".

Above the fire-places are handsome mirrors whose ornamentation of festoons of flowers forms an imposing spectacle. Upon one of these chimneys stands a bronze statue of Louis XV on horseback; on the second is a richly ornamented clock representing Louis XV, to whom in a dream Minerva is prophesying the destiny of France.

Girandoles over the fire-places and the side-table, candlesticks at the walls and a sparkling crystal chandelier complete the splendour of this apartment. The bust of Louis XV. on the top of the side-table of genuine Lapis Lazuli is made from white Carrara marble. The forehead in particular is very characteristic; the thoughtful expression of the great eyes, the eyelids and the aquiline nose executed in a most perfect fashion give us an idea of the talent of the artist. The position of the mirrors gives a remarkable appearance of immensity to this apartment, which is not in reality very large. Magnificent inlaid work decorates the floor.

If we are enchanted by this room, we are still more so on opening the door which gives an entrance to the

Dressing Room

which in its rosy brilliancy forms a pleasant contrast to the severe pomp of the preceding apartments with their abundance of rich and deep colours.

It is a boudoir full of a cosy charm and is wholly dedicated to the memory of the unhappy royal couple, to wit, Louis XVI and his consort Marie Antoinette enthusiastically admired by Louis II.

The gilded carvings on the walls in the flowery Rococo style display among group of little Cupids two bronze-

medallions of Louis XIV and Marie Antoinette. One corner
of the room is adorned with the bust of the Queen in white
marble, the principal ornament of the chamber. The lovely
ceiling painting (a creation of Widnmann) "little Cupids in the
midst of their play" enhances still the gay brilliancy. A fire-
place of rosy Tunis-marble is adorned with bronze ornaments.

DRESSING ROOM.

The arrangement of the mirrors again gives an appearance of
enlargement to the room with its beautiful furniture and curtains
of rose-satin damask, embroidered with nosegays of lilies.

One of the many surprises which Herrenchiemsee offers
in abundance to the beholder is presented by the thoughtful
homage, which is payed in this chamber by the royal builder
to the Emperor's lively daughter of the Danubian town. It
brings to one's mind the joyful days of the Trianon with the
idyllic pastoral play, brought to such a sudden and horrible
end by the days of Terror in the Great Revolution.

Already this room marks in its cheerful and comely decoration a transition from the strict classical style of Le Pautre towards the light and bright fashion of the pastoral time. We notice chiefly the discontinuance of "Gilding" as a decorative resource. In its place porcelain is employed for the ornamentation in sculpture and paintings; and the following rooms — with the exception of the studio — have in new and unsuspected magnificence real china employed as decoration in a most enchanting manner and resplendent with the fullest brilliancy of colour.

After the gorgeous bedroom in blue silk and glittering in its golden pomp, of which the impression seemed to be incomparable, and after the rosy gracefulness of the dressing room there follows again an apartment which, with green and gold as its primitive colour, affords a new and fascinating deception.

The Studio.

The equipment of this room appears at a first glance in its general outline as well as in many minor details to have resemblance to the Council Chamber. Yet the idea will soon be suppressed in sight of the peculiar ornamentation of the spacious chamber, the style of which is already entirely suggestive and eloquent of the transition to the Rococo.

Hangings and furniture are of green velvet with magnificent gold embroidery. Especially remarkable in their richness and magnificent ornamental work are the gold embroideries of the armchair standing in front of the writing table. It consists of rosewood with bronze ornaments (Pössenbacher, Munich). Particulary rich in its wonderful execution is the back to the chair showing, as it does, charming arabesques with the king's crown.

For the last time (in these apartments) does gold form the principal means of decoration, producing everywhere sparkling tones. Yet its application appears to be already more discreet and not any more predominant. The panels and door frames are kept in white; the frieze of the ceiling, richly adorned with stucco works, contains the following figures of the gods in rich gilding:

"Juno and Jupiter", "Venus and Mars", "Ceres and Bacchus", „Mercury and Minerva". The top pieces of the doors carry the royal initials with a crown; a rich arrangement of mirrors — two narrow mirrors in the corners above the

fire-places of red brown marble, two large mirrors in the
panels of the middle walls, exhibiting on their tops little
Cupids and lovely flower ornaments and two mirrors above
pier-tables by the window pillars — give again the fairy-
like effect of perspective enlargement to the room. A magnificent crystal chandelier, girandoles upon the pier-glass

THE STUDIO.

tables, wall brackets and two chandeliers (fantastically shaped
like palm trunks in wonderfully gilded carving work) stand
on both sides of the writing-table. They were meant to bathe
the room in magic illumination.

Upon both of the fire-places are standing two bronze
figures, on the right Juno, on the left Jupiter. In front of
the middle panel at the backwall, which shows in a richly
carved frame the image of Louis XV in life size, a copy by
Jules de Jury after Jan van Lon, stands the writing-table (so

much admired) of rosewood, inlaid with multi-coloured wood and magnificent metal fittings, a copy out of the Lonore Museum, of Parisian workmanship.

The five head-pieces of the doors by Jury, Rögge, Langenmantel and Schultheiss call to mind the victorious battles of French history. They are: "Arrival of the King at Havre de Grâce", "The Battle near Fontenay", "The Siege of Antwerp".

The floor is magnificently inlaid with rosewood, the walls and the ceiling radiate in white with rich gold ornaments; and the chain of the chandelier hanging from the ceiling is held by a Cupid.

Several easel pictures, which helped to add further to the ornamentation, have been taken away, yet without prejudicing the fine impression conveyed by the room. Still it offers in its finely harmonised brilliancy of colours an artistic and perfect ensemble of royal and splendid pomp.

The three precious clocks are supplied by Carl Schweizer (Munich), and form a valuable addition to the beauty of the chamber. Two of them are standing in front of the large mirrors at the side walls. A peculiar piece, giving testimony to the many-sided creative impulses of the royal builder, is the so-called Elephant Watch. The excellent representation of the animal in plated bronze carries on the gilded cover a tent containing the clock-work. Above it is a female figure, and upon the neck of the beast stands Love as Cornac. The Rock-watch, over 5 feet in height, shows upon the dial the sun. On the left is the moon and in front the earth; at the end the radiating sun partly covered with clouds.

The Astronomical clock (in the style of Louis XV and copied after that at Versailles with enamelled globe) shows the planetary system. In front is the date and the phases of the moon.

The following chamber is euphemistically called

The Light Blue Salon or Hunting Room.

What could be more delightful than the feeling of repose produced by this room, after eye and mind have been so busily engaged in the inspection of the apartments passed through?

Again the visitor is enraptured, as soon as he steps over the threshold. Even the most dispassionate mind, after having been able to pass indifferently through all the preceding room, must be carried away by a feeling of the greatest admiration — au admiration not only for the artists who created this splendid work, but also for the king, whose many-sided and cultivated artistic taste gathered together all the beautiful things in this room, like some fairy creation

THE HUNTING ROOM.

which enchants the eye by its magic perfection. The smaller the apartment, it appears, the more difficult becomes the task to give any idea in a description of all this stylish perfection of form, all this artistic manifestation in every detail, which is collected in these rooms in overflowing abundance. In the course of this description, reference has often been made to the conspicuous part played by Munich's art in the interior equipment of the whole castle. But here especially its importance again in a marked degree presents itself to the eye. This is evident in the graceful wood sculpture of the wall decorations, in its magnificent foliage — representing trees with birds sitting among the branches — which covers the walls in shimmering and golden brilliancy with their luxuriant growth and increases a thousand fold the fairy-like magnificence. The panels between, separated by narrow and broad mirrors, which give this apartment the appearance of stretching into infinite length and breadth, form arcades of trees. The curtains are of blue moirée-silk. In a really enchanting manner, this room must have unfolded its whole magic charm, when the girandoles upon the fire-places, the chandelier and the brackets by the mirror-walls spread their bright illumination of candles over it, reproduced a thousand fold by the arrangement of mirrors. Truly charming, and an astonishing performance of the highly developped China industry of Meissen are the fire-places and girandoles, as well as the festoons of roses with which the walls are inlaid. The garlands overhanging the mirrors are wood-carvings in multi-coloured paintings with a striking resemblance to China work. Of plaster casting is the chandelier, the execution of which was meant to be made in ivory; the smaller hanging over the couch is of Venetian glass.

The floor shows rich inlaid work of sycamore, cherry and ebony wood. The ornamentation of the ceiling in the rich flower style of the 18th century, animated by birds, consists of plaster sculptures and medallion-pictures with hunting scenes by Eibl and Schnitzberger.

The whole cheerful splendour of the pastoral and hunting life, which, at the French royal court formed the favourite pastime for ladies and gentlemen, the apparently peaceful idyls of farms with their idyllic shepherds and shepherdesses and the exciting mirth of the royal hunts with the sounds of the horns, the letting loose of the hounds and the shouts of Tally Ho! — all this is reflected from the delightful representations on the ceiling and from the paintings over the headpieces of the doors. In their interpretation and representation they speak of the Rococo style, which impresses this exuberant picture on the mind and gives to it the stamp of this idyllic aesthetic tendency.

The paintings (copies by Merk, Munich) represent:

"A pastoral Scene", "A Present to the Herdsman", "Returning home from the hunt".

The design of the decoration of this charming room originates from Professor Perron. Again and again the har-

6

monious beauty of this room arrests the eye. It is a pity
however, that the time allowed for the inspection is but a
short one.

Through a Corridor the way leads to the

THE OVAL SALON.

Oval Salon

otherwise called "The Porcelain Chamber".

It is in its noble and unobtrusive splendour the same
work of art as the Light Blue Salon.

In the most enchanting manner China has been used
here as the main decorative resource. Unmatched in delicacy
and elegance, cheerful and graceful in its splendour, sweet
and lovely in its colours, this room reflects the Rococo style
in its loftiest formations.

For the equipment of this apartment, in white and gold, the Castle of Fontainebleau gave the enchanting motifs.

A delicate fragrance of violets escaping from the floor inlaid with sandal-wood at once leads the beholder into the time of the powdered, Rococo. One may only observe the sofa (itself a masterpiece), the arm-chairs and the foot stools of which the white satin coverings display in relief embroidery (Bornhauser, Munich) small, magnificent landscapes, pastoral idyls, parrots playing (in different colours), little boys begging, and flower baskets. The hangings are of satin with wonderful silk embroideries. The arrangement of pilasters divides the room into doors, windows, mirrors and four large panels.

Exceedingly pretty are the bronze ornaments in the doors. The allegorical paintings in the panels are richly coloured sketches upon canvas, and were destined to be executed in porcelain. The pier-glass-table with vases and girandoles, the clock, the chandelier, the mirror frames and the brackets at the pillars are beautiful productions of Dresden China and give to the chamber a delicate hue. The fire-place comes from Brèche and is of Tunis marble.

The gaming table, a creation of the cabinet-maker Pössenbacher (Munich), consists of rosewood with bronze ornaments and shows on its broad surface artistically inlaid paintings in porcelain; the allegorical ceiling painting (an original composition by Munsch, Munich) represents "Light". The two charmingly-framed pictures above the doors treat in their lively representation and masterly technique of colour, of:

"A Hunt under Louis XV" and "A Theatrical Performance".

Especially pretty is the last in spite of the little space and figures: The King in the middle box and the public in the pit follow with much attention the love scene that is being performed on the stage.

The panels of both of the doors, of which the marble framework is richly adorned with gold ornamentation, contain each four magnificently coloured porcelain paintings, the four seasons and four allegorical figures — one of which in a medallion picture, representing History, contains the only portrait of King Louis II to be found in the castle.

A slight touch of the past breezes over this delightful chamber, of which the tasteful and noble brilliancy and the delicately executed ornamentation are but too little admired.

6*

Also in the

Dining room

that comes next, Dresden China playes a conspicuous part in the decoration. Once more this room exhibits the royal purple with gold as the predominant tone. Yet the grave and gorgeous pomp which is displayed yonder in the state bedroom, in the strict classical arrangement and in the architecture of the Italian High-Renaissance style, is happily avoided here in this room, where comfort is the primary object sought for. It is fitted up with a fine artistic understanding in beautiful and pretty shapes.

The rounded tops of the windows, the doors and the fire-places with the gigantic mirrors above them give to the architecture of this chamber an appearance of rich variety. Wood and plaster sculptures form magnificent frames for the paintings over the doors.

Little Cupids in lovely playful attitudes top the medallions over the windows, doors and head-pieces of the mirrors which are adorned with festoons.

From the purple of the panels between the doors, mirrors and windows, there beam forth from gilded wood carvings the emblems of gastronomical enjoyment, still-life objects drawn from hunting and fishing. The magnificently adorned arched wedges contain artistic representations from the life of Psyche by Professor Widnmann.

In wonderful busts upon the pier-glass tables and above the door panels appear Louis XV and the ladies who played a conspicuous part in his life's destiny: Duchess Ventimille, Countess Maily, Duchess of Chateauroux and Marchioness de Pompadour.

The two fire-places from Brèche de Vara support a clock and vases of Meissen porcelain. The narrow compartments between the fire-places and the door leading to the Oval Salon are inlaid with mirrors and produce together with the large mirrors a wonderful effect of perspective enlargement and extension.

The four tables standing along the side-walls show pictures of remarkable historical interest, executed upon Sèvres-porcelain by Grünwedel of Munich after the King's own directions. They carry the beholder into the midst of the splendid Court-life of Versailles and represent:

"A Fancy Ball in the Gallery of Mirrors at Versailles",
"A Court Ball at Versailles", "A Theatrical Scene with a

THE DINING ROOM

Ballet in Versailles" (especially remarkable for the charming
Rococo style of the architecture), "The Marriage-Ceremony of the
Dauphin (Louis XVI) in the chapel of the Castle at Versailles".

In the midst of the room, which is of an oval form, stands the fabled "Tischlein deck Dich" (little table cover thyself) as it is designated in all descriptions of it. It is expressive of the desire for sensation in our time, to find something uncommon in it, when every better-class household contains an elevator and every hotel a lift. Magnificent gold embroideries upon the red damask of the table-cloth, the arm-chairs, foot-stools and the hangings again charm the eye.

An extremely delicate nosegay of admirable beauty made of Meissen porcelain and of the highest artistic perfection stands upon the table.

The chandelier hanging from the ceiling with 108 candles is unparalleled in loveliness and delicacy; it consists of thousands of flowers in porcelain and gives to the chamber its peculiar character.

All the splendour of this room flooded with the bright daylight only received its full effect when the brightness of the candles was reflected in the mirrors and the magic gleam of light was flowing in from the adjacent rooms and the purple and gold were still more vivified.

In its interior decoration the dining room is in the style of Louis XV and the lustre of the porcelain is a fashion created by Augustus the Strong.

One step over the threshhold leads us abruptly back into the glittering magnificence of the Renaissance of Versailles, into the

Little Gallery.

This charming hall in violet and gold might almost be taken for a miniature edition of the great gallery, if it were not for the diversity of the pictorial and plastic ornamentation which contains no allusion whatever to French royalty.

The small gallery, resembling the staircase in richness and brilliancy of colour, contains only representations of mythological and allegorical subjects: Two small corner-rooms border the gallery on the east and west. Charming is the stylish arrangement of pillars and the coating of the walls with their magnificent stucco-work; but the principal charm of the whole lies in the gigantic plate-glass windows opposite the rounded tops of the windows, which divide the walls into broad panels inlaid with panes of plate-glass.

The wall decoration here also consists of stucco marble most perfectly wrought. Above the principal frieze richly adorned with gilded ornaments representing figures, we see the following:

"Wisdom, Peace, Justice, Heroic Virtue, History, Rhetoric and Perfection".

THE LITTLE GALLERY.

The ceiling forms a barrel vault, the architectural adornment of which consists of medallions and festoons. The paintings are happy creations by Rogge.

The following paintings stand out effectively from the beautiful gilded ornamentation, in their fresh brightness of colour. They represent:

"Apollo rewarding the Sciences and Arts", "Minerva crowning the Genius", "Divine Providence and Discretion with their symbols", „Prudence with its symbols", "Mercury as the most prudent of the Gods".

The benches and curtains of the corner-rooms are executed in lilac and gold; five magnificent crystal chandeliers with 36 candles each, wall brackets in front of the windows above the pier glass tables and girandoles serve for the fairy-like illumination of this gorgeous hall. Four magnificent figures in the niches represent the four parts of the Earth. The four negro figures on both sides of the entrance speak of the many-sided artistic tastes of the Royal Builder. They carry girandoles, and seem to criticise severely and with satirical mockery the foibles of many a petty sovereign of past centuries in the life at Versailles.

The floor of the gallery is inlaid with rose wood. Both of the corner-rooms of this gallery, shimmering in its comfortable beauty, contain as a further magnificent adornment the following ceiling paintings:

In the western corner Pavilion is "The heaven-assaulting Titan Prometheus carrying off the beneficial fire".

And in the eastern corner Pavilion:

"Vulcan, creating Pandora", by Munsch.

It appears to be intentional, that the interior decoration of the apartments in their finished state begins and ends with representations of the cheerful contemplation of the life of antiquity and of the world of the old gods.

The loveliness and cheerful splendour of the Little Gallery close the long suite of pompous apartments which we have been seeing.

Their inspection transports the visitor from amazing astonishment at the sublime magnificence to a feeling of relief, when the folding doors of the last-mentioned halls are opened.

To artists the castle of Herrenchiemsee offers in every detail of its interior equipment — known to everybody by the hundreds of excellent photographic views — a rich source for study of the newly-created models of a style, which in our days has again begun its victorious career through the civilised world.

In the preceding description all attempt to give an idea of the cost of everything has been desisted from. How can those sums mentioned in many guide-books give any idea of the immense artistic value of the articles, which at King Louis II 's command were collected in these rooms?

Our eyes are still wandering in raptures round the graceful brilliancy of the Little Gallery, overflooded by the sunlight penetrating the thick white hangings. Still are we looking down upon the broad ranges of trees bordering the avenue leading down to the lake, through which in purest azure blue its waters are gleaming, when the official opens the high, beautifully carved and gilded folding-door and — disenchanted we find ourselves (immediately after all this splendour) in the midst of the brick works of the unfinished construction.

In the second staircase, called the Prince's Staircase, the attentive beholder sees that all the marble magnificence with which walls, pillars and pilasters are invested, is artificial; here the brick masonry shows in prosaic nakedness every detail, which yonder charms the eye in its disguised form.

To separately conducted parties the unfinished rooms are also shown, where the only splendour exhibited lies in the pompous names, perpetuated upon wooden boards, uncompleted now for all time.

Once more, before the visitor leaves the Royal Castle, its magic beauty is displayed in the last finished space. Passing the machinery of the dining room table we arrive at the

Bath Chamber.

The swimming tank is made of iron and lined with marble; the circular walls with their red glowing illumination, display representations from the life of Venus.

"The Birth of Venus from the Foam of the Waves", "The Toilet of Venus", Dolphins, Nereids and Tritons are playing merrily on the rocky sea-coast; the ceiling painting shows: "Venus and Vulcan" by the historical painter Weiser (after Boucher).

The very realistic wall paintings have suffered considerably. The wall is also adorned with a pretty chandelier of Venetian glass. Renewed admiration is for the last time forced upon the visitor at the opening of the door to the

Bath Dressing-Room.

This apartment, extending beyond the field of vision, deceives even the most practised eye. The isochromic style of the decoration has created here a magnificent and bewildering picture. It seems as if once again the whole magic charm of everything that had been seen in the state rooms was to be summed up in this chamber.

The style is in the most charming Rococo, which by the cunningly executed arrangement of mirrors calls back to one's mind the sports of that epoch.

THE BATH.

The decorative style in conjunction with the richness in mirrors was meant to transpose a piece of nature into the interior of the castle — a labyrinth with straight and winding arcades. The many-shaped wall decoration, carved in wood, shows in glittering gilding a park, over-flooded by the glowing splendour of the evening sun.

Towards every side, wherever the eye turns, the boundless perspective deceives with regard to the extension of the room.

Standing in a niche and looking to the right and left, the arboured walk, formed by the mirrors standing opposite, extends in infinite length; whilst the mirrors, on both sides of the way out, show the arcade in a curved line.

The ceiling painting above the lovely ornamented frieze "The Water" presents itself full of charm and infinitely

THE BATH DRESSING ROOM.

repeated in the mirrors. It is an original composition by Geiser. The two pictures with beautiful frames above the door represent:

"Diana" and "Venus after the Bath", copies after Boucher by Geiger.

The wonderful sofa in the niche of the back wall and the foot stools are covered with rose silk and charmingly embroidered with silver. A chandelier is suspended in the midst of the room and a little one also above the sofa;

girandoles upon the pier-glass-tables in front of the mirrors by the side walls complete the enrapturing brilliancy of this chamber, to which the festoons above the mirrors and the birds sitting between the foliage bestow a particulary lively and delightful character.

It is with reluctance that we leave this chamber together with the two preceding, the Dressing Room and the Oval Salon, showing the whole loveliness of the Rococo in its sweet charm and glorified by the long-extinct and courtly splendour of the past century.

Hastily our thoughts are gliding back to the sublime magnificence of the Chambre de Parade, the sunny splendour of the Gallery of Mirrors and the pomp of the remaining apartments.

Only a few years were allowed to the king to rejoice in his wonderful creation, to enjoy the fairy-like splendour, the magic charm of his state-rooms and to dream away such hours as must have appeared to him bright rays in the midst of his restless life, over which the dark shadows of his doom only broke too soon.

The Castle of Herrenchiemsee will remain still in remote times the destination of thousands of joyful tourists; the artist, the industrial tradesman will gratefully praise the gifted monarch with enthusiastic words, having received anew stimulation to activity and new creative impulse; they will appreciate his highly developed artistic taste, which revived in new and lovely forms the art of a time long since vanished. The king deserves the gratitude of future ages as being the promoter of a closer connection between the industrial and the plastic arts.

The laying out of the gardens at Herrenchiemsee was faithful to the model at Versailles. The chief part of the general composition was in the style made famous in Europe by the horticulturist of the Sun-King, Le Notre.

According to the ingenious ideas of the same the garden had to form the transition between the stony mass of the building and the open nature, and to serve as an enlargement to the palace.

The broad terrace — the Parterre d'eau — arranged by Le Notre, is also found here in front of the castle. Beneath and connected by a flight of steps stretches the Grand Parterre, extending in rectangular form down to the lake, and animated at the beginning with fountains and statues in the midst of magnificently decorated lawns and flower-beds.

Broad walks extend to the right and left bordered with trellis work and ranges of trees. The gorgeous Apollo basin was made to form an agreeable point of rest for the eye, before the sight lost itself in the distance.

The canal going out into the lake and bordered with trellis work was meant to extend this perspective. The charming view from the porch of the castle upon the silvery glittering surface of the lake, the green hills covered with wood on the western bank of the Chiemsee and the mountains rising up behind them afford to the eye a most delightful picture.

The very ideal of a pleasure-ground such as the one designed by Le Notre's master hand presents itself here to the visitor. The royal superintendent of horticultural works von Effner has in an ingenious manner compressed into a narrow space the whole grandeur of the pleasure grounds at Versailles. The financial crisis interfered here with the completion of everything as we have seen it did inside the castle as well.

The chief attention in the immense water-parterre is claimed by the two large fountains. In the midst of two gigantic basins of 500 square meters rise groups of rocks 51 feet in height, which awake the highest interest with their allegorical representations and the human figures of more than life size and lovely Cupids along the edges of the basins.

The two fountains resemble the North and South Parterres at Versailles. A winged genius or Pegasus (without wings) surmounts the group of rocks in the North Basin, which is called the Fountain of Pegasus. Pegasus is depicted galloping towards heaven and announcing his glory; others, vainly struggling against Fate, throw themselves down upon the sharp rocks at the foot of which Clio (Destiny) on a Sphinx is marking the names of the victors.

The sculptor Maison was responsible for the creation of this group. Upon the rocks in the South Basin (called the Fountain of Fortune), that divinity sits enthroned, her head garlanded with flowers. She is surrounded by groups of little boys at play, whilst dolphins sport about round the rocky base. This group, created by the sculptor Rümann, whilst forming a strange contrast with the scene depicted in the Basin facing it, yet enchants us by its grace and fulness of life.

In the corners of the water-parterre looking towards the west are little basins similar to the Fountain of Diana and

Le Point du jour at Versailles. Each of these smaller basins consists in its turn of an upper and a lower basin in marble. Upon the wall (also of marble) separating the two, we observe groups of animals about to fight with one another. In front of each stand 2 statues in white marble on pedestals of grey marble. The North Basin contains a fine example of the artistic talent of Hauptmann the sculptor in the magnificent statues of Diana and Venus; the latter of whom is receiving from Love an arrow of gold; as well as in the savage groups representing: "A Lion subduing a Wolf"; "A Lion with a defeated wild Boar". We remark the talent of the master equally in the statues representing "Flora" and "Fountain" in marble at the South Basin, as well as in the following animal groups: "A Leopard overcoming a Bear", "A Dog with a Stag".

The art of the gardiner, by planting flourishing bays with the richest variety of colours, has succeeded in compensating us for the want of the fountains, originally intended to throw to the heavens vast radiating jets of water. We feel the want of them even less, because the grey figures about the fountains are in such complete harmony with the colour of the rocks. On the other hand one cannot help lamenting the want of the jets of water for the Fountain of Latona, where, from the parterre, a staircase leads up consisting of 22 steps. (At Versailles the number is 103).

Five great steps in marble of different colours surround the enormous basin. On the four lower stages are 72 figures representing frogs, gilded and sparkling; as well as lizards and all sorts of monsters one finds in the waters, as well as men changing into frogs. But the chief ornament of this basin is formed by the figure on the highest step. This figure represents:

Latona drawing towards her and protecting her children Apollo and Diana.

Hauptmann, the sculptor has executed this group — a master-piece of modern sculpture — in the finest white marble. The additional charm it would have had from the sparkling jets of water is lost for ever like that of the fountains on the Parterre. "The waters were fizzling and whistling from the mouths of the monsters in a vast circle round and above Latona, so that this splendid statue seemed to be hidden in a watery veil, but the goddess was not touched by it. She only seemed to emerge from it as another victory of the Beautiful in art." This statue is best when viewed from the north. It rises radiant in whiteness. Behind one perceives the dark and tranquil forest, whilst further away still appears the zig-zag summits of the Kampenwand glistening against the blue sky.

The vast exterior of the Castle stretches out once again in mournful silence before the spectator. It seems to be played round by the rays of the sun and lulled to sleep by the murmur of the forests and the perfume of flowers borne by zephyrs from the mountain slopes. A purple twilight glimmer plays round the beaming figures on the fountains, and is reflected in the high windows of the castle, which throw their light out upon the broad surface of the lake.

What peace and tranquillity reign in this mysterious country, where one is far removed from the noise and bustle of the town!

Everyone quitting Chiemsee on a summer's evening when the sun is sinking to rest, and bidding farewell to this spot of earth so full of the charm given to it by a distant past, will return with a light heart to the work that lies before him, and will find less irksome the turmoil and stress of the life of to-day.

THE END.

RESTAURANT

ON THE

LADYS ISLE

HOT MEALS AT ANY TIMES OF THE DAY.

Specialities:

Chiemsee Fish.

Roasted Chicken. //// ////

Excellent beer
from the Royal Castle Brewery
of Herren-Chiemsee. ⚮⚮⚮⚮⚮

**Pure wine on draught
and in bottles.** ⚮⚮⚮⚮

Post and Telephone.

The Chiemsee.

Neuschwanstein.

Preface.

The most romantic of all the castles built by Ludwig II. of Bavaria is undoubtedly that of Neuschwanstein.

This building stands on the ancient boundary line between Bavaria, Tyrol and Swabia, far distant from the island castle of Herrenchiemsee, that "royal unfinished dream of gigantic proportions."

Here in Schwangau King Ludwig, from the golden days of childhood until his unhappy end, spent his life, and this fact adds much to the interest and romance already interwoven round this spot by legend, poetry and history.

In every description of Hohenschwangau and Neuschwanstein the unparalleled beauty of their situations, amid the solitude of mountain and forest country, is mentioned with rapture and enthusiasm.

The brilliant memories of these noble mansions cling like a halo round their walls and nothing, not even the empty prose of our present age, can ever alter or detract from the romance by which they are surrounded.

The Castle of Neuschwanstein arose out of the ruins of Castle Vorderschwangau.

It is built in the style of the 12th century and with its gables, turrets and pinnacles, towers up from the mighty Tegelfelsen proudly into the air.

The beauty of its site and the pomp and grandeur of its interior decorations strike all who see it with admiration, and it is this pomp and the imposing building itself, which reflect the romantic age of chivalry and minnesingers.

"Powerful and defiant outwardly,
"Sweet, lovely and sublime within."

If, in the Castle of Linderhof and in the enormous buildings of Herrenchiemsee, the German visitor is struck with pained astonishment at seeing that the fundamental idea was to glorify the great monarchic age in France, he must first completely divest himself of his patriotic feelings before being able to admire with an unprejudiced mind the wonderfully productive power of industry and art in harmonious union.

Here, on the contrary, in this Castle of Neuschwanstein, everything is purely German. It recalls before our eyes a mighty epoch of German history, and set in the serious frame of that period it stands as a "monumentum aere perennius" to German thought, habits and customs.

As in all the buildings erected by King Ludwig, so in Neuschwanstein, fine art and applied art strive together for the palm, and it is difficult, well nigh impossible, to decide to which of the two it should be awarded.

Art was offered a large field in the entirely original decoration of the walls in the rooms and halls with scenes taken from the old German legends. These, after years of industrious work, were converted by Munich artists into masterpieces of art.

Here in Neuschwanstein, the importance of applied art seems to be less prominent than at Linderhof and Herrenchiemsee. And yet it is just this visible, tasteful and harmonious subordination of applied art to the brilliant accomplishments of fine art, which forces, not only the laity, but also the expert, to feelings of astonished admiration at the combined productions of both branches.

A description of the Castle of Hohenschwangau (which owes its present form to the ideal romantic taste of King Max II. of Bavaria) seems at first sight out of place in this book, which treats mainly of the castles erected by Ludwig II. These two buildings, however, are so inseparably united the one with the other, that it becomes a duty for him, who is endeavouring to do full justice to King Ludwig's artistic taste, to enter into the impulses and youthful impressions received within the walls of Hohenschwangau, which led eventually to the carrying out of the plan for building the stately royal castle high up on the summits of the Tegelfelsen.

In one respect, at least, all these castles built by King Ludwig bear resemblance to each other and that is in the wonderful natural beauty of their positions and surroundings. In this neighbourhood of Schwangau, even the most indifferent of natures must be struck and impressed by the majestic splendour of the lofty mountains, the deep blue of the alpine lakes, peeping out from their frame of dark forest trees, and the luxuriant, brilliant green of wood and meadow.

A wonderful peacefulness seems to reign over the entire country.

A few steps from the frequented road leading to the castles bring the wanderer within sight of numberless winding paths. Following any one of these, he will soon find himself amid the seclusion of mountain and forest, the quiet and calm of which can hardly fail to have a beneficial effect.

Here he is enthralled by the indescribable charm which the thousand gone-by eventful years have cast over this place, poetry and legend weave brilliant, bright-hued pictures in the peaceful idyll—and the impressions here received, do not die away when mountain and lake are no longer visible, the mysterious whisperings of the forest trees no longer audible —or the wild rushing sounds of the mountain streams, as they hurry on their downward course, are no longer ringing in his ears but last—through long, long years—through a whole lifetime—when after bidding a reluctant farewell to this beauteous spot, the wanderer returns once more to the routine of ordinary, every-day life.

Routes by which to reach the castles.

The enormous rush of visitors to the Castle of Herrenchiemsee is due, to a great extent, to the convenient railway communication with Munich. It is only a short two hours run from here, and after a few hours, travellers are enabled to continue their journey in whichever direction they please.

In visiting the Royal Castles in the Schwangau, the modern up-to-date rage for rapid travelling must content itself with a greater expenditure of time, for even by the express, the shortest route takes four hours, that is to say four hours there and back from Munich. And on all other lines, travellers are dependent on hired carriages. The most practical and convenient means of connecting the visit to the Schwangau Castles with that of Linderhof is to make use of the official carriage connection, supplied by the local Railway Company, which plies twice daily between Füssen and Oberhof.

The General Direction of the State Railway has met the wishes of the travelling public in the most obliging manner by the issue of circular tickets. Munich (Central Railway Station)—Füssen and Oberau—Munich. The price of the 2nd class ticket is 12 Marks, and of the 3rd class 7 Marks 30 Pfennigs. This includes the use of the quick train without additional payment.

The charms of the country are as numerous as the routes leading to it.

That already mentioned, the line Munich—Füssen, is the most convenient and shortest of all these routes. The distance covers 132 kilometers viâ Buchloe, Kaufbeuren and Biessenhofen, from here the branch line leads to Oberdorf and Füssen. Quick trains do not stop at Biessenhofen.

Trains must be changed at Kaufbeuren, from whence direct local trains run to Füssen.

Tourists travelling from Munich across the undulating Bavarian plateau to Buchloe, are charmed by the lovely panorama which meets their eyes by the station of Grafrath. The dark forest stretches out to the shores of the glittering Ammersee, and the Karwendel, Wetterstein, Zugspitz, Plansee and Lechtalberg form a glorious mountain background. Crossing the river Lech, on the left the gables and towers of the old town of Landsberg become visible.

On the way from Buchloe to Kaufbeuren, the mountains become gradually more and more distinct and prominent. The Zugspitz, Hochplatte, Aggenstein and Säuling forming a most imposing spectacle.

The side-line, which branches off at the station of Biessenhofen, runs through the Wertach valley, which is pretty, but the views to be obtained on the journey from Oberdorf to Füssen are far more imposing. On the Watershed between Lech and Wertach a grand sight meets the eye of the alpine chain of Edelsberg, Alpspitz and Falkenstein across to the Zugspitz. The following mountains standing out distinctly in the picturesque scene: the Aggenstein, Schlicke, Säuling and Hochplatte.

The train passing along by the side of the Hopfensee, suddenly brings the traveller within sight of a lovely picture. High up on the mountains the white building of Castle Neuschwanstein becomes visible and to the right of this, the old Castle of Füssen.

Linderhof can be reached from the stations of Oberau or Oberammergau, either on foot through the Ammerwald across the Jägersteig and Blöckenau direct to Neuschwanstein, or by carriage through the Ammerwald along the shores of the Plansee to Reutte. Here this way divides, walkers going viâ Pflach across the Kniepass on to the Fürstenstrasse to the "Schluxenwirt", und then through lovely woods along the shores of the Alpsee to the village of Hohenschwangau, the other road leading viâ Pinswang to Füssen.

A third route, which however since the opening of the local railway to Füssen and Garmisch, is only little used, leads from the station of Peissenberg, viâ Peiting, Steingaden and Trauchgau, past the pretty Bannwald lake at the foot of the mountains and the village of Schwangau to Füssen or Hohenschwangau. Visitors arriving from Switzerland can travel from Kempten to Pfronten by the local trains. There they will find Post and Diligence in waiting to convey them on to Füssen (14 kilometers) and Hohenschwangau (20 kilometers).

This route is much frequented, as it not only abounds in views of great and varied beauty, but also because it tends to acquaint the visitor with the more distant neighbourhood of Füssen and Hohenschwangau.

For the sake of completeness, we will still make mention of the route from Innsbruck on the Arlberg line to Imst or Telfs, and from there with the Post viâ Nassereit to Reutte and Füssen, or from Nassereit across the grand Fernpass to Lermoos, Ehrwald and Griesen to the Plansee and Reutte.

This way leads through some of the most beautiful alpine scenery, and forms a fitting entrance to the Schwangau, which is undoubtedly one of the most charming and beautiful spots in the German Alps.

FÜSSEN WITH THE SÄULING. Drawing by H. Grabensee.

Schwangau.

The tourist, after a long drive, descending from his carriage at Füssen, is greeted by a scene of charming beauty and splendour.

A few steps from the station, which is surrounded by buildings of a modern type, lead to the town. The gabled houses, surmounted by the church towers, have an almost southern appearance, and far above, enthroned on its high rocky seat, crowning and commanding, as it were, the town beneath, is the Castle of Füssen.

This place, situated at the entrance of the pass of the Julian Alps and close to the beautiful, wildly romantic rapids was called at the time of the Romans "Jauces Julias." Here the Lech breaks madly through the mighty rocks, which look as if they would fain hold the waters back, and prevent them from forming a wide open stream in the plain beyond.

Destroyed by the great migration of people, Füssen was rebuilt, and here St. Magnus, the Apostle of Algäus, erected a monastry. The St. Magnus Church, which was restored in the 18th century by Jacob Herkomer and rebuilt in charming Rococo style, contains in the Byzantine-norman crypt under the High Altar the relics of the Holy Magnus; the adjoining Chapel of St. Anna, otherwise called the "Freyberg Chapel" contains as its most precious ornament a highly interesting painting, entitled the "Totentanz" or "Dance of Death" by Jacob Hiebeler 1610, after Holbein.

One of the chief ornaments of the town is the monument to the Prince Regent Luitpold of Bavaria, which represents the Prince attired in the simple garb of a citizen; medallion pictures of the two Kings, Max II. and Ludwig II. of Bavaria, bear testimony to the gratitude felt by the inhabitants of Füssen toward the reigning house.

The castle with its four towers occupies a position high above the town; it was erected by the Bishops of Augsburg, and is an imposing building.

Here it was that the Emperor Maximilian, when visiting Füssen for the purpose of heron-hawking, constantly took up his abode, and its apartments witnessed the end of the short, fateful dream of the Emperor Karl VII., when in the year 1745 peace was concluded between Austria and Bavaria.

A beautiful view is to be had from the Storchenturm (Stork Tower) of the castle, not only of the glorious highland world alone, but also of the plain beneath and valley of the Lech. This landscape, so rich in variety and unspeakable beauty, charms the beholder and makes his first impression to be one of never-to-be-forgotten pleasure and delight.

The entire neighbourhood of Füssen is rich in beautiful scenery. Hardly a path but leads to some point from whence a glorious view may be obtained. This fact enables one to fully comprehend the preference which King Ludwig II., that ardent lover of the alpine world, felt and showed all his life long, for the Schwangau.

Towering above the beautifully wooded mountain foreground the grim, rocky summits of the Tyrolese ranges gaze down at the little town of Füssen and at the plain beneath with its sprinkling of sparkling lakes and its bordering range of hills. Extensive forests form the frame-work of this wonderfully charming picture, the beauties of which are so manifold, that it is impossible to mention them all. We choose out from others, the walk leading to the "Magnustritt"—a legendary footprint of the Saint; where, from a high rocky platform, according to one account, St. Magnus cast the burning brand into the robber castle of Rosshaupten, whereas another account accredits him with having sprung from this spot over the terrible rocky ravine in order to escape from the savage forest animals which were pursuing him. The view from the iron bridge "König Max Steg" at the roaring waters of the Lech passing over the rapids in the narrow ravine beneath, is grand and romantic beyond description.

A charming walk is through a pretty valley to the neat little village of Faulenbach, and then on to the dreamy looking Alat Lake and the little town of Vils (this latter situated in Tyrol) or along the Kobelweg across the Scharte to Lände, from this spot an extensive view is to had of the Lech valley and the following mountains of Tyrol: the Gern and Köllespitze, Thaneller, Schlicke, Vilserkogel, Rossberg and Aggenstein.

Here we only make mention of the charming and beautiful views to be obtained on the road from Reutte to Füssen, as it is by this route that most of the visitors to the castle leave Schwangau in order to proceed, either by carriage or on foot, to Linderhof.

Amongst the numerous mountain excursions, which can be made either in the next vicinity of Füssen or from a greater distance, we recommend the excursion to the Falkenstein.

Three roads lead to this summit from Füssen in three hours. The most beautiful of these three ways is undoubtedly that through the forest, which leads from the Alat Lake across the Saloberalpe (glorious view, particularly of the Zugspitze) to Zirngrate and from thence by a newly laid out path to the picturesque ruin of Castle Falkenstein.

Here in former times stood the castle of the Bishops of Augsburg. This, in the rough days when "might was right" not unfrequently served them as a place of safety and refuge; towards the end of the Thirty Years War, it, as well as the neighbouring castles of Eisenburg and Hohenfrevberg, was burnt down—only the ruins remain to bear witness to the glories of chivalric life in the middle ages.

Creepers cover the walls; a lovely view is to be obtained from the windows of the green valley beneath, sown as it were, with numberless villages and hamlets, in and out of which winds like a glittering serpent, the silver stream of the Lech; beyond stands the royal Castle of Neuschwanstein

ALATSEE NEAR FÜSSEN.

and then towards the south are the idyllic valleys of Pfronten. Ach and Vils. A mighty circle of mountain giants gazes down in solemn carnestness at the witnesses of an age long since past.

As at Neuschwanstein, the brilliantly coloured, almost fairy-like picture-decorated Hall conjures up before our eyes the Legend of Parzival, so it had been the intention of King Ludwig II to erect on the precipitous, rocky summits of Falkenstein, a „Montsalvat" in honour of the Holy Grail. This was te have been in the Gothic Style and ornamented with mosaic work, and from a purely artistic point of view, it is much to be deplored that this building (a model of which by Oberbaurat Max Schulze of Regensburg, is set up in the Castle of Neuschwanstein) was never carried out. Like to an eagle's eyrie, this was to have grown out of the rocks, the summits of which hang over a precipice of terrific depth and steepness. Like the castles of the robber knights, it wat to occupy a very limited space. The castle buildings grouped round the "Burgfried" (or inner keep), the entire construction in the picturesque charm of numberless powerful towers, artistically ornamented with high gables, graceful alcoves, threatening pinnacles and loopholes, and with one entrance, well guarded and defended, on the east. This building — the interior fitted up with true royal luxury and pomp — would have occupied a more isolated position than Neuschwanstein itself, but like it, it would have presented to the world an expressive picture of long past centuries.

The only reminder of the intended structure that remains intact is the beautiful winding Königstrasse leading up the mountain side. The high pressure water supply also dates from this time. A summer restaurant on the top of the Falkenstein forms a pleasant resting place for the numberless tourists who are attracted to this spot.

The first really comprehensive view of Schwangau is to be obtained from Mt. Calvary. This summit, on which are erected the Three Crosses (distinctly visible from a considerable distance) can be easily reached in 45 minutes from Füssen.

The road to it leads from the station up through the town, passing the Spitalkirche (Hospital Church) to the Lechbrücke. Even from here, the mountains present a beautiful view, a view, which from the summit of Mt. Calvary, becomes an extensive and glorious panorama.

Far beneath in the foreground, are the town and Castle of Füssen, the broad stream of the river Lech hurrying on

RUINS OF FALKENSTEIN.

with its green waters into the wide open plain beyond, endless church towers and villages, and the three lakes, Bannwaldsee, Hopfensee and Weissensee, sparkling like ore in the rosy light of the morning sun.

The view on the east and south is of overwhelming beauty — in the valley beneath, the green Schwansee lies glistening in the rays of the sun — above it, towering over the tops of the high forest trees, is the Castle of Hohenschwangau, with its turrets and gables, and higher still — in the background — the enormous buildings of Castle Neuschwanstein in solitary and stately beauty — the whole surrounded by mighty mountains and forming a picture of enthralling splendour.

The mountains are all, more or less, of grotesque formation. The Tegelberg, Straussberg, Pilgramschrofen, and the Säuling, silver gray, concealing in the folds of their rocky garments sparkling lines of snow, whilst beneath, in wood and meadow, the May beauty of an alpine spring has already become apparent. Deep blue, steel green, the summits of the mountains are faithfully represented in the clear waters of the Schwansee, no breath of wind ruffles its surface, no rough sound of human life destroys the peacefulness of the Sunday morning, only from Füssen ascends now and again the melodious music of the church bells.

On the south, rising above the wooded ridges of the Schwarzenberg, the long crest of the Schlicke, Vilserkofel, Rossberg, the three pointed Aggenstein, the Breitenberg, Edelspitze and Alpspitze become visible.

A glance back at the wide valley, through which the river Lech is wending its way, and at the Vilstal, Weisshaus, and the former free city of Vils will amply repay the trouble.

A little path from Mount Calvary conducts through a quiet, peaceful, wooded valley past a quarry to a slight elevation, from which a lovely glimpse is to be had of the noisy Lech Fall, and from there to the prettiest of all the ways leading to Hohenschwangau. This path is called the "Alpenrosenweg", (lucus a non lucendo), from the formerly luxuriant growth of the Alpine Rose — this plant, unfortunately, has long since fallen a prey to the collecting rage of the travelling public.

The Alpenrosenweg begins, branching off from the Füssen — Reutte road, at the much frequented "Weisshaus" (situated in Tyrol) and continues along the incline of the

FÜSSEN FROM MT. CALVARY.

wooded Schwarzberg, offering frequent glimpses of great beauty of the country beyond.

A charming walk may be taken along this road, so carefully kept by the civil authorities, in the pleasant shade of the dusky firs past a group of rocks on to the Fürstenstrasse and from thence, by the side of the Alpsee, to Hohenschwangau.

The view from the Alpenrosenweg of the blue glimmering surface of the Schwansee is strikingly beautiful.

A second equally delightful road, the "Kienbergweg" leads from Füssen, gradually ascending through the forest to the hollow between Kienberg and Kalvarienberg. The road then crosses the Fürstenstrasse, (which leads through the park) continues, in deep shade, along the west bank of the Schwansee, and in zigzag up the Fischersteig to the Alpenrosenweg.

A third way from Füssen to Hohenschwangau leads along the road past the Lech Fall to the Bavarian Custom House Schwarzbrücke. Here the Königstrasse branches off to the left into the Royal Park, passes over a hilly ridge between Schwarzenberg and Kalvarienberg, and brings one suddenly in view of the buildings of Neuschwanstein. Directly afterwards, on the right hand side, far above the tops of the trees, appears the Castle of Hohenschwangau. Passing the Schwansee, the Königstrasse joins the direct road leading from Füssen to Hohenschwangau. Whoever coming from Reutte leaves the high road at the Ulrichsbrücke and takes the easternly direction towards Pinswang, going on to the "Schluxenwirt" (inn) will experience great satisfaction at the route he has chosen and thoroughly enjoy the drive or walk, as the case may be.

One can rest, provided with good and ample refreshment, very comfortably in the little garden belonging to the "Schluxenwirt." The Gernspitze, the Schlicke and the Rote Wand stand out in sublime beauty in the sultry heat of the sun, towards the south the Säuling appears, rising up over the heads of the forest trees enveloped in a pale gray mist. All around is the idyllic valley of meadows filled with busy life and the sweet sound of the bells of the grazing cattle. From a slight eminence a view can be obtained of the silver gray rocks of the Planseeberg, the wooded Tauernkopf, Zingerstein and Jochberg, the green Mähberg, the Gartnerwand and, as mighty commander, as it were, over all this confusion of mountain peaks, domes and ridges, the Thanellerspitze, which stands out more prominently on account of its wonderfully beautiful formation, than any of the others.

The capitally laid-out Fürstenstrasse winds up the side of the mountains with a charming view of the wide spreading Lech valley and its chief summit, the Passhöhe (883 meters = about 2943 ft), then crossing the frontier, it leads into a lovely beechwood in which the dark green waters of the Alpsee soon become visible. A lovely view is to be seen from the upper path, which has branched off from the road, of the lake surrounded by wooded mountains and the great towering Säuling, which, with its jagged companion, the Pilgerschrofen, are faithfully reflected with all their minutest details, in the unruffled waters of the lake.

The Alpenrosenweg soon joins the road, and the two ways now united, lead under the shadow of beautiful beeches to the village of Hohenschwangau.

How unspeakably delightful to wander on a summer's day under the shade of these trees, the air full of a cool, balmy sweetness! Beyond, the lake unruffled in the sultry midday sun and the summits of the mountains trembling in uncertain light, testifying to the heat without!

This neighbourhood is most suitable for a stay of longer duration. There is hardly any part of the Bavarian Alps which presents such a number of charming views as Hohenschwangau. For days and weeks the tourist can wander about in the peaceful woods and mountains. The beauty of springtime likens the country to a paradise, the air is full of nerve-strengthening, bracing qualities. He will be unceasingly greeted by fresh beauties. A picture already seen, surprises him by appearing before his eyes set in a new frame. Every hour of the day, every tone of light altering or intensifying its charm. The invigorating air of the woods is mingled with the sweet scent of the trees laden with blossoms and of the innumerable lilies of the valley which grow so luxuriantly all around.

Naturally the most frequented road is that which leads direct from Füssen to Hohenschwangau. This also has its charms, although not in such variety as those possessed by the routes already described.

At the Lechbrücke near Füssen, the road follows the right bank of the river towards the north. Wide spreading trees overhang the way and in the early morning hours, the countless dewdrops on the firs on the steep rising hills, when caught by the sun, glitter and shine like so many jewels.

2*

FÜSSEN FROM THE NORTH.

On the left, tossing and foaming in its stony bed, the wild mountain torrent rushes along, and one turns round with pleasure to look back at the pretty, picturesque view formed by the town of Füssen, surmounted by its castle worn gray with age, the windows of which are glittering in the rays of the bright sunshine.

Almost imperceptably the road enters the park grounds and one is greeted by the sweet scent of the trees and flowers.

History and tradition have combined to sanctify this spot. The first glimpse of the Castle of Neuschwanstein, looking down from its steep rocks, is hailed by every tourist with exclamations of delight. The situation of the Castle of Hohenschwangau, which on the hill to the right rises up over the tops of the beech trees and on whose highest gable stands the swan, the heraldic bird of the gau (or district), seems almost to suffer when comparing it with the site occupied by Neuschwanstein. But the beauties of the spot are not yet all visible. The lakes, in whose still surface the Castle of Hohenschwangau is depicted in all its proud beauty, are not yet in sight and the trickling of the fountains and the gentle mysterious whisperings in the summit of the mighty lime tree in the courtyard of the castle have not yet been heard, and, nevertheless, the spectator is moved to feelings of awe and admiration, feelings, which, in the apartments of Hohenschwangau and still more in the halls of Neuschwanstein, are intensified and deepened.

Every voice is raised in praise of the sublime sentiments displayed by the two Kings, Ludwig II. and Max II. of Bavaria, who created here these castles as monuments to old German history and tradition, which give so eloquently expression to the past of the Schwangau, a past so variable and rich.

Few of the German castles exhibit such a wealth of proud historical reminiscences and few are equally closely connected with the most important moments of German history as Hohenschwangau. The brilliancy and power, sorrow and distress of the German empire, the minnesingers and brave warriors, the enthusiasm for the crusades, and the new birth of German intellect, the humanitarian age, the misery and wretchedness of the Swedish war and the decline and fall of splendour—all these inspiring and sorrowful remembrances hang around these walls, which like those of a hundred other noble mansions, were consecrated to decay and ruin, and which, notwithstanding, arose again in fresh brilliancy and splendour out of oblivion and destruction.

The bright-hued beauty of their interior decorations reflect the histories of the Guelphs, the Hohenstaufen and the

HOHENSCHWANGAU FROM THE VILLAGE.

Schyren, of the German chivalric age and the rich folk lore of those days. And the atmosphere seems filled with a sad spectral sound, a bitter moaning for King Konradin, the last of the Hohenstaufen, and for King Ludwig II. of Bavaria.

The road leading to the pretty village of Hohenschwangau winds round the castle rocks, here it is joined by the road from Peissenberg; on the latter, a charming villa colony has sprung up in the last few years; the village of Hohenschwangau itself consists merely of a few smart coun-

Drawing by H. Grabensee.

try houses built by the road-side, some buildings belonging to the castle and the two well-known inns, "Zur Liesl" and "Zur Alpenrose", both occupying enviable and charming positions.

The view from the shady garden of the inn "Zur Alpenrose" of the adjoining Alpsee can never be forgotten. The lake stands out like a deep blue jewel set in a spring green frame of trees. The mountain peaks towering up behind the forest on the south, the Gernspitz, Köllespitz and Schlicke, are, with their precipitous inclines and sharp ridges, faithfully reflected in the smooth waters, over which swans, with snow white plumage, are gliding hither and thither. A dreamy and charming peacefulness lies over this spot, which at every advancing hour of the day unfolds some new and peculiar charm; in the morning the lake appears like a dull, dark green looking-glass, at noon, when the mountains are enveloped in sultry heat, it shines deep blue out of its surroundings of trees and the ripples sparkle and glitter like gold—and again, in the evening when the mountains are reddening under the kisses of the sinking sun, then the emerald waters reflect, in purple and rosy tints, the beauty of the Schwangau. And yet how dark and wild this same lake can appear, when on the Tannheimer mountains heavy thunder clouds collect, from out of which dart, every now and again, vivid flashes of light!

Snow-white, the Castle of Neuschwanstein stands out in bold relief from its dark back ground of forest trees and gray, grim rocks.

Piled on the summits of the Tegelfels, whose sides descend with startling precipitancy into the valley beneath, this majestic castle, with its powerful towers and turrets, might almost have been the work of Cyclopean hands.

Even in the face of nature, glorious as she here is, Neuschwanstein holds her own. And in the interior, where the beauties of pure architecture and decoration have vied with each other, this stone shrine of the German heroic age inspires the visitor with endless admiration and delight.

The charm of this lovely neighbourhood draws one more and more within its spell. The wide, slightly ascending Königstrasse is overshadowed by the spreading branches of lofty trees. Nothing, save the murmuring of the mountain streams flowing into the valley beneath, disturbs the perfect peacefulness of this secluded spot.

Suddenly a partial glimpse is caught of the enormous castle rising high above the branches of the forest trees—and—partial and imperfect as the view is, yet its beauty fills one with amazement. Two paths on the right lead—the one to a "look-out" called "Jugend" from which a lovely view is to be had—the other to the "Marienbrücke".

NEUSCHWANSTEIN.

Printed by Franz Humal, G. m. b. H. in Munich.

From Steinberger's "Royal Castles".

Castle of Neuschwanstein.

Another view of the castle is to be obtained from an inn standing on the left hand side of the road, yet this also gives no adequate idea of its vast dimensions.

The "Herrenbau" or lords' building, of the castle reaches up to an enormous height, yet is overtopped by the slender Hauptturm, or principal tower, on the north side of which is placed the enormous stone figure of St. George and the Dragon.

Above the inn, the wood on the left becomes less dense, the road follows the edge of the steep incline and a lovely and extensive view becomes visible of the gleaming course of the river Lech, of the Bannwald lake and of the thickly inhabited plain beneath.

A few steps farther on, a glance over the breastwall discloses a sight of the Pöllat Gorge, down into which the Pöllat river rushes and thunders, and from which the steep walls of the Tegel and Neudeck rocks arise. Gracefully, like a delicate web, the Marienbrücke spans the tremendous precipice.

On the right stands the imposing building of the royal castle. Now for the first time this edifice shows itself in all its beauty as described by R. Wagner.

NEUSCHWANSTEIN TOWARDS THE N. E

"Completed the immortal work;
"On mountain's summit the castle of the Gods,
"The beautous building displays itself in all its glory.'
And really, as if grown out of the rocks, from which the space was wrested after years of arduous work, and as if

destined for eternity, so stands this castle before our astonished eyes.

Great towering walls form the foundation of the gate building, its pinnacle-covered round towers seem small and low in comparison with the enormous dungeon (the square tower) whose huge supporting pillars project, as do also those of the adjoining castle buildings.

The beautiful symetry of the entire construction is brought out most prominently by the cleverly and artistically arranged gradation of height in the various buildings.

The gate building may be taken, so to speak, as the basis of the whole edifice, this is followed by the knights' building, or "Ritterbau", this is succeeded by the gigantic palace, which again in its turn is overtopped by the slender principal tower or "Hauptturm."

In agreeable contrast to the Norman castles of medieval ages, which had merely small loop-holes, this castle has innumerable windows, but at the same time the endeavour to carry out the characteristic feature of that style of architecture is well demonstrated by the narrow windows in the towers, opening to the inside. The grandest view of the castle is from the Marienbrücke, from which bridge the mighty building shows itself in all its beauty.

The castle structure occupies the entire top of the Tegelfelsen, an isolated rocky head, projecting from the main mountain. On three sides the rocks descend precipitately into the depth beneath, and are, naturally, quite inaccessible. Brick walls, 50 meters in height, were needed to make space and a secure foundation for the castle buildings, as well as for the wide road, which had to be hollowed out in zig-zag.

The only accessible side to the castle would have been from the south, where the Tegel rocks are united with the mountains, but this connection has been destroyed by blasting. Here the walls of the palace tower up, like a real "Rock Castle", without moats and outer walls, so that this edifice of proud, kingly glory is on all sides completely inassailable. The entrance to the castle is at a spot rendered awe-inspiring and terrible by nature, at the precipitous descent to the Pöllat ravine and to the valley beyond.

The spectator feels himself transported back to the medieval times of chivalry and minnesingers, when he crosses the threshold of this castle, in which however all the arrangements and requirements of modern times have been so well and tastefully adopted.

Amongst the building creations of Ludwig II. of Bavaria, the prize of honour undoubtedly (if only on account of its outward perfection) belongs to Neuschwanstein be-

NEUSCHWANSTEIN TOWARDS THE S W.

cause of the perfect carrying-out and personification of German sentiment, which are here united in the unusual harmony of art and nature.

The plans for the entire castle buildings were made by Hofbaudirektor von Riedl after sketches by the Hoftheater-

maler Jank, whose designs (after numerous alterations), formed the foundations of this singularly beautiful building.
The laying of the foundation stone, which was preceded by
several years work at the gate building, took place on
Sept. 5th, 1869. In the year 1892 the superintendence of the
building was undertaken by Hofoberbaudirektor von Dollmann, who was succeeded in the year 1884 by Hofbaurat
Hofmann.

After the king's death, the already commenced or partly
roughly finished buildings, the square tower, knights' building and women's apartments, were all completed, whereas
the inner tower and chapel remained untouched.

The name of Hofmann is always closely connected with
the peculiar, tasteful beauty of the castle; in addition to
superintending the architectural part of the building, he
worked indefatigably at the original motives for the designs
on the walls and ceilings, as well as at the furniture.

Fine and applied art vied with each other in creating
the castle apartments with such bewitching beauty that
the atmosphere of real medieval poetry seems to cling around
these walls.

The castle buildings which were completed consisted at
that time, of the gate building or Torbau, the knights'
building or Ritterbau, palace and women's apartments or
Kemenate.

The knights' building unites the gate building with the
palace, which, on the south side, is joined to the women's
apartments, by which arrangement, the large courtyard is
formed. Broad outside steps lead from this to the lower
courtyard and also to the gate building.

The rich construction of the entire building here becomes apparent, and in the palace it is made still more
striking by the breaking of the straight line in the blunt
corner, by the charming projecting balconies and alcoves, the
delicate little corner towers, the enormous two-storied high
loggia on the southwest side (with a roof of dull gold) and
the slender round towers on the north and south sides. These
towers exhibit an entirely different formation to that of the
square tower; the north principal tower, which stands 65
meters high above the upper castle courtyard, has, at the
height of the palace roof, a gallery with a stone balustrade
running round it, and above this a cornice with battlements,
out of which a small side-tower projects.

A colonnade above the cornice decorates and embellishes
the south low chief tower.

The enormous square tower, which like the other towers, contains the staircase, is constructed in the interior as a round tower, with a gallery running round it and a lean-to roof, whereas the principal towers all terminate in slender points.

The entire castle building is of bricks and is ornamented with marble squares from Alterschrofen (on the road between Füssen and Hohenschwangau). The façades are carried out in Nürtinger sandstone.

The enormous palace building is five stories high, and is crowned by a huge copper covered roof.

On the south-west side of the palace, a knight with shield and spear is enthroned, and the Bavarian heraldic lion gazes down from the top pinnacle into the courtyard beneath.

The front of the castle buildings, especially that of the palace, is brightened up by the alcoves and balconies, as well as by the dome-shaped Norman windows.

The inexpressible dreamy charm which this castle, built in the pure Norman style, casts over every spectator, is impossible either to explain or define. The charming themes which the mighty monuments of the Norman Architectural Period have left over to our times have again assumed shape and form, and stand here as a lasting monument to the proud past for the Country of Bavaria.

The last turning of the road leads to the

gate building.

The red brick façade is richly ornamented by the cupolas of the Norman arched windows, by the battlements of the projecting balconies, and by the leaning roofs of the middle erection and side fighting towers.

The gate archway of Nürtinger sandstone bears on it the Bavarian coat of arms. Over the cleft made in the rocks by blasting, it had been intended to place a draw-bridge. This however was not carried out, and a stone bridge now occupies the site, which leads to the splendid castle gate, richly ornamented by carving. The gate building contains on the ground floor to the left

the porter's lodge.

This is now used as the ticket office. Above the door is a stone figure of a dog (symbol of fidelity), beneath it, the inscription

„Bei Tag und Nacht,
die Treue wacht.“
(Faithfulness keeps guard by day and night.)

Adjoining the porter's lodge are the kitchen departments and the winding stairs leading to the first floor.

An inspection of the royal dining room awakens in one a presentiment of beauty and splendours that are to come. (It is unfortunately impossible, owing to the inconvenient entrance, to open this apartment to the general public, but the castle steward shows it willingly to a small number of visitors.)

The massive oak furniture is richly carved, the doors and presses are decorated with costly fittings, the wooden sofa has a high carved back, the cushions covered with pressed leather. The beautiful paintings on the walls form the chief ornament of the apartment.

These pictures represent scenes out of the life of a giant in the middle ages.

A connoisseur will at once remark the difference in the conception of the persons and scenes. "Youth" was painted by Schwoiser, "Manhood" and "Old Age" by Hauschild.

The various pictures represent; —

"The Son bidding farewell to his Mother."

"The Steward instructing the Youth in quoits and shooting."

"Pagan Worship."

"Love-making in the ballroom."

"Enlisting for the war."

"The defence of the Knight thrown from his horse during the Tournament."

"The marriage of the Squire."

The tournament is depicted in brilliant colouring, the squire holds the stirrups of the powerful war horse, while his knight receives the "Thanks" from the hand of a lady bending over the balustrade of the platform. On the departure to the crusades, the squire receives the blessing of the Bishop, his mother waves her last farewell, and his wife and child bid him a sorrowful adieu. The battle scene with the unbelievers is full of life and colour.

The last picture shows the squire as a worthy old man, noting down the history of his life.

The small room adjoining this apartment served the king, during the building of the Castle, as his bedchamber.

The view from the balcony of the dining room over-
looking the upper courtyard, is beautiful in the extreme.
To the right the enormous building of the square tower is

THE CASTLE COURTYARD.
After an original photograph by Franz Hanfstaengl.

visible, to the left, the graceful building of the "Kemenate"
or women's apartments with its Norman arched windows
and colonnaded balcony, and finally the huge palace, in all
its grand and imposing beauty, completes the picture.

The façade is constructed with elegant simplicity, which is also preserved in the columns and arches of the high windows, in the projecting balcony of the upper floor, in the charming alcove turrets and in the powerfully delineated decorations of the top story.

The pinnacles, zig-zags and domes of the round towers with their galleries and balustrades intensify the grandeur of this building. Enormous frescoes, by Hauschild, ornament the east pediment of the palace. These paintings represent "St. George and the Dragon" and "Maria with the Infant Jesus, surrounded by Angels", and exhibit fresh brilliant colouring and much artistic talent.

Wide outside stairs lead from the upper court to the first floor of the palace.

The enormous brick wall, which separates the lower court from the upper, is the foundation of the inner keep, or "Burgfried" which it had been intended to build.

The façade of the inner side of the gate building is made of Bayreuth sandstone and its warm yellowish-red tone forms an agreeable contrast to the glittering light colour of the rest of the building, which, owing to the total absence of vegetation in the courtyard, has nothing to relieve it.

A deathlike stillness surrounds the white walls, the castle stands before one like a fairy picture created by spectral hands and it strikes one with a dull sensation of regret, that here in summer no fountain is trickling, no lime tree is standing in which the soft south wind could gently murmur. The utter stillness of the spot is only broken by the thundering roar of the Pöllat Falls.

The abundant symbols of the middle ages are carried out in the smallest details of the architecture. The brilliant figures of German tradition and of the German hero and minnesinger age meet the eye on all sides, which, since the mighty compositions of Richard Wagner, have become the property of the German people, and although these representations treat exclusively of the old fables, yet here the word and art of the great musician seem to be the apt and true accompaniment to them.

One state room follows another, all in their beauty certainly quite different from those of Herrenchiemsee or Linderhof, nevertheless possessing equal charm and splendour, so that the eye is delighted, and the spectator inspired with endless admiration at the many-sided artistic talents of the royal architect and of those artists who worked under his supervision and direction. The entrance to the palace apartments is by the outer stairs in the upper castle court. These lead up to the corridor on the 1st floor. Before entering the

CORRIDOR ON THE 1st FLOOR.
United Art Establishments, Munich.

State Apartments a glance should be cast at the simple beautiful architecture of the knights' building, whose high gabled centre-building with its pure-styled window and door arches lend to the long extending front a most imposing appearance.

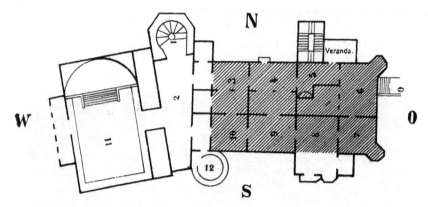

GROUND PLAN OF THE 3rd FLOOR.

0. Ground floor and outside stairs (palace).
1. Turret with a winding staircase.
2. Vestibule.
3. Aides'-de-camp apartment.
4. Workroom or study.
5. Grotto with veranda.
6. Sitting-room.
7. Dressing-room.
8. Bed-room with oratory.
9. Dining-room.
10. Servants' room.
11. Throne-room.
12. South turret with a winding staircase.

N.B. The counter-hatched surface shows the extension of the State Hall or Fest-Saal on the upper floor.

The walls of the enormous corridor are decorated in bright colours. Huge pillars of Salzburg marble support the vaulted roof, the plinths of which are also ornamentally painted. The capitals are ornamented with foliage and other designs, such as dragon, swan, fighting cocks, bear, wolf, heron, owl and finally the charming head of an angel.

The principal passage, which joins the corridor, is likewise painted in brilliant colours, the capitals of the pillars and the piers being decorated with the following subjects: dragon, cat, dog, imps, etc. as well as a humorous figure of a peasant, supporting a pier and perspiring under the weight of the heavy burden.

Four enormous lanterns hang supported by chains from the centre of the vaulted ceiling, each a masterpiece of art.

3*

The window arches are ornamented with artistic capitals. The long row of servants' apartments opens on to the corridor of the first floor.

On the landing of the same, two models are set up, the one is the representation, true to nature, of the Falkenstein plateau at the time of the king's death, with the ruins of the Castle of Falkenstein, the other represents the Castle of Falkenstein, as the king had planned building it.

Two stair-cases lead from here to the floor above; the rectangular is for the domestics, the other the principal stairs, which is continued in the great tower as a winding stair-case.

The walls of the principal stair-case are painted in brilliant colours, the panels being decorated with designs of dragons. Passing by the 2nd floor (on which are the visitors' apartments and still unfinished) the 3rd floor is reached. Here the king's apartments are situated. Passing through a glass door, over which are painted in brilliant colours the arms of Bavaria, of Schwangau and the Pfalz, we reach

the landing.

the peculiar beauty of which immediately excites the greatest interest. The open space is resplendent with brilliant colouring, enormous pillars support the wide vaulted ceiling, whose plinths are richly ornamented in coloured designs. The apex of the plinths support three mighty chandeliers with designs of swans by Wollenweber, others are decorated with coats of arms.

The capitals of the columns of Falkenstein marble are decorated (by Perron) with designs of animals, bearing a symbolical connection to the pictures in this room. The narrow surfaces of the pillars are likewise decorated with animal designs; i. e. raven, stag, cock, boar etc. A richly carved wooden wainscot ornaments the base of the wall.

The architecture of the landing is rendered most effective by pillars with beautiful capitals which lead to the apartments and Throne room. Heavy silk curtains with designs of animals interwoven in gold (Brussels work) drape the entrance to these rooms.

The settees with exquisitely carved feet—the arms and backs of the same covered with cushions of pressed leather, on which are designed in gold and surrounded by ornamental work, the swan and the Bavarian lozenge coat of arms. The walls are embellished by ten dramatically executed pictures,

CORRIDOR ON THE 3 rd FLOOR.
United Art Establishments, Munich.

illustrating the Legend of Sigurd. These are by the hand of the artist Hauschild.*)

The greatest hero of the Germanic folk lore was Sigurd or Siegfried. He belonged to the Wälsungens, a race which owed its origin to Wotan (Odin) and was the son of the brother and sister Siegmund and Signe (Sieglinde). Being thus the offspring of an unholy alliance, he was condemned to an early death. Sigurd's father had received from Wotan a sword of the Gods, which at his death broke on the God's own spear. These pieces were inherited by Sigurd.

Siegmund as he fell in battle with the sons of Hunding, was protected, against the will of Wotan, by Walküren (Valkyr). Brünhilde, the Walküre or Valkyr, was sent into a charmed sleep by Wotan, from which only Sigurd could awaken her. Sigurd's fate is prophesied to him by his uncle Gripir. He will avenge his father's death on the "hard, agile sons of Hunding," will kill the "worm Fafnir," will seize the "brilliant treasure," break the "charmed sleep of Brünhilde, the royal maiden" who will tell him about the runic treasure. He will exchange vows of love and fidelity with Brünhilde, break and forget them after Gudrun has handed him the drink of forgetfulness, woo Brünhilde for King Gunar (the brother of Högni, Gudrun and Gutorm), by assuming the form of Gunar will usurp the king's rights on the wedding night, and Brünhilde, enraged at the deception, will incite Gunar, Högni and Gutorm to avenge her wrongs upon Sigurd.

The first painting represents
"S i g u r d w i t h G r i p i r."
The horror felt by Sigurd at the unlucky prophecy is clearly expressed on his face.

The second picture shows
"T h e D w a r f R e g i n" forging the sword "Gram" out of the pieces belonging to Siegmund. The dwarf tells Sigurd the origin of the treasure guarded by Fafnir, and excites him to do battle with him. The scene is placed,—free from theatrical effect—in the full glare of the forge, which throws the two principal figures into bright relief.

The dwarf-smith Regin is executed with great skill and perfection.

---

*) The German and northern folk lore with its rich world of ideas is, unfortunately, not the common possession of the German People; and as the pictures in Neuschwanstein representing scenes out of the same differ from those set on the stage by R. Wagner, a short description will be given of each, in the order in which it appears.

Equally beautiful is the representation of
"S i g u r d's f i g h t w i t h t h e D w a r f F a f n i r."
The "Light Hero of the Sun" strikes down the dragon
with the sword, Regin watches the struggle from the background.

REGIN MAKES THE SWORD "GRAM" FOR SIGURD.
United Art Establishments, Munich.

The part that in Richard Wagner's "Siegfried" is sung
so sweetly by birds, is here in the legend told to Sigurd,
after the death of Fafnir, by the eagles, whose language,
after he has drunk of the heart blood of Fafnir, Sigurd
understands. Their advice leads him to kill Regin, they
praise the maid Brünhild, who lies in the charmed sleep.

The next picture shows
"S i g u r d r i d i n g t h r o u g h t h e f i r e."
The Valkyr lies in a deep sleep clothed in complete armour. Sigurd cuts with his sword "Gram" the cuirass in two. Brünhilde hands her rescuer the love potion in a horn filled with mead and relates her history, and tells him of the vow she has made not to marry any man who knows fear, and divides with him the runic treasure.

Above the window hangs the painting of
"G u d r u n h a n d i n g S i g u r d t h e D r i n k o f F o r -
g e t f u l n e s s a t t h e c o u r t o f G u n a r."

The paintings now skip over the events prior to the prophecy of Gripir and show in a large picture
"T h e m u r d e r o f S i g u r d b y G u t o r m."

A bright spot in the woods, on a sunny May day, forms the scene for this deed: Gunar and Högni are standing in the foreground waiting, full of expectation, for Sigurd. Sigurd sitting unsuspectingly under a high spreading tree, entices his unsaddled horse to his side, and at this moment, Gutorm spears him in the back.

The following pictures are full of passionate emotion.
"G u d r u n a w a i t s t h e r e t u r n o f S i g u r d" and
"B r ü n h i l d e m o c k s G u n a r o n a c c o u n t o f S i -
g u r d's m u r d e r."

Then follows the touching picture
"G u d r u n's l a m e n t."

On the veil being lifted, which had concealed the body of Sigurd, Gudrun breaks out into painful lamentations. The passionate emotion of Gudrun and her women at the sight of the dead body is excellently depicted.

The fable makes Brünhild, on hearing of Sigurd's murder, lose all feeling of revengeful hatred and in new awakened love to Sigurd, she spurns his assassins and stabs herself with a sharp iron.

Her last request to her hated husband Gunar was to build an enormous funeral pile, roofed over with shields, on which she, and Sigurd and all those who should follow her in death (5 maids and 8 men attendants) were to be burnt.

"Place between us the beautiful weapon,
"The sharp iron, as it once before was placed,
"When we two lay upon one couch,
"And one named us man and wife."

Gunar however prophesies to her the end of the Gibichungen in the hall of Alti, his own end in the Serpent's tower and the revenge of Gudrun on her husband Atli.

The last picture demonstrates the
"B u r n i n g o f t h e b o d i e s o f S i g u r d a n d B r ü n-
h i l d o n t h e f u n e r a l p i l e."
The noble pair are represented in the rigid stillness of
death. The flames devour greedily the wood of the scaffold.

ADJUTANTS' APARTMENT.
United Art Establishments Munich.

What grand thoughts lie in all these representations,
what rich forms they have been given by the fresh-hued, artistically designed and executed paintings, so full of warmth
and passion!
If, illuminated only by the light of day, these pictures
present such a striking and beautiful appearance, how much
might their beauty be enhanced, if one were only able to see
them under the light of thousands of candles burning in the
chandeliers!

The first apartment of the king, which opens on to this landing is the

business room or adjutants' apartment.

This room is divided down the centre by columns of Salzburg marble. The walls are wainscotted with beautifully carved wood, and decorated with brilliant coloured paintings.

The columns are ornamented by blue woollen curtains, with interwoven designs of animals in gold; beautifully carved tables, chests, sofas and chairs complete the furniture of this simple and comfortable apartment. The pillars at the windows are likewise of Salzburg marble; the division of the room by the columns and arches impart to it a particularly comfortable and snug appearance. This style has also been adopted in several of the other apartments and the light and brilliant colouring of these pillars add much to the beauty and symetry of the room. The panels of the doors are ornamented with beautiful carving and fittings.

There is in this room nothing whatever to betray the beauty concealed in the adjoining apartment

the King's study.

This room is divided in the same way as the above, only an alcove on the northside is added. Round each pillar is a narrow brass band, set with sparkling stones, which gives the appearance of a bracelet round a full white arm.

The carving of the wainscotting is splendid, as is the decoration of the ceiling.

The portières and curtains are of green silk trimmed with gold embroidery, in the centre of which is the crowned lion and the Bavarian coat of arms, the silver and blue lozenges, standing out in prominent relief from the rest of the work.

The object which naturally attracts the most interest on entering the room is the king's writing table. The chair standing before it is a masterpiece of artistic workmanship. The high back is ornamented with charming embroidery, which surrounds the heart-shaped shield with the Bavarian Lozenge, the beautiful carving is surmounted by two crowned lions which support the crown and the Bavarian arms.

The cushion on the seat is richly embroidered in gold with designs of lions.

The table cloth is of green velvet, with gold fringe and embroidery.

STUDY.
After an original photograph by Franz Hanfstaengl.

The inkstand is a masterpiece of goldsmith's work from Harrach and Wollenweber. It stands between two branched candlesticks and lamps in the Normanic style. Dragons form the feet of this artistic object.

Stands for ink and sand are set with glittering stones and terminate in crown-shaped cupolas.

A Norman arch supported by columns, in the recess of which are lions bearing the Bavarian arms with the royal crown, is surmounted by the figure of Lohengrin with the swan nestling against him. A group of remarkable life-like beauty. The writing map is open-work gold embroidery set with jewels and filled in with lapislazuli.

Equal perfection and artistic beauty are shown in the paper-cutter, seal, penstand and letterweight, the latter on a high pedestal with the Bavarian arms.

The large bookcase in the corner is a charming piece of furniture. Four Norman arches with beautifully carved arched panels and capitals, support the head-piece, the front of which is constructed of seven entwined columns with beautiful capitals, and which is rendered still more effective by the projection of the centre division. The panels of the cupboard doors are ornamented with artistic fittings, the top of the same crowned by pinnacles, gables and towers.

The stove standing opposite the bookcase is a fine specimen of ceramic decoration.

To enter into details, we will mention the artistically carved feet of the table, which are of a strict Norman design. The chandelier which hangs above the writing table is a beautiful example of technical work, it is most artistically designed and executed and would prove an ornament to any ecclesiastical building.

A second chandelier with eighteen candles hangs from the centre of the recess.

In the panels of the wall which connect the Norman arches with the side walls are the two portraits of
"D u k e   F r i e d r i c h   t h e   Q u a r r e l s o m e   o f   A u s t r i a"
and
"D u k e   O t t o   t h e   I l l u s t r i o u s   o f   B a v a r i a."

The pictures stand out well from the decorative-painted wall-surface, which was created by Aigner to represent gobelin and has for subject, the well-known Legend of the Knight Tannhäuser. This Legend, now brought by Richard Wagner before the whole world, treats of the adventurons life of the Minnesingers and connects the luxurions court of the Goddess Venus (old-german Holda) in the forest-surrounded

Hörsel Mount with the most brilliant event of medieval court life, namely "The Singers' Fight on the Wartburg".

Reminiscences of the ancient heathen times and of the power of Christendom are introduced into this Legend and one is reminded by the chief figures of Tannhäuser and Elisabeth of the deeply stirring song of the "Happiness and Despair of Love".

STUDY: WRITING TABLE.
United Art Establishments, Munich.

Tannhäuser, after leaving the Minnesingers in a quarrel, goes to the Venus Mount and there spends an entire years in vain sensual lovemaking.

The longing
"For the world of the earth,
"For the breath of the forest,
"For the heaven's clear blue,
"For the fresh green of the meadow,
"And the birds' sweet song,
"And the dear sound of the bells,"
takes him away at last from the charms of Venus.

The Goddess does her utmost to keep him. but a prayer to the Mother of God delivers him from her satanic charm.

He meets in the forest the knights and minnesingers on their way to the Wartburg and these invite him to take part in the Singers' War. There he sings with warmth and

STUDY: RECESS.
United Art Establishments, Munich.

passion in praise of sensual love, arousing in those present a storm of indignation against him, only Elisabeth, the niece of the artistic-minded Landgrave, who carried Tanuhäuser's image in her heart, protects him. Outlawed and banished, Tannhäuser wanders about, stays for a time at the Castle of Trausnitz with Duke Otto the Illustrious, and goes then as a penitent to Rome to seek absolution for his sins: he is excommunicated by the Pope. who hurls at the repentant sinner, the words: "Sooner should the dry staff in his hand break forth into leaf and bud, than that Tannhäuser could hope for forgiveness of his sins."

Three days later, the staff broke into leaf and blossomed and the joyful news was told to Tannhäuser, who lay at the point of death, as the last ray of light from the world.

The pictures illustrating this legend begin with "Tannhäuser on the Venus Mount."

This hangs above the large bookcase in the recess.

Weary of the charms of the Goddess of Love, Tannhäuser reclines moodily at her feet, cupids engaged in play hover round the group, which includes also the Three Graces.

The painting above the door leading to the business room or adjutants' apartment represents "The Ride to the Wartburg."

On the pillar between the window of the balcony doors hangs the charming picture entitled "The shepherd boy blowing on the shawm."

This picture seems to bring before us the rustling of the trees and the beauties of spring.

"Now blow I merrily on the shawm,
"May is here, the dear month of May."

And the earnest, sorrowful tones of the pilgrims' chorus break in in the joyful music of the old folk's song of "The noble Tannhäuser."

The next painting represents "Tannhäuser's Reception on the Wartburg."

This hangs above the second exit, and gives a glimpse at the court life during the middle ages.

Landgrave Hermann of Thüringia offers his princely greeting to the knights and minnesingers, arriving at the Wartburg.

The following picture displays much life-like animation. "The Singers' War on the Wartburg."

Then follows the picture to the left on the back wall. "Tannhäuser striking up for the Dance in the open."

This picture is so true to life, one almost expects to hear the music which Tannhäuser is drawing from his violin;

and the next picture, by the contrast. strikes one all the
more impressively.
"Tannhäuser as Penitent before the Pope."

TANNHÄUSER STRIKING UP FOR THE DANCE IN THE OPEN.
United Art Establishments, Munich.

"———My head bowed low,
"I accuse myself with a gesture of despair
"Of the ignoble passion———
"And for deliverance from the scorching fetters
"I cried out to him, overwhelmed with pain."
Then follows the charming painting illustrating
"Pegasus being crowned with roses by
cupids."

The door now opens on to the

grotto

which is an artistic imitation of a stalactic cave by the landscape sculptor Dirrigl.

TERRACE (FORMERLY WINTER-GARDEN).
After an original photograph by Franz Hanfstaengl.

The waterfall, which in former years added much to the beauty of the grotto, has long since dried up and deprived the cave of its poetical charm; and the adjoining terrace, roofed over with glass, in which was formerly a pretty flower garden with fountains resembling the Hanging Gardens of Semirimus, is now likewise empty.

The view from the windows embraces the broad plain lying far beneath, out of the fresh green of which shine the sparkling waters of the Bannwald and Hopfen Lakes, and the river Lech.

The adjoining apartment is decorated in beautiful light blue and silver and is the

sitting room.

This apartment, by its beautiful architectural construction, by its light brown panelling and furniture of pure artistic form impresses one with a sensation of comfortable warmth, from which the really royal splendour of the arrangements in no wise detract. The entablature of the ceiling, supported by splendid piers, is ornamented with artistic wood carving, and on the frieze glitter the arms and names of the persons and countries connected with the Legend of Lohengrin. The curtains and portières are of royal blue, embroidered in silver with garlands of flowers surrounding the crowned swan.

The armchairs, seats, and the enormous sofa are beautifully carved in wood, the cushions being likewise embroidered with floral designs and the crowned swan, which emblem is also interwoven in the splendid carpet and table cloth.

The elegant appearance of this apartment is greatly improved by the clever division of the same by columns (with beautiful capitals) which give to the recess a most comfortable and snug appearance.

The alcove serves as a look-out and cosy corner.

The artistic fittings of the doors are of beautiful ornamental work, and like all other ornaments in this apartment, carried out in the Romanic style.

The frame of the large table standing before the sofa is of wood, carved in designs of swans, the arch supported by eight pillars on which rests the enormous table. The handsomest ornament in the sitting room is the wall-cupboard, an imitation of the celebrated Wartburg press; divided into three, the lower division consists of delicate columns, beautifully carved, the doors decorated with ornaments of foliage.

The handles of the centre drawer represent lions heads.

The top division with its graceful columns and arches is particularly beautiful. Little doves are seated on the

CEILING FRIEZE.

capitals. The three panels of the Norman arches contain
pictures by Piloty, which are allegorical representations,
symbolising scenes out of the three poems "Tristan and Isolde,"
"Parzival," and the "Nibelungenlied," and bearing the following inscriptions:

"Tristan hands Isolde the Love Potion,"
"The Miracle of the Grail,"
"Siegfried and Kriemhilde,"
and beneath

"Gottfried of Strasburg composing poetry,"
"Wolfram von Eschenbach and the Landgrave Hermann of Thuringia,"
"Bishop Piligrin of Passau with the poet
of the Nibelungenlied."

The enormous chandelier in the centre of the apartment
is formed like a crown and set with sparkling stones. The
swan is again brought into prominence, being introduced
into the iron work.

Another handsome ornament is the candalabra which
stands on the table in the recess.

The pictures in this apartment illustrate the Legend of
Lohengrin (after Garin le Lorrain).

This legend, like that of Tannhäuser, is much better
known than the others belonging to court poetry. Naturally
Richard Wagner has in no small degree contributed to this.

Elsa, the daughter of the Duke of Brabant, is, at his
death, presented to the Count Telramund as his wife. The
Count, not satisfied with her alone, also wishes for her lands,
and in order to obtain possession of them, accuses Elsa before
the Emperor of breaking her marriage vows. In the cathedral Elsa beseeches God to send her a champion to establish
her innocence at the trial assigned to her by her judges.

The mystical power of the Grail is here introduced into
the legend. In the Grail temple, to which on every Good
Friday a dove brought down from heaven the Host, whereby

4*

SITTING ROOM

United Art Establishments, Munich

the sanctity and miraculous power of the holy Grail was renewed, the following inscription appeared on the Grail vessel

WARTBURG-CUPBOARD.
United Art Establishments, Munich.

"The Grail would send Elsa a champion" and while the Grail
knights were disputing for the honour of rendering this service, the temple was illuminated with a supernatural light.

The white dove flies down with the Host, and to the astonishment of all, appoints Lohengrin, the son of the Grail-king Parzival, to be Elsa's champion. In an equally miraculous manner a swan appears on the Lake Brumbane with a skiff, into which Lohengrin steps, and after bidding a sorrowful fare-well to his relations, hurries off.

At Antwerp he leaves his miraculous conveyance, with which the swan instantly disappears. Lohengrin, in the presence of the assembled court, makes Elsa promise never to inquire his name or antecedents. Elsa acquaints him through a knight of her distress, where-upon Lohengrin presents himself as her champion. The broad field between Mayence and Oppenheim (where the meetings of the Imperial Diet were held) formed the scene of the contest between Lohengrin and Telramund. After a hot encounter the latter was defeated, and according to the King's decree, beheaded.

The brilliant marriage of Elsa with Lohengrin took place at Antwerp. Two sons were born to them, and the pair lived together in devoted love, when suddenly Elsa, incited to the act by a false friend, put the fatal question to her husband. Lohengrin, in the presence of the Emperor and assembled court, satisfied her curiosity. The entreaties of Elsa, of the King and court, all were in vain. The swan re-appeared with the boat to fetch Lohengrin on his return journey.

The series of pictures by Hauschild commence with "E l s a g o i n g t o C h u r c h," which is to a great extent, hidden by the large press before it.

Then follows;
"T h e M i r a c l e o f t h e H o l y G r a i l."

A supernatural light is shed upon the sacred object over which the dove is hovering—children and virgins kneel in amazed adoration —. The aged Grail King and his knights gaze in reverent terror at the holy object, on which appears in flaming characters, the name "Lohengrin."

Above the door hangs the picture entitled
"L o h e n g r i n ' s d e p a r t u r e f r o m t h e G r a i l M o u n t a i n."

On the left from the entrance;
"L o h e n g r i n ' s a r r i v a l a t W o r m s."

Indescribable joy and happiness are expressed in this picture by Heckel, which represents the landing of Lohengrin in the bright fresh spring-time in the Rhine country.

Two pictures on the wall of the recess represent "Lohengrin's journey to, and arrival at Worms" and the "Landing of Lohengrin."

SITTING ROOM WITH RECESS.

United Art Establishments, Munich.

The back of the recess contains the picture of
"E l s a ' s L a m e n t."

And above the door in the Norman arch:
"T h e D e i f i c a t i o n o f t h e S w a n."

Which is represented by a charming figure of an angel
rising out of the waves.

Another large picture in the recess represents;
"L o h e n g r i n ' s c o m b a t w i t h T e l r a m u n d."

A brilliant throng gazes from the island at the struggle,
and the joy of the spectators and happiness of Elsa are
beautifully depicted.

The next painting is of
"L o h e n g r i n a n d E l s a w i t h t h e i r C h i l d r e n."

All unsuspecting, the children play happily at their
parents' feet, when Elsa, nestling lovingly against her husband, questions him about his birth and name.
"Alas! Now all our happiness is o'er!"

Then follows;
"L o h e n g r i n ' s R e t u r n."

Lohengrin, overcome by grief at his lost happiness, sits
in the skiff which is racing over the stormy waves.

The recess also contains pictures representing scenes from
the Lohengrin Legend.

The charming tone of colour which prevails in the apartment agrees so perfectly with the bright-hued, life-like representations of the Swan-Knight Legend, that the romantic
charm of the long past glorious age of chivalry and court
life during the middle ages is brought most vividly before
our eyes.

The dressing room.

The furniture of this apartment is covered with violet,
embroidered in gold. The peacock, the heraldic bird of the
room, glitters on all the embroideries, both of the furniture
and of the portières, and is introduced in the richly ornamented frieze. The walls are tastefully covered with simple
wooden panels.

The cheerful appearance of this apartment is heightened
by the paintings on the ceiling, the room being in this
respect quite unlike the others, in which all the ceilings are
of wood.

The subject of the painting is a thicket formed by the
luxuriant trails of the vine, in which singing birds of brilliant plumage are flying hither and thither.

The enormous toilette table and the beautifully carved oak frame of the large glass hanging on the wall are in strict artistic keeping.

The toilette set of faience, bearing in enamel the crowned swan and Bavaria's lion upon, it is a real work of art.

Seats, stools and armchairs are covered in violet velvet heavily embroidered in gold—the design being the peacock surrounded by floral decorations.

The most beautiful ornament of this apartment is the jewel box, a graceful and splendid piece of carving. The picture on the front of this box, or rather chest, illustrates "The Seignorial Rights of Medieval Times" by Spiess, who has painted the delicate subject so decently and with such charm, that one is tempted to forget the objectionableness of the theme.

The door fittings are of beautiful workmanship.

From a charming alcove a view is to be seen of the Pöllat ravine and the giant mountain summits of the Schwangau.

Pictorial decoration in this apartment is devoted to the greatest lyric-poet of the middle ages—Walther von der Vogelweide, and to Hans Sachs, the Meistersinger, these two men who have most nearly touched the chords of German hearts and souls.

"The Honour of Germany", the "Price of her men and women"—no poet has immortalised these subjects more than has Walther von der Vogelweide, and music, like the note of a nightingale, proceeds from the poetry of the talented shoemaker of Nürnberg, who with his song greets the dawn of a new era.

The fresh, poetical wall paintings on gobelin linen are the work of E. Ille.

Above the door leading to the sitting-room is the picture of
"Young Walther at the birds' decoy."

Beneath the shady trees in his father's courtyard Walther sits surrounded by his feathered favourites, and with the tame falcon on his wrist.

The large picture above the glass represents
"How Walther sings his song at court."

At the court of the old Duke Wolf the singer praises enthusiastically the customs and habits of the German people.

The assembled knights and ladies listen full of admiration to his song.

Then follows

DRESSING ROOM: PORTIÈRE.
United Art Establishments. Munich

"Walther, in an enthusiastic speech, demands the services of a number of knights to take part in the crusades."

The intense fervour felt by the knightly singer for the Holy Object, (the delivering of the Saviour's Grave out of the hands of the unbelievers,) is shown by his whole attitude, as embracing a stone cross, he extols the purpose of the Holy War.

DRESSING ROOM: JEWEL CHEST.
United Art Establishments, Munich

Above the entrance to the recess are portraits of Walther and Hans Sachs by Ille.

The following picture is full of the poetry of the middle ages

"Walther riding past a castle, fiddling
merrily."

DRESSING ROOM.
United Art Establishments, Munich.

and the philosophical moment out of the life of the Minnesingers is well shown by the picture of
"Walther sitting on a stone, musing."

This last is an illustration of his poem „Ich sass auf einem Steine," the plaintive song treating of the dispute between Emperor and Pope and the unfortunate Interregnum.

Above the door hangs a picture of
"Walther with Duke Friedrich of Austria as Crusaders."

In the crusade hymn as well as in the song entitled "In the promised land" Walther shows his deep religious sentiments, and the powerful impression which his vocal talent makes upon his listeners is vividly expressed in the picture.

The last painting shows a pair of lovers, and has for title
"Beneath the lime tree,"
this is founded on Walther's song, bearing the same name.

This picture is full of charm and one can almost fancy one hears the low whisperings of the lovers mingled with the rustling of the tree, laden with its spring blossoms and foliage, above them.

On the wall of the alcove Ille has painted-artistic scenes taken from the life of Hans Sachs, namely
"Hans Sachs receives the chain of honour of the Meistersingers,"
"Hans Sachs, as youthful Meistersinger, singing his first song in public,"
and the third and last:
"The grey-haired Hans Sachs collects his works."

It is difficult to decide what captivates the most in this apartment, whether the light brilliancy of its furniture or the real poetical atmosphere which hovers over its pictorial decoration. The conviction that none of those rooms which still remain to be visited can possibly surpass, or even come up to this apartment in splendour or regal pomp, is speedily disproved as the door is opened which conducts to the

sleeping apartment.

This room is in the strict Old-Gothic style, the ground colours dark blue and gold.

At the first glance the room gives the impression of being an oratory, did not the charming wall paintings and articles of furniture dispel the idea.

This sleeping apartment is a masterpiece of art—art belonging to medieval ages and yet, even in its smallest details of furniture, meeting the requirements of modern times, so that the most critical eye has no fault to find.

The beautiful blue, in unison with the rich mingling of gold, sets off and increases the impression of warmth and comfort which this room imparts. The style of architecture here employed necessitates a complete alteration in the formation of the apartment. A slender column supports the vault of the ceiling, and the absence of the usual division by columns and arches gives an appearance of additional size, which is not a little added to by an alcove, as well as imparting an air of greater comfort and cosiness to the apartment.

The alcove opens on to a balcony from which is a glorious view of the Pollät ravine, the graceful Marienbrücke and of the gigantic steep sides of the Säuling.

The high wainscot is of beautiful carving in the Gothic style and surmounted by garlands of vine and finials, the ceiling and its girders are equally artistically ornamented. The modillions are of cedar wood. The beautifully formed supporting column in the centre of the apartment has suspended from it a graceful candalabra for eight candles. Above the capital allegorical figures are introduced, and the top of the pillar terminates in the figures of gnomes supporting the ceiling.

Equally rich decoration is exhibited on the buttresses on the walls, which being of wood, stand out very prominently from the same.

The chief object of interest in this apartment is naturally the state bed.

If, in the Castles of Herrenchiemsee and Linderhof one is filled with amazed astonishment and admiration at the fairy-like splendour surrounding the state bed, here in Neuschwanstein one is struck by the brilliant achievement of applied art which created this, in every respect, masterpiece of art—it has almost the appearance of a tabernacle, such as the old Gothic masters created in such perfection in the cathedrals in Germany.

A charming feature in this apartment is the openwork carving on the side wall above the artistically executed picture in relief, by Perron, which represents the "Ascension of Our Lord."

The carving of the canopy with its beautiful ornaments of grapes on the top of the roof, and the delicate finials, is carried out in its most minute details with the utmost artistic perfection. The roof is a remarkable piece of work and one of the finest specimens of wood-carving belonging

SLEEPING APARTMENT.

United Art Establishments, Munich

to the present day. In perfection of work and design, it far surpasses the richest Gothic soundingboard.

The finials, resembling the most delicate flower buds, reach right up to the ceiling of the lofty apartment.

The two curtains of the bed exhibit embroidery of high artistic taste, the gold on the blue ground being extremely charming and effective. The border is a conventional pattern of flowers, and the centre panel is ornamented in embroidery work, by the royal crown, the Bavarian lozenge—formed coat of arms, and the heraldic animals of Bavaria and Schwangau, the lion and the swan.

The coverlet of the bed is equally handsome.

The ceiling of the canopy is sown with gold and silver stars.

The head-piece of the bed is ornamented by the wonderfully beautiful picture (by Julius Frank, in the Byzanthine style) of the Madonna with the Child Jesus. The face of the Mother of God, who holds the Child upon her lap, is full of earnestness and dignity, the Babe raises His right hand in blessing, the left holds open the Book at the words.

"Peace be with you, I am the Light of the world."

The beauty of this picture surpasses that of all others in this apartment.

By the side of the bed is a huge armchair, the covering of which is charmingly embroidered, the back is beautifully carved and the posts of the same are crowned by lions.

Also the washingstand, stove and reading desk are striking examples of applied art.

The washingstand is evidently, as far as is possible, the imitation of a Gothic altar, and in spite of its enormous size, is a splendid piece of furniture. The slab of the table, into which the basins are sunk, rests on large fluted columns. Above the basins are silver swans from which flows crystal clear water from the Säuling mountain.

A simple method is employed for emptying away the water, it being merely necessary to tip up the basins.

In the front are two pillars which act as supports to the roof of the canopy. The back of the canopy contains a shelf for toilet requisites and in the glass, which occupies the entire back wall, one sees reflected the artistic stove and reading desk.

The crowning of the canopy with the most delicate ornaments of grapes and finials is strikingly beautiful, two swans with out—spreading wings decorate the foreposts of the shelf.

SLEEPING ROOM: BED.
After an original photograph by Franz Hanfstaengl.

The wall above the Gothic archway of the door to the dining-room forms a recess which contains the standing figures of the Tristan Legend, King Marke, Rivalin and Blanche-fleur, and the Gothic arches of the recess are themselves crowned by beautifully formed finials.

The enormous stove standing between the door and the reading desk has a decidedly monumental appearance. Two twisted columns with beautiful capitals flank the centre panel of the lower construction, which contains two windows with Gothic arches. The upper part is built on to this, containing in the centre a broad Gothic window with a double row of columns and a richly formed rose window, and at the side stand the statuettes (by Hirt) of Tristan and Isolde under graceful canopies. The top of this artistic piece of workmanship is built like the pointed roof of a Gothic edifice.

The walls on each side of the stove are ornamented with charming floral decorations. The reading desk by the side of the stove is a copy of the choir-stalls in the Gothic cathedrals. A handsome Gothic canopy overhangs the splendid armchair, the cushions of which are ornamented with glittering embroidery.

The back wall, formed like a Gothic arch, is ornamented with splendid carvings, between which are introduced in relief, the arms of Bavaria and Schwangau and the swan. The high back of the chair is crowned by delicately carved finials.

On the reading desk are two branched candlesticks in bronze, each for four candles.

The alcove with its embroidered benches forms a most cosy resting place. The windows are ornamented with the arms of Bavaria, the Palatinate and Schwangau.

A blue glass lamp is suspended from the ceiling.

The door opening into the oratory is a splendid piece of workmanship, it is beautifully carved, has artistic fittings and beautiful tracery work above the Gothic arches.

The chandelier for 24 candles, which hangs suspended from the ceiling in the background of the apartment, is profusely ornamented with carvings, grapes and vine leaves, and the centre is formed like a small tower with finials and pinnacles. The air of luxury and comfort is intensified by the graceful stools standing by the walls and the sofas, in the alcove, the embroidered cushions of which bear the designs of the crowned lion in gold, the swan in silver, and the lozenge of Bavaria.

The swan is also interwoven into the handsome carpet by the bed-side.

The decorations of the sleeping apartment have far surpassed those of all the other rooms already described and

SLEEPING ROOM: PICTURE OF THE MADONNA (AT THE HEAD OF THE BED).
United Art Establishments, Munich.

inspected and have changed the mood of the spectator from
delighted astonishment to solemn earnestness, to which

5*

SLEEPING ROOM: STOVE.
United Art Establishments, Munich.

have contributed in no small degree, the beautiful series of paintings by A. Spiess.

The artist, with an innate comprehension of the earnest, indescribable Love and Sorrow in the world of the Tristan and Isolde Legend, and imbued with the deepest feeling in the spiritual deliniation of the figures represented, has been successful in reflecting the legend by masterly-executed pictures. Masterly in the workmanship, and especially so as regards the ideal comprehension of the subject and the real severe, but nevertheless so sweet romance—and in the presence of the life-like, fresh-coloured beauty in which these paintings, treating of the great epic poem of Love, are represented, words seem cold and empty.

Next to Wolfram von Eschenbach's "Parzival" no other epos of German medieval literature is of such importance as this Legend of Tristan and Isolde by Gottfried of Strassburg, and into this also is introduced the wonderful song of Love in the allpowerful strains of Richard Wagner's music, who describes with immortal beauty in his musical drama, this Rapture of Love and Sorrow of Love.

As the most precious bloom from the rich garland of legends which surround King Arthur and his Round Table, this Legend of Tristan and Isolde has been left over to us as a true and faithful picture of chivalric and court life. Tristan, the son of King Rivalin and his wife Blanche-fleur, (a sister of King Marke of Cornwall) lost his mother at his birth, his father fell in battle against Duke Morgan, who possessed himself of Tristan's lands. The marshall of Rivalin, Rual le Foitenant, brought up the orphaned Tristan and had him instructed by Kurwenal in all knightly accomplishments, in harp playing and hunting and in the manners and customs of the court.

Tristan was enticed by Norwegian merchants on to their vessel and then carried off, but as their ship seemed about to go down in a terrific storm, they, acting up to the sailors' superstition, placed him in a boat and set him adrift. The waves carried the bark on to the coast of Cornwall, where Tristan met some hunters, who conducted him to the court of King Marke. Here he speedily became the king's favourite, until Rual after much searching, at length discovered him and revealed his noble birth to the king. Receiving knighthood, Tristan avenged his father's death on Duke Morgan, placed Rual as ruler over his recovered possessions, and returned to Cornwall. When the Irish warrior Morholt arrived to demand the shameful tribute from King

Marke, Tristan killed him in a hot encounter on an island, whereby his sword broke and a piece of the blade remained

SLEEPING ROOM: WASHING-STAND.
United Art Establishments, Munich.

embedded in the head of the fallen man. Tristan received a wound from Morholt's spear, which was poisoned, and his health slowly waned and broke.

At his request he was placed in a boat and left to his fate, with no companion save his beloved harp.

SLEEPING ROOM: READING-DESK.
After an original photograph by Franz Hanfstaengl.

Drifted on to the coast of Ireland, Tristan was taken on land by some fishermen, who were enchanted by his wonderful music. Queen Isot and her daughter, Isolde the Golden-Haired, who possessed a knowledge of magic potions, nursed him back to health. Tristan gave himself out as the musician Tantris, whose ship had been plundered by pirates, and out of whose hands he had escaped with difficulty, being severely wounded, in a small boat.

No one recognised in the pale musician the conqueror of Morholt, against whom the whole of Ireland cherished a deadly hatred.

Fully restored to health, Tristan returned to Cornwall and spoke enthusiastically of the wonderful beauty of the Princess Isolde.

The Cornish knights, jealous of Tristan, persuaded the grey-haired King Marke to woo her, and the foolhardy Tristan undertook the dangerous journey to court the princess for King Marke.

Tristan landed in Ireland with a brilliant following, all being disguised as merchants.

Full of the love and excitement of adventure, Tristan killed a dragon which was the terror of Ireland, and in consequence of this heroic deed his courtship was received favourably by the king.

All hatred seemed to have disappeared, he mastered only Isolde, for had she not made the discovery that the piece of sword blade left in Morholt's head fitted into the sword of the guest, and had hoped that Tristan would woo her!

Before the departure for Cornwall Queen Isot concocted a love potion, which she gave to Brangäne, the playfellow of Isolde, to take care of, with the injunction to let King Marke and Isolde drink of it on their wedding night, so that they might be united to each other in faithful and true love.

Richard Wagner's "Tristan and Isolde" commences at the journey to Cornwall, and at this point the series of paintings in the sleeping apartment also begin.

In the panel of the Gothic arch above the exit to the dining-room is the figure of a woman attired in the medieval patrician costume reading out of a book. Round the picture are the words of Gottfried of Strassburg taken from his "Tristan and Isolde."

"We hear to-day still gladly,—sweet and ever new,
    of their deep faithfulness,—their love, their sorrow,
    their joy and their distress."

Isolde's lamentation and home sickness and her hatred for Tristan, who treated her with great deference and respect as his mistress, increased from day to day. When Tristan entered the women's apartments on board ship, in order to comfort the complaining Isolde, a waiting woman unintentionally handed to him the love potion, instead of the wine which Isolde had demanded.

This action forms the subject of the first painting. "T r i s t a n h a n d s I s o l d e t h e L o v e P o t i o n."

TRISTAN HANDS ISOLDE THE LOVE POTION.
United Art Establishments, Munich

Tristan's respectful demeanour, and the spurning indifference of Isolde are excellently represented in this picture. Although acquainted by Brangäne of the mistake, both forget honour and duty—the fatal drink accomplishes its work, they love each other with heart and soul, in life, in death and in eternity—

Nothing suspecting, King Marke makes her his wife. Brangäne takes Isolde's place on the wedding night.

Tristan and Isolde lived happily in their love, but treachery obtained at last possession of their secret. Tristan fled from the rage of King Marke, and Isolde was placed under strict surveillance. Brangäne, moved by the distress and grief of Isolde, adrised Tristan to throw pieces of bark into the stream which flowed through the royal castle, and she would conduct Isolde to the great pine tree in the courtyard to see these messengers of love.

The second painting represents the love scene of "T r i s t a n a n d I s o l d e i n t h e g a r d e n."

The scene is placed in a beautiful garden with the proud castle occupying the back ground, the flowers are in full bloom, the little stream flows past with its tiny silver waves—moonlight sheds a fairy-like charm over the whole picture. Tristan is sitting at the foot of an enormous tree holding Isolde in his arms—Brangäne is keeping faithful watch in the distance.

Tristan is banished, is obliged to fly in order to escape from the certain death with which King Marke's terrible anger threatens him.

The third picture shows "T r i s t a n a n d I s o l d e b i d d i n g e a c h o t h e r f a r e w e l l."

With great delicacy of feeling the artist has represented this scene as taking place in the garden of the second picture.

In deepest sorrow, their hands tightly clasped, their gaze fixed on each other full of grief at the impending separation, so stand the lovers there—Brangäne, their faithful guardian, comes hurrying towards them, and in the back-ground King Marke, the Dwarf Melot, and the Lord High Steward are visible, all coming to surprise the unhappy pair.

From now on Tristan led the adventurous life of a travelling knight, but still he could not banish Isolde from his thoughts. In Bretagne he assisted the Duke in fighting against his enemies. The Duke's daughter, Isolde Blanchefleur, captivated his heart, and he hoped to free himself from his love for Queen Isolde by an alliance with her.

As he on the wedding day, slipped the green jasper ring, in which a lock of Isolde's golden hair was concealed, unobserved from his finger, his love for Isolde awoke again, and his heart was filled with sorrow at his faithlessness to her—. He lived with his wife in celebacy and now the fate which awaited him could no longer be diverted. Confined to his sickbed by a wound from a poisonous arrow, he hoped to obtain healing and deliverance from Isolde the Golden-Haired. The faithful Kurwenal has gone to Cornwall, a white

ISOLDE, BY THE DEAD BODY OF TRISTAN.
United Art Establishments, Munich.

sail on the returning vessel is to announce to Tristan that Isolde is on board, a black one. that Kurwenal is returning alone.

Isolde Blanche-fleur, devoured by jealousy, has listened and overheard this arrangement made between Tristan and Kurwenal. The beautiful picture over the entrance to the Oratory represents
"T r i s t a n , a w a i t i n g I s o l d e's A r r i v a l."

Partly raised up on his sick bed, Tristan looks pale and wan as he gazes through the open alcove window of his castle into the distance beyond, anxiously hoping for a glimpse of the white sail. His wife gazes darkly and gloomily at him. Kurwendal's pleading was not in vain — he persuaded Isolde to accompany him and together they set out on the homeward journey. As the white sail shone out in the distance Tristan's wife stood up before him with the words, "Your ship is in sight, a black sail is at the mast."

Tristan uttered the beloved name "Isolde" and sank back dead.

His faithful followers, filled with sorrow, attired him in full armour—and Isolde Blanche-fleur, beside herself with horror, wandered half distraught about the Castle.

The overwhelming passion of the loving woman, who regardless of everything had cast off every bond, is wonderfully expressed in this painting of
"I s o l d e ' s L a n d i n g w i t h K u r w e n a l."

And the last picture of these series is most impressionable.
"T h e D e a t h o f I s o l d e a t t h e B i e r o f T r i s t a n."

The majesty of the Monarch Death is shown with wonderful pathos in this picture.

The womanly figure of Isolde, as she embraces Tristan in the dying agony of love, seems to possess a supernatural beauty. Bragäne kneels praying beside the bier, and King Marke, who has hurried after Isolde, stands with the faithful Kurwenal, both filled with grief and sorrow, before the "abode of true love in Life and in Death."

The "Allegory of Love" is completed by the ideal female figure (on the right by the door) representing a Queen with wings, bow and arrow in her hands, and the "Allegory of Faithfulness" by the charmingly beautiful earnest figure of a woman in the costume of a citizen in the middle ages, with roses in the plaits of her hair, glancing down at a little dog, the symbol of faithfulness. Here in the bed-room, as also later on in the state hall, the spectator is unconsciously driven to form comparisous between this and the other castles.

ORATORY.
United Art Establishments, Munich.

In Linderhof and Herrenchiemsee it is the brilliancy of magnificence which impresses the visitor—here in Neuschwanstein, it is the charm of real German emotional beauty which imposes and impresses. The most important age of the Teutonic race is here represented in charming beauty by the style employed in these apartments. By the illustrations of the Song of Love and Faithfulness — these two most noble qualities of the German people,—a lasting monument has been raised to them.

Adjoining the sleeping apartment is the

oratory

which also is in the Gothic style. The capitals of the columns support charming heads of angels. The hanging lamp, in which burns the Eternal Light, is suspended from a dove representing the Holy Ghost.

A splendidly carved ivory crucifix is on the Altar, and behind it in the picture panel, is a painting of St. Louis of France, the folding doors decorated with charming figures of angels bearing palms. The reverse sides of the doors are beautifully carved

The back wall of the peaceful Sanctuary is ornamented with Gothic tracery. The glass paintings, which are from Maier's Royal Art Establishment in Munich, represent the last days of St. Louis.

On the walls are scenes from the crusades of the same saint. The king's praying desk, which stands before the Altar, is covered with violet cloth, (the colour of penitence) ornamented with embroidery in gold.

Passing once more through the bedroom, we come to the

dining-room.

The ground tones of this apartment are purple and gold. The portières and cushions on the comfortable armchairs are of purple with designs of foliage and flowers embroidered in gold.

The door fittings are of handsome iron-work. The Norman style of architecture is again adopted in this room, this being particularly apparent in the graceful double pillars by the doors.

The panels in the wainscotting are of charming ornamental carving, likewise the frame of the enormous table.

A striking ornament in this apartment is a table centre-piece in gilded bronze, a representation of Siegfried's Fight with the Dragon, and a masterpiece of work of the Munich

applied art by Wollenweber. The design represents the
gnarled stem of an oak tree, wonderfully true to nature,

DINING-ROOM.

United Art Establishments, Munich.

placed on a high marble pedestal — the enormous branches
are covered with dense foliage—; at the foot of the tree is
a rock, from under which the Dragon has crawled out, and
rears up its horrid figure.

DINING ROOM: TABLE ORNAMENTS.
United Art Establishments, Munich.

The strong stalwart figure of Siegfried is supported by his left hand against the tree, the right hand he lifts up to give a powerful death-blow to the Dragon beneath him.

This group is a remarkable piece of artistic work; to

DINING ROOM.

United Art Establishments, Munich.

be convinced of this, one need only remark the beautifully formed figure of the Dragon-Killer, clothed in a bearskin, then the limbs of the Dragon, and above all, the ferns and flowers growing at the foot of the tree, the branches of the same, and the formation of the rock.

The ceiling, which is of wood in this apartment, is not flat, but slanting, and the supporting beams are beautifully carved.

Splendid cabinets are placed round the walls, the shelves of which are supported by twisted columns.

The stove, on which rests an enormous china swan, is constructed with Norman arches and columns.

Two candalabra beautifully ornamented with enamel work on the centre of the table, a splendid chandelier for eleven candles, and a coloured carpet interwoven with arabesques, complete the elegant furniture of this apartment.

The pictures are by J. Piloty and are set in beautiful frames ornamented with flowers, the simple drawing of which harmonises so well with the coloured lines of the portières and curtains.

The pictures themselves are on gobelin linen and represent scenes taken from the life at the court of Landgrave Hermann of Thuringia. This brilliant court rises again out of the cloud of the past, the remembrances of the minnesinger age being refreshed and revived by the charm of legend and myth. Wolfram von Eschenbach, Gottfried von Strassburg and Reinmar von Zweter gaze down from out of the paintings over the three doors. The other pictures deal with scenes from the life on the Wartburg and from the legendary Singers' War, in which Klingsor, the magician from Hungary, with his protegé Heinrich von Osterdingen, in spite of his knowledge of magic, fell a victim to the vocal talent of Wolfram von Eschenbach.

The first picture presents

"Klingsor, disguised as a merchant, propounds his riddle before the court."

The sorcerer, attired in rich oriental costume, stands before the steps of the throne as he gives his riddle, full of deep learning and intent, to be solved. The Landgrave and his assembled court listen in amazement at his oratory, of which the theme is the heated disputes of the singers. This scene is shown by the second picture

"The Singers' War on the Wartburg."

Wolfram, unperturbed by the scholarly cleverness of the worsted Heinrich von Osterdingen and his friends, extols in his song the Landgrave as the noblest of princes. The scene represented is one of the most striking of the Singers' War. How powerfully Wolfram stretches his figure to its full height, as he, by his musical talent, conquers his opponent! The furious expression on the face of a singer pointing to a document, and the defeated breakdown of the conquered man, show the artist's perfect comprehension of his subject.

According to the conditions agreed upon, Osterdingen should forfeit his life; the supplication of the Landgravine

MENSERVANTS' APARTMENT.
United Art Establishments, Munich.

procures for him the favour of calling upon Klingsor as judge.

The third picture represents, with great artistic imagination

"The magic flight of Klingsor with Osterdingen through the air to the Wart-

6*

b u r g which lies deep below, bathed in the light of
the moon."

The following pictures present the Landgrave as the
patron and encourager of art and science.

"T h e L a n d g r a v e c o m m i s s i o n s W o l f r a m
v o n E s c h e n b a c h t o t r a n s l a t e t h e "W i l l e-
h a l m e."

"T h e L a n d g r a v e p r e s e n t s g i f t s t o t h e
s i n g e r s."

"L a n d g r a v e H e r m a n n r e t u r n s t o H e i n r i c h
v o n V e l d e g g e h i s l o n g - l o s t m a n u s c r i p t
o f t h e A e n e i s."

The astonished delight at the gift is depicted to the
life in the expression of the singer, and overcome with joy
Heinrich von Veldegg accepts from the hand of the Landgrave the manuscript of his work, which he had long given
up for lost.

The last of the charming and brilliant-coloured paintings is the

"I d y l l o n t h e W a r t b u r g."

This picture gave the artist opportunity to display his
skill to the utmost in the brilliant colouring of the gorgeous
attire of the ladies and gentlemen represented.

After the grandeur of the dining-room, the room we now
enter, namely, the menservants' apartment, strikes us at the
first glance almost with a chill, but here also, the delicate harmony of the profusely carved wooden panelling of the ceiling-
rafters and the articles of furniture, with the many coloured
wall-paintings, imparts to this room a comfortable, homely
appearance.

On the stools and chairs are cushions which bear in
pressed leather the lozenge and the lion of Bavaria.

Unlike the adjutants' apartment, this room is without
curtains, but this is amply atoned for by the glorious view
from the windows.

The large landing is now again reached by passing
through a small anteroom, which contains on the left the
entrance to the south turret with its winding staircase.

As is the case in all the splendid buildings erected by
Ludwig II. of Bavaria a full inspection of the Castle of
Neuschwanstein inspires the visitor with the sentiment of
delighted enthusiasm and admiration. One would imagine
that all the splendour exhibited in the apartments already
visited could hardly be exceeded, but the one we now are
about to enter possesses a really almost supernatural beauty.

THRONE ROOM (THRONE-DAIS.)
United Art Establishments, Munich.

The throne room.

Here everything speaks of greatness, solemn dignity and sublime splendour.

The comprehensive love of art exhibited by the royal architect is made most prominent in this hall.

As has been seen, the style employed in the bed-chamber is pure Gothic. On the floor beneath it was planned to build a Moorish Hall, a plan, which unfortunately, owing to circumstances, was never carried out. Here in the basilica structure of the throne room, the ideal beauty and gold and coloured splendour of the Byzanthine style has reached its summit of perfection. Art has succeeded in creating in this enormous hall the pearl of the entire building. Architecture and painting have worked together in harmony.

Professor Hauschild, in his beautiful and unique fresco paintings, demonstrates the relation borne from earliest times by the kingly office to religion, also the kingly office at the introduction and establishment of Christianity. These pictures by their depth of thought, grandeur of composition, and splendid grouping, raise in the spectator sentiments of the highest admiration.

To whatever part of this apartment the eye wanders, it is everywhere greeted by perfect harmonious beauty.

The architecture of this hall, which stretches through two entire floors, is grand in the extreme. The double row of pillars form the colonnade and passage leading to the platform, besides appearing to reduce the gigantic size of the apartment and afford at the same time space for the long row of fresco paintings.

The narrow north side, which is rounded off to an oval, was destined to receive the dais for the throne. An enormous archway separates this apse from the body of the building. Sixteen brilliantly polished, red porphyr pillars with gilded bases (placed six on either side of the hall, and four on the narrow north end) support the gallery. This is on a level with the top floor, and makes an almost magical impression by its equal number of columns of imitation lapis-lasuli, with gilded bases and profusely sculptured capitals. Above these pillars is the upper gallery with Norman arches. These ornament the walls and form a connecting link with the wood-panelled ceiling.

The floor is of rich mosaic work representing the vegetable and animal world, a master-piece of art by Detomas.

THRONE ROOM FROM THE THRONE-DAIS.

The border alone, of ornamented and linear designs, is a work of art of the highest rank. The light from the windows shining through the galleries illuminates the gold and gorgeous coloured beauty with a magic brilliancy. All the arches, recesses, and corners are profusely covered with frescoes, the parapets and surfaces of the arches with bright coloured ornamental decoration in powerful and decided tones.

Nine steps of snow-white marble conduct up to the dais.

It had been intended to erect a throne of ivory and gold beneath the canopy which is supported by four pillars. Lions were to have been employed as pedestals to the beautifully simple architectural balustrade.

The back wall of the throne-recess is decorated (after a design by the Court Architect Dollinger) with paintings on a gold ground, representing palms and crowned lions. This has been carried out within the last few years. Above this, likewise on a golden background, are the portraits of the six holy kings, separated from each other by narrow palms. These are:

> Casimir of Poland,
> Stephan oi Hungary,
> Henry of Germany,
> Louis of France,
> Ferdinand of Spain and
> Edward of England.

And above these is the beautiful painting of
"Christ as the First Lawgiver and King
of Kings,"
surrounded by a halo of cherubs' heads and twinkling stars. St. John the Baptist and Mary kneel at either side in adoration, with groups of angels in space.

The archway serves as a completing frame and is resplendent with ornamental decorations, between which the symbolical representations of the Seven Gifts of the Holy Spirit are introduced in medallions.

The side walls of the dais are furnished with the powerfully imposing figures of the Twelve Apostles supporting the commandments.

Here, as in all the other pictures in this hall, the artist has fully understood, by the measured quiet, solemn earnestness and superior dignity of his figures to impart to them the severe ecclesiastical tone, without falling into the lifelessness and stiffness which characterise most Byzanthinic originals. The view of the long hall from the throne platform

is one of overpowing beauty—the brilliant colouring, the
reflected glitter of the splendid pillars and the gorgeous

THRONE ROOM.
United Art Establishments, Munich

marble of the mosaic floor, all tend to charm and delight
the eye.

The panels of the Norman arches display idealised
eagles, and the south narrow wall is decorated with paintings, the designs being hares pursued by ravens. From the

colonnade of the lower gallery the following beautiful picture is visible

"S t. G e o r g e i n b a t t l e w i t h t h e D r a g o n."

The swan crowns the helmet of the knight, and the Castle of Falkenstein stands in the back ground of the picture.

With architectural skill the widened embrasure of the Norman arch which is before this picture and also before that of "St. Michael" (which hangs above on the back wall of the upper gallery) is employed as a kind of frame to the same.

The large painting of "St. Michael" represents the Archangel with shield and sword doing battle with Lucifer, the Prince of Darkness. Armed angels surround the victor who sets his foot on the neck of Lucifer, from whose head the crown falls off and beneath whom the abyss of Hell opens.

On the front wall, above the picture of St. Michael hangs the painting of

"T h e M a g i."

The star in the east is shining before them as their guide. The picture is full of life and animation and executed with a fairy-like oriental splendour.

The painting on the east-side-wall characterises the lawgivers of the pre-christian era.

Manu, Zoroaster, Hermes, Solon and Augustus, each with his national characteristic. A picture of Moses hangs on the opposite wall, a fiery halo round his head, the Table of Commandments in his left hand, the right raised with a gesture of sublime grandeur pointing to Heaven. The Jewish people have sunk upon their knees and listen to the words of their heroic and brave deliverer. The history of Christendom is represented in the brilliantly coloured paintings which decorate the walls of the colonnades.

On the west wall in the upper colonnade is the picture of "S t. L o u i s f e e d i n g a n d c l o t h i n g t h e p o o r."

In the lower colonnade:

"S t. C a s i m i r e n g a g e d i n P r a y e r b e f o r e t h e A l t a r."

"S t. C l o t i l d e, Q u e e n o f F r a n c e, i n s t r u c t s h e r h u s b a n d i n t h e C h r i s t i a n F a i t h."

"S t. E l i s a b e t h o f T h u r i n g i a n u r s e s t h e s i c k."

On the east wall of the upper colonnade:
"St. Stephan converts the Hungarians to Christianity."
"St. Heinrich builds churches and monasteries."

Again in the lower colonnade:
"St. Edward as Judge, protecting the rights of the serfs."

CORNER FIGURE.

"The Holy Ferdinand in battle with the Moorish unbelievers."

The corner angles of the cupola vault are ornamented by four charming figures of angels with the crown insignia—sceptre, globe, sword and crown.

Six monumental candalabra, two of which stand upon the dais, the remaining four along the sides of the walls, were intended, together with the chandelier, (which latter was never constructed) to shed the mellowed, softened light of candles over all this beauty.

If in this hall the eye has been captivated by the grandeur of its construction and decoration, it seems on opening the door to

the loggia

as if nature herself had striven with the work of men's hands in creating all this splendour. It is well-nigh impossible to describe the charm of the wonderful scenery. The Castle of Hohenschwangau, far below between the two lovely lakes, the deep-green foliage of the woods, the mighty mountains and the alpine foreground, all these lie before our eyes, and words are wanting to express the beauty of the picture. Most striking is this scene in the evening hours when the shadows of twilight are softening the gorgeous colours of the lakes and castle, and the mountain giants, under the farewell kisses of the departing day, are blushing in purple, violet and rosy rays, when from Füssen the sounds of the evening bells grow, like an Eolian harp, fainter and fainter until they die away, then it seems as if a quiet mysterious whisper ran through the peaceful mountain forest, and nothing but the rush and roar of the Pöllat falls disturbs the calm of the evening.

Our mind is still occupied with the splendour of the throne room. A thousand details spring up before our eyes, which we would fain remember and retain in our memory.

The fourth story is now reached by the main staircase. The termination of the staircase is richly and beautifully constructed. Eight pillars of Untersberger marble, the bases and capitals of the same handsomely sculptured, divide the rotunda into panels with charming decorative painting-designs of animals.

The sockets of these pillars are beautifully sculptured.

The frieze round the top of the walls is an ornamental design of dragons. The ceiling vault is blue, studded with innumerable golden stars. The Norman arches are embellished by floral decorations. The wrought-iron supports to the lanterns are artistically constructed in the form of dragons.

The attention is attracted by a remarkable piece of sculpture. This represents an enormous dragon angrily rearing itself up towards the middle column, which is sculptured in the form of a palm tree. Instead of a capital the upper end of this column, or tree, is ornamented by golden dates. It lies like a deep shadow on this keystone of the enormous building. What a fantastic appearance it must have presented when illuminated in the evenings by the subdued light from the candles in the coloured glass lanterns! Then the dragon appeared as the grim guardian of the state hall, that Holy of Holies of the castle.

The door now opens on to the

landing.

Like the landing on the third floor, this is equally beautiful in decoration and colouring.

The sculpture work of the capitals and porches which are constructed out of marble from Falkenstein, from the Tegel Rocks and from Untersberg, is very beautiful and profuse. The portières to the porches are of rich colours intermingled with gold—a wooden wainscot, richly carved, covers the base of the walls—also the backs of the seats are of handsome wood carving—the cushions belonging to the same are of pressed leather with designs of the swan, lion and the lozenge coat of arms.

The enormous frescoes, painted by Hauschild, are the continuation of the Sigurd Legend, the beginning of which is in the third story. The paintings here illustrate the Gundrun Legend after the Edda.

After the death of Sigurd, Gundrun went to live with Thora, the daughter of the Danish King Hakon, and with whom she remained for seven years. With Thora she embroidered and wove in the endeavour to dispel her grief.

"German Halls and Danish Swans, Heroes' Games and Hosts of Heroes, Red Shields of German warriors, Princes' followers in full armour."

From her mother Griemhilde, Gudrun received the Drink of Forgetfulness, which took from her the memory of Sigurd, and she permitted King Alti (Etzel) to woo her. She lived with him at his court, in spite of great riches and the blessing of children, in discord and unhappiness.

Accused by Helke, one of Etzel's maids, of having an intrigue with Dietrich of Berne, Gudrun was condemned to death—; uninjured, she drew the stone out of the boiling kettle and the well-deserved punishment fell upon Helke.

With great cunningness Gudrun interpreted to her unloved spose his dream, which he related to her in the following words:

"I fancied that you, Gudrun, ran me through the breast with a shining dagger. I saw twigs torn down in the garden, dipped in blood and brought up to me that I should cat them," as of no importance or meaning.

Alti sent messengers to Gunar and Högni to invite them to his court and in order to insure their coming, he offered them grants of land.

Gudrun, understanding the true wicked intentions of Alti, sent her brothers warning letters in the Runic writing, also the wives of the two kings, made anxious by dreams

STAIRCASE (DRAGON AND PALM).
United Art Establishments, Munich.

and understanding the writing, warned their husbands against taking the journey. The reception of the brothers, who arrived together with a large following at Alti's court, fulfilled the warning.

Atli greeted them with the words: "It was long since intended to rob you of life."

In spite of all Gudrun's endeavours to keep the peace, a savage struggle broke out betweeen the Huns and Gibichungs. Gunar was first overpowered, after him Högni, and Gudrun, filled with wild grief, stepped in between the men.

Atli commanded Gunar to be thrown into the Serpent Tower, and Högni to have his heart torn out of his body.

Gunar, thrown into the tower, sent the serpents into a sleep by the music of his lute—nevertheless an adder stung him and caused his death.

When Atli mocked Gudrun about the death of her brothers, her heart was filled with pain, anger and hatred, notwithstanding she gave orders for the funeral repast for the fallen Huns to be prepared. During the meal she disclosed to her husband that he had eaten the hearts of his two sons, whom she had killed, and had drunk wine out of their skulls.

Overcome by wine, Atli, who had ordered Gudrun to be stoned, was stabbed by her in his sleep.

She gave his treasures to the people and cast a burning brand into the castle. Gudrun then sought death in the sea, but the waves would not swallow her, and carried her across the Sound to a new life, in which she, married to King Onacher, was forced to see her sons and daughters all carried off by death.

Every verse of this ancient legend speaks of murder and death. One must regard it as great merit on the part of the artist that he was able to disguise the wildest scenes of this Heathen Song.

The series of pictures begin on the right of the entrance with the painting

"Gudrun goes, after the death of Sigurd, to join Thora in Denmark."

The next painting illustrates

"Thora and Gudrun embroidering the heroic deeds of their ancestors."

The two Princesses, surrounded by busy women, are engaged in their artistic work, which hangs in riehly embroidered carpets, on the walls of their apartment.

The third picture leads the spectator into the hall of the castle to the

"Courtship of Gudrun by Atli."

Three Princes in golden armour, their helmets glittering with precious stones, demand the hand of Gudrun, who

CORRIDOR ON THE 4th FLOOR (THE GUDRUN LEGEND)
United Art Establishments, Munich

sitting on the throne, attired in mourning, gazes sternly at her suitors. Thora, dressed in lighter coloured garments, converses with her in a friendly manner, and tries to persuade her to listen to their suit.

Then follows
"G u d r u n's w e d d i n g j o u r n e y."

This illustrates the entrance of Atli and Gudrun into the king's castle. The rich garments of the pair display royal splendour, and the astonished people and the charming group of virgins, assembled to meet them, are aptly depicted as showing great life and animation.

Above the window is a painting of
"A t l i r e l a t i n g h i s d r e a m t o G u d r u n."

This picture commences the dark side of the drama.

The following picture hangs on the long wall
"A t l i's m e s s e n g e r s a t t h e C o u r t o f G u n a r."

Above the door
"G u d r u n g r e e t s G u n a r a n d ' H ö g n i i n t h e H a l l o f A t l i."

The following masterpiece of art represents
"T h e s t r u g g l e o f t h e G i b i c h u n g w i t' h A t l i's f o l l o w e r s."

A fight rages in the hall, and Högni with herculean strength, dashes a conquered foe into the roaring flames.

The regal splendour of the royal table is dimly visible through the dense atmosphere of the hall, caused by a night of debauchery. In this picture, in which
"A t t h e F u n e r a l R e p a s t, Gudrun informs Atli
that he is drinking out of the skulls of his sons, and
has devoured their hearts,"
the horror of Atli is clearly expressed by his distorted face, and a shudder of disgust at the unsexed woman goes through the drunken guests.

The picture above the door illustrates
"G u n a r i n c h a i n s, i n t h e S e r p e n t T o w e r."

On the right of the principal door is the picture of
"G u d r u n c a s t i n g t h e b u r n i n g b r a n d i n t o
t h e c a s t l e."

The white garments flutter about the tall figure of Gudrun, who is hurriedly descending the marble stairs. Her hair, streaming over her neck and shoulders, shines red gold; enraged fury burns in every vein of the woman, who is casting the burning brand into the castle.

The last painting illustrates
"G u d r u n   c a r r i e d   b y   t h e   w a v e s   a l i v e   o n   t o
t h e   s h o r e."
Numbed and stiff, the marblelike white figure floats on
the top of the waves, which will not mercifully close over
the unhappy woman, but bear her to the shore, there to suffer
new, and inexpressible sorrows.
We now come to

The State Hall.
(27 meters long — 10 wide.)

which, with the corridor leading to the dais, occupies the
entire space allotted in the floor beneath to the apartments
of the king.
Architecture, art and technical industry have vied with
each other in making of this apartment a masterpiece of
beauty.

The Corridor leading to the Dais

is built into the state hall, and provides thereby a spacious
gallery for spectators. Charming glimpses can be obtained
through the Norman arches at the wonderful splendour of
the state hall. The corridor itself, separated from the hall
by the wall of the platform, is artistic and beautiful.
The sun, shining in through the Norman arches, forms
wonderful effects of light and shade. The seven handsome
chandeliers suspended from the ceiling sparkle and glitter.
The prevailing colours of the corridor, red and gold, are reflected in brilliant hues on the ceiling. Scrolls, on which
are inscribed the names of the German minnesingers, are
secured by charming linear ornaments. The panels above the
arches display endless riches in the shape of chromo paintings,
and the ornamental formation of the picturesque decoration
on the parapet of the side walls is full of variety.
Each arch is supported by two enormous pillars with
beautifully sculptured bases and capitals.
The corridor terminates in a comfortable, cosy alcove.
And now we come to the paintings. These treat of the
Legend of Parzival, an epic poem of the middle ages, which
illustrates the fate of Parzival's father, Gamuret, and the
adventures of Gawan, a knight of King Arthur's Round
Table.
Two classes of legends are united into one in this Legend of Parzival, the Legend of the Holy Grail with its
mystically spiritual, and the Legend of King Arthur and his

Round Table, with its worldly chivalric character. Into this
also is interwoven the Fable of Lohengrin, that of the Priest

PASSAGE LEADING TO THE THRONE-DAIS.
After an original photograph by Franz Hanfstaengl.

Johannes (by whom the idea of a Christian Grail knighthood was introduced into the East), and lastly that of the
Sorcerer Klingsor.

7*

Gamuret, the son of King Gantius of Anjou, left his home in the search of adventure and in his wanderings came to Bagdad. Here he won for himself distinction and honour in fighting on the side of the Kalif against the Fatimites.

He was shipwrecked near the town of Patelamunt, which was being hotly besieged by the enemies of the Moorish Queen Belakane. His offer of assistance was accepted, and followed by a splendid suite, he entered Patelamunt, whither the fame of his former heroic deeds had preceded him. He defeated the leaders of the besieging army in a hot battle, and won the crown and hand of Queen Belakane.

His love of adventure drove him, after a period of wedded happiness, to take secret flight. Shortly after, a son was born to him and Belakane, who was named Feirefiz.

In Valois (Waleis) Queen Herzeloide reigned.

At a grand tournament, at which the prize of honour, constituted the lands and hand of the Queen, Gamuret appeared, clad in splendid armour glittering with gems, as the honoured victor, and the judges awarded him the valuable prize.

At Babylon, Gamuret, for whom Herzeloide was watching and waiting, lost his young life. A posthumous son was born to Herzeloid, whom she named Parzival. Him she brought up in the solitude of the forest, far from the brilliant court of the king. She had him carefully instructed in every branch of knightly warfare.

When one day out hunting, Parzival saw for the first time three knights. These inspired him with such awe and reverence, that he sank before them on his knees. At his earnest entreaty, Herzeloide permitted her son to leave her, and he set out, attired as a jester and seated on a sorry nag, in search of adventure.

After the parting with her beloved son, Herzeloide's tender heart broke.

In his wanderings Parzival met Sigune, who was supporting the fallen Knight Schionatulander, who had been killed in a combat with spears, on her lap.

Sigune disclosed to Parzival the secret of his noble birth.

Sigune's love for Schionatulander forms one of the most touching and pathetic themes of this epos.

Parzival's first combat took place before the town of Nantes and in the presence of King Arthur and his knights, with the red knight Ither von Gahawis, and in this encounter, Parzival proved victorious. He took from his fallen foe his armour and warhorse.

Parzival received instruction from Gurnemanz in the outer forms of chivalric arts and customs, and was cautioned by him against asking too many questions.

Parzival continued his journey to Belrapeire, the residence of Condviramour, whom an impetuous wooer was besieging with an army. The lovely young couple fell hotly in love with each other. Parzival engaged the suitor in a combat with swords and overpowered him. The reward for this victory was the beautiful Condviramour. In spite of his love for her and his wedded happiness, Parzival's love of adventure again asserted itself, also the longing to see his mother, of whose death he had not heard. So once again, he set forth on his travels.

When passing the lonely mountain lake Brumbane, Parzival observed a boat nearing the shore in which a pale faced man, beautifully attired, was seated. Parzival asked him if he could direct him to a lodging, whereupon the stranger pointed out to him a castle near at hand— the Grail-burg. He wended his way thither, and met with a cordial reception. When seated at table in the hall, Parzival suddenly recognised in the suffering King Amfortas, the lonely man he had met on the lake.

Filled with astonishment, Parzival perceived the mysterious wonder of the Grail, which was worn by Repanse de Schoye, the sister of the Grail-King.

Remembering the warning given to him by his instructor, Gurnemanz, Parzival forbore to ask any questions about the king's illness.

Sorrow reigned over the whole assembly, for had Parzival only put this question, Amfortas would have been released from his suffering. (Parzival, however, would have succeeded him as Grail-King.) On taking leave of Amfortas for the night, Parzival, out of pure etiquette, still refrained from putting the momentous question. Knights conducted him to his rest, and virgins brought to him his night-potion. Falling into a heavy sleep, he saw revealed to him in a dream his future life, a life full of fighting and trouble. On awakening, Parzival, to his astonishment, found the castle deserted, only the Squire who drew up the draw-bridge after him, scolded him for having neglected to ask the all-important question.

Wandering about, he came across Sigune in a hermitage, with the embalmed body of Schionatulander. Sigune explained to Parzival about the castle and the illness of the king. She also, scolded him for having failed to ask the question.

Parzival, shortly after, met King Arthur and was admitted by him as a knight of the Round Table. Thereupon Kundry, the sorceress, rode up on a mule and abused Parzival in no measured terms for not having put an end to the sufferings of King Amfortas. On taking her departure, she demanded the adventure—loving knights of the Round Table to fetch from Chatel-Merveill (the magic castle of Klingsor) the Prize of Love.

A strange knight accused Gawan, a knight of the Round Table, of assassination and challenged him to a duel. Sorrowfully, Parzival took leave of King Arthur. After him, Gawan also left the Round Table in order to present himself at the scene of the forth-coming duel. From now on, Gawan's adventures occupy a prominent place in the poem. One of these adventures is the participation in the fight against King Melianz, who, having been rejected by Obie, the Duke's daughter, as a suitor, appeared with a large army before Bearosch.

Melianz was overpowered in a combat with spears and forced to surrender to Gawan. Parzival fought, unrecognised, on the side of Melianz.

Gawan succeeded in reconciliating Obie with Melianz, and the bloody fight ended in a joyful wedding feast.

Continuing his travels, Gawan suddenly perceived a lady's saddle-horse standing by a tree, and beneath the tree itself sat the owner, holding a severely wounded knight on her lap. Gawan, who had a knowledge of medicine, treated the wound and succeeded in restoring the sick man to health. Riding on, he met the Duchess Orgelouse von Locrois, and then and there, fell violently in love with her. This love, however, was not reciprocated by the Duchess, who replied to all his entreaties with disdain. Nevertheless Gawan served her faithfully and lovingly.

A ferryman warned Gawan against attempting to enter Castle Chatel-Merveill. As however, he was not to be deterred from his purpose, the man gave him some clever advice as to how he should conduct himself when there. Scarcely had Gawan entered the castle before a series of the severest trials began. On retiring to rest, he was prevented by the glass—like condition of the floor from gaining his bed, the magnificent "Lit-Merveill." At length, by dint of springs, he succeeded in alighting upon it, whereupon the bed sprang round and round the room, as though in furious anger, and only ceased after Gawan had offered up a pious prayer.

Now he was assailed by a storm of stones and bolts so that he could only protect himself with the greatest diffi-, culty by his shield. When this at last ceased, an enormous lion sprang into the room. Gawan, nothing daunted, at once courageously began to attack him and succeeded in culting off one of his paws with his sword. The blood flowing from the wound afforded Gawan a firmer footing on the floor, and he was able to kill the lion. Overcome by the terrible exertion, Gawan sank fainting over the dead body of the lion. The women who were kept prisoners by Klingsor in his castle, brought him back to life. Gawan, by his courageous conduct, had become possessed of the castle and enormous riches. Orgelouse, however, demanded a further proof of his bravery, and that was to fetch a branch from the tree of King Gramoflanz, to whom she bore a deadly hatred. Gawan set off on his trusty warhorse for the forest of the king, reached it in safety and broke off the branch. While in the act of doing this, he was surprised by Gramoflanz and arranged a tournament with him.

When Gawan returned in safety, bearing the branch, which he presented to Orgelouse, she was quite overcome by his faithfulness and courage, and she sank on her knees before him.

Their marriage was now celebrated with much pomp and splendour, and King Arthur honoured it by his presence. In the meantime, Parzival had been travelling about for years and had met the old Prince Kahenis with his wife and two daughters, all dressed in the garb of penitence and going on a pilgrimage. The old man severely rebuked Parzival "for omitting to observe the day of the Lord's Passion, and for not having, as the pious custom demanded, doffed armour and weapons." Parzival expressed himself as indifferent about honouring God, whereupon the princely pilgrim exhorted him to take self-communion.

Riding on, Parzival came to the lovely forest hermitage of Trevrizent. Trevrizent likewise scolded him for riding in complete armour on the Holy Good Friday and Parzival then and there before the simple altar in the hermitage, made confession of his sins, and received instruction from Trevrizent about the Holy Grail. On Parzival acquainting Trevrizent with his parentage, the latter revealed himself as the brother of Herzeloide and the Grail-King.

The day arrived for the meeting between King Gramoflanz and Gawan. The king was on the ground, waiting for his adversary. Suddenly Parzival, decorated with a twig from Gramoflanz's tree, appeared on the scene. A few days previously Parzival had overcome Gawan in knightly combat, and now he succeeded in likewise overcoming Gramoflanz.

The encounter between Gramoflanz and Gawan did not take place, as the former was engaged in paying court to Itonje, Gawan's sister.

During the days of feasting the hero Parzival disappeared secretly and met a richly armoured knight, whom he engaged in combat with the spear and sword. As Parzival's sword broke, the stranger knight generously threw his aside. The combatants made themselves known to each other. The strange knight proved to be King Farefiz, Parzival's stepfather. They returned together to King Arthur, and Feirefiz was appointed a knight of the Round Table. In the midst of the festivities, Kundry, the Grail messenger, arrived, and flinging herself at the feet of Parzival, she implored of him to pardon her for having formerly insulted him.

She brought the joyful news:
"Thine was the highest happiness,
"The inscription on the Grail was read,
"As King of the Grail thou art chosen,
"Now thy question shall release
"From suffering, misery and pain King Amfortas."

In the Grailburg Parzival released King Amfortas from endless sufferings, and after long years of waiting Condviramour saw Parzival again, and his two sons, Lohengrin and Kardeis, rejoiced at the return of their father, whom they now saw for the first time.

Once again Sigune and Schionatulander come into prominence. Parzival found Sigune in the hermitage on her knees, dead, before the coffin of her beloved. They were both laid to rest in one coffin.

At the Grail Table Feirefiz fell deeply in love with Repanse de Schoye. When all present reverently bowed down before the Grail, Feirefiz alone remained erect, for to him as a heathen, the wonder of the Grail was not disclosed. Not until he had become a Christian and received Baptism, did the glory of the Grail shine upon him.

The marriage of Feirefiz with Repanse now took place with much ceremony and pomp. From this union a son was born—known later as the Priest Johannes.

ALLEGORY OF THE "SÄLDE".

CENTRE OF AN ARCH (IN THE
PASSAGE TO THE THRONE-DAIS).

United Art Establishments, Munich.

With a short description of the Legend of Lohengrin the heroic poem now ends.

The paintings in the dais-corridor serve to complete the Legend of Parzival (the illustrations of which are in the state hall) and to symbolise the virtues of chivalry.

The first painting, on the wall to the right, represents "T h e M e e t i n g o f P a r z i v a l w i t h t h e P i l g r i m P r i n c e K a h e n i s."

The contrast between the hairy garb of penitence worn by the Prince, and the steel armour worn by Parzival, is admirably expressed.

Although the scenery of the picture is deliniated in the garb of winter, yet it seems as if the charm of Good Friday lay on it and one heard the angry tones of Gurnemanz's rebuke:

"Doff quickly the armour,
"Insult not the Lord, Who
"To-day, laying aside every weapon
"Offered for the sinful world,
"His Holy Blood as reparation."

The first picture on the left wall is one of Kolmsperger's excellently thought-out allegories called "Die Sälde."

This is a female figure simply attired in the dress of the middle ages. Her hair is adorned by a wreathe of full-blown roses, and in her left hand she holds a sheaf of lilies, the flower of innocence. Roses are strewn on the ground at her feet.

The next pictures illustrate scenes from the Legend of Gamuret and Gawan.

"G a m u r e t's e n t r y i n t o t h e b e s i e g e d m o o r - i s h c i t y o f P a t e l a m u n t."

"G a m u r e t's v i c t o r y o v e r t h e e n e m i e s o f B e - l a k a n e."

"G a m u r e t w i n s i n t h e T o u r n a m e n t t h e h a n d a n d c r o w n o f H e r z e l o i d e."

The entrance to the state hall in the centre of the corridor is ornamented by the following allegories,

On the left

"D i e S t ä t e" or "Constancy and Patience."

On the right

"D i e T r i u w e" or "Faithfulness."

The following pictures form the continuation of the illustrations of the epic poem.

"G a w a n's m a r r i a g e w i t h O r g e l o u s e."

"Gawan plucks a branch from the tree of
King Gramoflanz."
"Gawan succeeds in bringing about a re-
conciliation and promise of marriage between
Melianz and Obie."
"Gawan saves the life of a wounded knight."
"Gawan's adventuros at Chatel-Merveill."
Next to these hangs the picture of the allegory "M ä -
z e" or "Moderation," which inspires one with admiration
and wonder. An ideal female figure, splendidly attired, is
poised on a globe, holding up a goblet in her right hand.

The wall decorations at the commencement and end of
the corridor are by Schultze, and are well worth notice.
Small, slender trees, to the stems of which are fastened
lyre, bow and quiver, are set in the narrow panels. Two
white doves are perched at the foot of one of these pictures,
and birds of brilliant plumage are flying hither and thither
amid the branches of the trees.

The alcove, which forms the end of the corridor, contains the charming picture illustrating the allegories
"Strength and Justice." The former holds a powerful lion by a chain, the second, beautifully dressed, holds in
her right hand a naked sword, and in the left, the weights.

A glance through one of the windows of the corridor
discloses, on the outer wall, a gigantic statue of the Madonna in sandstone.

The centres of the Norman arches are embellished with
numbers of brilliantly coloured paintings, the subject of
which are symbolical designs bearing on the Parzival Legend.

Each arch contains two of such representations, which,
surrounded by profuse ornamental painting, display the following characteristic figures:

a) A chained Sea-cat, snatching at a bunch
of grapes.

The centre-piece is an imp, above which are the flaming
fires of Hell.—The Symbol of Impure Desire.

b) A Falcon, swooping down upon a goose.

This is surrounded by swamp and water plants, the
centre a cherub's head, with wings. Above, are the sun
and stars and also a Hand, raised in the act of taking an
oath. This represents Parzival's Dream on the Plimizol.

c) A Phoenix, rising up out of the flames.

A bat forms the centre-piece, above which the sun is rising.

This symbolises the eternal youth of the Phoenix
through death in the flames.

d) A C r o c o d i l e , surrounded by ornamental foliage.

A dragon occupies the centre, and above stands a castle, struck by lightning—the Symbol of Sin.

e) S y r e n s. (Half fish, half woman.)

In the centre is a bear, greedily devouring honey, and above this are poisonous plants and toadstools. This represents the temptation to immoderate desires.

f) A B i r d o f P a r a d i s e , surrounded by charming foliage. Over this is a lamb, conventional lilies and a dove. The bird of paradise is flying in the higher and purer air above.

g) A S a l a m a n d e r , rising out of the fire on garlands of green leaves. The centre picture represents prison windows, through which flames are bursting—above these are tongues of fire, and amid foliage a black cross, on the beam on which is the word "Fides" (i. e. Faith); symbolising the Purified Souls. (Salamander purifying itself in the fire.)

h) A P e a c o c k with a wheel, floating on the clouds.

Above this the sun, and two Feet bearing the marks of the Crucifixion. The centre pikture represents a banner with a cross and palm branches, and again above these are cherubs' heads, medallions, a hand lifted in the act of taking an oath, globe with cross, and a dove taking flight.

The peacock is the Symbol of Blessedness and Immortality.

i) A M a g p i e , sitting amid conventional foliage.

The centre picture represents a quarrelling dog and cat; the Symbol of Instability and Inconstancy.

j) A W i n g e d D r a g o n , in a densely starred sky, surrounded by floral ornamentations. Above are designs of dragons.

Herzeloide's dream, indicating Parzival's Misfortuness.

k) A S n a k e , winding itself round a tree—an apple in its mouth.

The centre-piece is a fox, dragging a goose into its hole. The Symbol of Cleverness, Temptation and Cunning.

l) A C r o w i n g C o c k.

The centre-picture a barking dog.

Symbol of Watchfulness.

The entrance to the state hall is ornamented by (on the left) a lion, and (on the right) a stag.

A charmingly pretty figure of an angel. looks down from the middle of the Norman arch, holding in its hands

BANQUETING-HALL WITH THE SINGER'S "ARBOUR".

United Art Establishments, Munich.

a scroll, on which is inscribed the ancient greeting "Salve" or "Hail!"

The beauty and profuseness of the decorations in this corridor must perforce strike everyone, and yet, gorgeous as this splendour all is, the state hall cannot fail but to impress still more. Bright daylight streams in through the ten enormous windows on the south and east, and on the north through the Norman arches of the corridor leading to the throne platform.

The splendours of court life in the middle ages are here brought before our eyes. The ceiling follows the formation of the roof, whereby the hall gains considerably in height. The forty-two panels of the wainscotted ceiling are richly ornamented, in gold and brilliant colours, with conventional

STATE HALL: BREASTWORK PAINTING.
United Art Establishments. Munich.

designs and with the signs of the Zodiac—Ram, Bull, Swins, Crab, Lion, Virgin, Weights, Scorpion, Marksman, Capricorn or Ibex, Water-carrier and Fish.

The chandeliers suspended from the ceiling, in spite of their massive workmanship, impress one by their apparent lightness and elegance, and the ten candalabra, placed at intervals by the side of the long wall of the apartment, are especially remarkable, being set with sparkling stones, which, in their setting of gold, glitter and shine with all the colours of the rainbow.

On the east side of the hall, the light streams in through the sixteen gorgeous glass painted windows, illuminating the beauty of the apartment with thousands of colours.

The corridor wall supports a gallery, the parapet of which is so constructed above the entrance as to form a balcony, and, as supports to the same, the figures of Kliot. the book-writer and Fleietanis, the astronomer, are characteristically employed.

A glass-door in the east wall leads out on to a balcony, from which a lovely view is to be obtained. This embraces

STATE HALL (LOOKING TOWARDS THE CORRIDOR TO THE THRONE-DAIS),
After an original photograph by Franz Hanfstaengl in Munich.

the castle courtyard, the women's apartments, and the massive square tower, and beyond and above this, the mighty mountain giants and the green splendour of the surrounding woods.

The alcove in the south-east end of the state hall corresponds with the alcove in the tribune or dais corridor.

This is adorned by (Kolmsperger) the allegorical female figures of Wisdom and Truth, the former with her attributes, the winged serpent and looking glass, and the latter holding a lighted candle in her hand. The space before the window-wall on the east side is raised from the floor by a step, and opposite to this little platform, the singers' arbour is erected, which is reached by mounting four steps.

The Norman arches of this "arbour" are supported by four slender porphyr pillars, the capitals of the same being richly ornamented by sculpture, symbolising the minne song. Above the "arbour" there is a "box" supported by four pillars. Two doors, beautifully carved and with handsome fittings, form the side entrances to the singers' platform.

The architectural frame work of this splendid hall is filled in by the numberless and beautiful paintings on the walls. Court Architect Hofmann created, with untiring energy, the designs for these decorations, which represent, in hundreds of variations, blossoms, buds, fruit, conventional foliage and animals. Even a superficial inspection shows an endless riches in design and colouring. Here, one sees vine branches with conventional leaves and splendid fruit, there, linear and foliage ornaments, eagles and dragons, which, in unison with the symbolical animal figures in the embrasures of the arches, on the parapets and binding-vaults, lend their brilliancy of colour and beauty to the stately hall. The capitals on the window-wall deserve mention as masterpieces of wood carving, which, by their delicate and plastic construction, stand out prominently from the brilliant coloured background.

These carvings represent serpent with anchor, Satan, angel with the Grail-Paten, pillar bearing designs of dragons, two armed knights, pillars with ornaments of plants, bear climbing a tree, squirrel, and the wizard Klingsor. The escutcheons of the persons connected with the Parzival Legend are introduced on to these pillars. The beams of the ceiling rest on beautifully sculptured animal forms, which crown these, architecturally and plastically, beautiful capitals. The portraits of the persons in the Parzival Legend are placed above the windows and arches of the singers' "arbour", surrounded by buds and blossoms, intermingled with designs of animals (dragon, swan etc.).

STATE HALL, FROM THE LOGGIA.

United Art Establishments, Munich.

Engl Neuschw.

8

On the east window-wall are the entire figures of Titurel, Frimutel and Amfortas, on the south window-wall and above the singers' arbour, (in medallion form) Repanse, Feirefiz, Sigune, Schionatulander, Ginovra, Artus, Herzeloide, Gamuret, Belakane, Kardeis, Lohengrin, Elsa, and Johannes. The Bavarian coat of arms, in brilliant colouring, is placed over the doors on either side of the singers' arbour.

The series of paintings representing scenes from the Legend of Parzival are full of poetical feeling and sentiment.

STATE HALL. HERZELOIDE, PARZIVAL'S MOTHER.
United Art Establishments, Munich

The first painting hangs on the window-wall to the right and is entitled

"How Parzival, when out hunting, first heard of Knighthood."

The pretty fair curly-haired boy has sunk on his knees in awe at the brilliant spectacle which the knights present on their war-horses.

The second picture illustrates

"Parzival bidding his mother farewell."

This represents Parzival dressed as a Jester and seated on a sorry nag, a spear in his hand. Herzeloide kisses him, filled with grief at parting with her son.

The third picture
"P a r z i v a l's f i g h t w i t h t h e R e d K n i g h t"
represents Parzival meeting with his first adventure. His
wretched nag has broken down before the furious onslaught
of the powerful warhorse, but with youthful agility, Parzival has regained his feet, and poises his spear for the
death-bringing thrust.

The next painting is full of charm:
"P a r z i v a l's m a r r i a g e w i t h C o n d v i r a m o u r."

The noble pair, hand clasped in hand, gazing lovingly
at each other, leave the church, preceeded by two pages.
Their road is strewn with roses.

Then follows
"P a r z i v a l's m e e t i n g w i t h t h e s i c k A m f o r -
t a s b y t h e l a k e."

An atmosphere of gloom envelopes this picture. The
Grail-King is seated in the boat—pale, and with an expression of intense suffering on his face. Parzival, on the contrary, is represented as full of youth and vigour.

On the front wall is the picture
"P a r z i v a l i n t h e G r a i l C a s t l e."

The architecture of the Grail Hall is magnificent, it
seems as if the sublime beauty of the state hall were reflected in the picture. All the wonderful mystery during the
meal has failed to draw the momentous question from Parzival's lips. Erect and immovable, he stands on the throne-
dais, with the sword presented to him by Amfortas grasped
in his hand, gazing after the virgin who is carrying away
the Grail Vessel.

Amfortas, his head sadly resting on his hand, points,
with the left, to his painful wound.

Above this picture is the representation of
"P a r z i v a l b e i n g s e r v e d b y v i r g i n s, a n d
c o n d u c t e d t o h i s r e s t,"
and also
"P a r z i v a l's d r e a m i n t h e G r a i l C a s t l e."

"It wove for him a picture
"Of an encounter with spears,
"Its frame was as the blades of swords,"
"Horses wildly stamping, all eager for the fray—.
"A dream, so full of storm and woe—
"That should, in wakeful life, his death be thirty-
fold intended,
"It would be as nought compared with the agony of
the dream."

8*

THE APPOINTING OF PARZIVAL TO THE OFFICE OF GRAIL-KING
United Art Establishments, Munich

By the side of the balcony window hangs the picture of
"P a r z i v a l   l e a v i n g   t h e   G r a i l   C a s t l e   and
being scoffed at on the drawbridge."
The door-porter calls after him roughly
"Thou gander———
"Why hast thou not opened thy mouth,
"And thy host here questioned?
"Now is the most coveted of prizes denied to thee!"
"T h e G r a i l m e s s e n g e r K u n d r y c u r s e s P a r -
z i v a l."
This picture is true to the life. The artist has painted
Kundry from the description given of her in the epic poem,
making her possessed of intense ugliness. She hurls her
curse at Parzival, abusing him in terms of violent anger.
Parzival stretches out his right hand as if to ward off the
words.

King Arthur watches the scene with amazement. A
beautiful girl standing in the foreground of the picture,
covers her eyes, weeping bitterly.

The picture in the dais-corridor
"P a r z i v a l   m e e t s   t h e   k n i g h t l y   f a m i l y   on
Good Friday going on a pilgrimage"
ought, by rights, to have been placed here in order to complete the series.

The next painting is
"P a r z i v a l   r e c e i v e s   i n s t r u c t i o n   about   the
Miracle of the Grail."
The branches of the firs are white with frost. The fire
before which Parzival is seated, is crackling merrily. The
scene which represents Parzival with his gaze sadly fixed
upon the ground, and the earnest old man clothed in a
monk's habit, is full of reality.

Uttering words of consolation, Trevrizent points to the
picture of the Crucified.
"P a r z i v a l   r e c o g n i s e s   h i s   s t e p - b r o t h e r
F e i r e f i z."
This is the subject of the next picture.

The two brothers, who have just been engaged in a hot
conflict, gaze at each other, full of astonishment. The
broken fragments of Parzival's sword lie on the ground. In
the background their warhorses are grazing peacefully side
by side.

The last painting shows
"P a r z i v a l   s u m m o n e d   b y   K u n d r y   t o   b e   t h e
G r a i l - K i n g."

Kundry kneels before Parzival and King Arthur:

"In garments richly fashioned,
"And after Paris fashion
"Of costly velvet was her cap."

Parzival stretches out his hand in forgiveness to Kundry, King Arthur raises his hand in blessing. On every countenance joy is written. A squire blows the happy tidings on the horn.

THE STATE HALL. THE GRAIL WONDER.
United Art Establishments, Munich.

The following picture hangs on the front wall, above the singers' arbour:

"P a r z i v a l i n s t a l l e d a t t h e G a l a F e a s t a s G r a i l - K i n g."

Parzival is seated on the throne in the lofty hall of the Grail Castle. Repanse solemnly carries in the "Grail;" and a supernatural light proceeds from the Holy Vessel, which seems to envelope the picture in an atmosphere of sanctity.

With this corresponds
"L o h e n g r i n's d e p a r t u r e f r o m t h e G r a i l C a s t l e."

Lohengrin, seated in the boat drawn by the swan, looks back at the Grail with an expression and gesticulation of distress and sorrow.

The most beautiful of all these pictures is the splendid representation of the Miracle of the Holy Grail, which hangs on the east wall above the gorgeous colouring of the Norman arch window.

"Each year descends from Heaven a dove,
"Its wondrous power to strengthen and renew.
"It is called the Grail, and to its knights imparts
"Blessed, purest Faith."
    Angels bow down in adoration before the Grail Vessel,
on which the white dove, bearing the Host, alights.

STATE HALL. SIDE VIEW OF A CUSHIONED BENCH.
United Art Etablishments Munich.

    Nothing now remains to be inspected but the singers'
"arbour."
    A forest landscape covers the background, in which is
visible the gigantic ashtree of the Edda, "Ygdrasill." The
foreground is light green, amongst which squirrels, deer and

woodpeckers are disporting themselves. The side walls of the arbour are covered with luxuriant ornaments, plants and mythical animals. The portraits of the minnesingers Wolfram von Eschenbach, Bitterolf, Reinmar von Cweter, Walther von der Vogelweide, Heinrich von Osterdingen and Klingsor (this last seated on a dragon), appear amongst the tendrils of the ornamental foliage which decorates the walls.

The benches and seats placed along the sides of the state hall are beautifully carved, and the coverings of the cushions very handsome. These are of beautiful silk, interwoven with gold, and in delicate red and green tints. The arms of the sofas are fashioned to represent dragons, with ornaments of foliage and vines, idealised eagles and syrens.

Passing through long corridors, which serve to unite the palace with the knights' building, and which also show off to advantage the enormous space occupied by the latter, we come to the lower court.

NB. Here it is possible to obtain souvenirs, in the shape of pictures, photographs or books treating of the castles built by King Ludwig II.

Should visitors care to visit and inspect the kitchen offices it is permissible to do so. These are practically arranged, and built in accordance with the style of the whole castle.

A walk of about fifteen minutes leads to the Marienbrücke, from whence a lovely view of the castle may be had, showing the imposing building in its entire majesty.

The enormous building of the west castle front, with the loggia, gleams through the branches of the trees, presenting a wonderfully striking picture from this bridge, which, at a height of 90 metres, forms a graceful span across the 44 metre wide Pöllat ravine.

When the "Föhn" or southwind, stirs up the mountain water, slumbering under its cover of snow, then the Pöllat, as it rushes madly on its downward way, roars and thunders, echoing again and again in the peaceful stillness of that mountain spot.

High up on its rocky platform stands the castle. Those who have wandered through its apartments, and seen from alcove and balcony wonderful glimpses of the view beneath, can fully understand and appreciate this building, borrowed, so to speak, and yet in a style peculiarly its own, from the times of the middle ages.

From the "Jugend" ("Youth" a favourite look-out already mentioned), the entire beauty of the Schwangau, with

CASTLE-NEUSCHWANSTEIN, FROM THE MARIEN BRIDGE.

After an original photograph by Franz Hanfstaengl.

its charming lake and woodland scenery, is displayed before one's eyes. This well-known and much frequented spot is

reached by a shady path leading from the Marienbrücke.
This view corresponds with that seen from the loggia of the
throne room. Here also the ivy-covered Castle of Hohenschwangau adds to the dreamy beauty of the scene, and the
blue mist of the summer's day hovers like a thin veil over
the lakes, and forest, and mountain giants.

The following words express the beauty of this far-
reaching view

"Who on the "Jugend" becomes not young,
"Came with gray hair into the world."

After having duly visited and inspected the two royal
castles, one is tempted to linger on in this beautiful neigh-
boorhood, which so abounds in charming walks and excursions. Space does not permit of a description of all of these.
Only a few of the most beautiful can now be mentioned.

1. The road to the Ammertal, passing the shooting
lodge Blöckenau (Jagdhaus Blöckenau) and the Schützensteig.
(This is the shortest route for walkers between Hohenschwangau and Schloss Linderhof.)

2. The lower Winterzugweg, this beautiful walk branches
off from the road leading to the Blöckenau and, at a height
of 50 meters above the level of the Alpsee, leads round the
whole lake and joins, just before the Fürstenstrasse, the
Gnomensteig (with its grotesque group of rocks), which
winds up in 40 minutes to the Marienruhe and Marienbuche.
This is a beautiful shady walk.

3. The Tegelbergreitweg, with beautiful views of the
Castle Neuschwanstein.

NEUSCHWANSTEIN FROM THE PÖLLAT RAVINE.

United Art Etablishments, Munich.

Hohenschwangau.

Printed by Franz Hanrar, G. m. b. H. in Munich.

From Steinberger's "Royal Castles."

VIEW OF HOHENSCHWANGAU FROM "THE JUGEND"

Published by I. Speiser at Prien on the Chiem Lake.

The Castle of Hohenschwangau.

Pleasantly shaded by lofty beech trees, the broad carriage road leads on from the Inn or Gasthof „Zur Alpenrose" to the Castle of Hohenschwangau. Every now and again beautiful views of the Alp Lake and Sänling become visible, and at one spot, a break in the woods affords a glimpse of the enormous buildings of Neuschwanstein.

Before long, Hohenschwangau itself appears in sight—. High up, enthroned on the summit of the rocks, the lordly mansion towers up above the battlements of the castellated gateway and the encirding walls.

The picture is completed by the corner towers and graduated battlements by which the roof is ornamented, — the whole is like a dream which one has long seen in one's mind, but which now for the first time assumes shape and form. The outer castle gate bears the Arms of Bavaria and the Palatinate, sculptured in stone. Passing through this gateway, one enters the lower courtyard, which is only wide enough to afford room for the approach. The massive walls, growing, as it were, out of the rocks, present an interesting example of solid masonry. The large panel of the inner gate is ornamented (by Nehers) with two knights in armour, bearing a floating banner, on which are emblazoned the Arms of Bavaria and Schwangau —; a tablet bears the inscription: „Hohenschwangau zum Schwanstein, erected by the Nobles of Schwangau, restored by the Crown Prince Maximilian of Bavaria in the year of our Lord, 1836. — Carried ont by Dominic Duaglio."

In these few words is contained the eventful history of this noble mansion.

The upper courtyard is reached by passing through the gateway, the splendid Norman arch of which is ornamented by architraves enriched with Gothic tracery.

Ivy grows luxuriantly on the castellated walls, shrubs and green moss clothe the rocks, out of which the castle seems to have grown. This spot, so peaceful and still, seems to resemble more the cloister of a monastry, than the precinets of a royal castle. The road leads round the west and north sides in a gentle ascent up to the buildings.

After an original impression by H. Grabensee.

THE OUTER CASTLE GATE.

From the castellated walls, which conceal the precipitous incline of the mountain, and contain pleasant alcoves, a charming view is visible. This embraces the park and grounds, the deep blue waters of the Schwan Lake, shining

THE CASTLE GATE.
United Art Establishments in Munich.

through the trees, and beyond this, the wide Alpine foreground, with the glistening silver thread of the River Lech, the basins of the Hopfen and Bannwald Lakes, while on the right, stands the Castle of Neuschwanstein, overtopped by the high mountains of Schwangau.

The ivyclad courtyard, shaded by the wide spreading branches of the lime trees, forms, with its surrounding walls, the immense round towers and the graceful alcoves and balconies, a most charming and fascinating picture.

THE PRINCES' BUILDING.
United Art Establishments in Munich.

    This courtyard is bounded on the east side by the princes' building (Prinzenbau) the alcove of which is ornamented with frescoes by Glink. On the left, gnome with wooden sword and beer mug; on the right, gnome in a dancing attitude, holding sausage and knife — in the centre, rising out of the calyx of flowers, appear the half —

THE MARY FOUNTAIN.
United Art Establishments in Munich.

length pictures of an old man and a girl in medieval costume (with escutcheons).

On the left, by the wall, is the charming "Mary Fountain" (Marienbrunnen), the painting, a representation of the

9*

"Madonna with the Holy Child Jesus", is by Glink; beneath this are the heraldic arms of Bavaria and Schwangau.

The utter stillness of this spot, which presents such an excellent view of the castle, is only broken by the trickling of the water, which, flowing from the mouth of a lion, empties itself into the basin of the fountain beneath.

THE LION TOWER.

Two large castellated towers flank the facade, which, with its numerous windows, balconies with balustrades of stone, and alcoves, is impressively, if simply, constructed. Broad outside steps, the balustrade of which forms a terrace at the top, lead up to the castle entrance and serve to enhance the beauty of the architectural picture. The small

garden is situated on the west side of the castle, and on the
way leading to it, a glimpse over the low parapet of the

THE LIOM FOUNTAIN.
After an original photograph by Franz Hanfstaengl.

wall discloses a fine view, which from the balcony on the
upper floor, is still more beautiful and extensive.

The "Swan Fountain" (Schwanenbrunnen) is close to the entrance of the garden. On the right, in the same rocks on which the castle itself is built, the marble bath is hewn out, which, by the purple-red glow cast upon it by the coloured glass door, presents an almost magical appearance.

This is followed by the "Little Goose Man" Fountain (Gänsemännchenbrunnen); a copy of the Fountain bearing the same name on the market place in Nürnberg.

The "Lion Fountain" (Löwenbrunnen) the splashing and murmuring of which alone disturb the dreamy stillness of this quiet corner, presents a beautiful sight. The projecting terrace wall in the right hand corner of the garden, afforded space for this handsome erection, which, executed by the master hand of Schwanthaler, is a copy of the celebrated "Lion Fountain" (Löwenbrunnen) in the Alhambra.

Four lions in cast iron support an enormous basin, out of which the fountain rises, the spray emptying itself through the throats of the lions into the lower basin beneath.

The view from this spot is well worth noticing. The Alp Lake, surrounded by its frame of green trees, the mountains covered with a thick growth of fir, with here and there a sprinkling of beech trees to relieve the sombreness of the former, and the summits of the Gern and Köllespitze, all combine to form a lovely and charming picture.

This is perhaps the most delightful spot which the castle offers. Not only the view, but the sweet scents from the flowers and lime trees, the distant harmonious music of the bells ascending from Füssen, all tend to make the visitor inclined to linger on and dream awhile, before wending his way to seek new and interesting scenes elsewhere.

Narrow stairs lead from the right of the "Lion Fountain" up to the kitchen offices, above the entrance to which is an al fresco representation of a tankard surrounded by vines with the inscription

"When eating and drinking, forget not God."

The first room is

The Armoury (with chapel).

The figures of knights in full armour, visors closed, sword or lance in their hands, are placed round the walls, on which are arranged in picturesque groups shields, battle swords, darts, crossbows, arrows and hurlbats.

The background forms the chapel. Artistic glass paintings ornament the windows to the right and left of the Altar,

THE ARMOURY AND CHAPEL.
After an original photograph by Franz Hanfstaengl.

which are representations of the following ancestors of
the builder of this castle, the Emperor Ludwig of Bavaria

in coronation robes with sword and globe—and the imperial crown upon his head; and the Elector Maximilian 1. in a

BILLIARD ROOM.
Atfer an original impression by Eranz Hanfstaengel in Munich.

coat of mail. Above the entrance to the hall is the following verse:

"Welcome Wanderer, lovely women,
"Dispense with sorrow and entrust your souls
"To the joyful sense of poetry."

Then, over the door leading to the wine cellar:
"I salute thee, thou noble body salve,
"Thou doctorest me on every side
"Thou art a wholesome syrup.
"The Emperor of Constantinople,
"The Grand Khan of Wallachia,
"The Priest Johannes, all these understood and appre-
"Thy nobility;   [ciated
"Why then should I scorn thee?"

Enormous tankards ornament this room.

Passing up the windingstairs, the visitor arrives at the
first floor. A glass door opens on to

The Billiard Room.

Valuable old articles of china fill the cabinets, which line
the walls. In one corner of the apartment is a picture by
Murillo, "St. Joseph with the child Jesus".

The centre of the spacious room is taken up by the
large billiard table. The ceiling is ornamented by profuse
Gothic tracery. A door, embellished by paintings on glass,
leads on to the veranda, which is surrounded by a high
stone parapet. From this spot a lovely view is seen of the
Lech valley, Baumwald Lake and the Castle of Neuschwanstein. The side doors which open on to the adjoining

Swan Knight Hall (Schwanenrittersaal)

are ornamented with valuable glass paintings, dating from
the XVI and XVII century.

The emblem or symbol of the castle is the swan, and
this design is introduced into every apartment in all sorts
of artistic variations.

The histories of the three ruling races of Schyren,
Guelph and Hohenstaufen, stand out prominently from the
background of local and German legend and history which
form the subject of the wall paintings. These again are surrounded by scenes taken from the life of chivalry in the
middle ages; proverbs and verses express in amusing terms
the earnestness of the old sayings and events.

The ornaments on the tables and brackets, the light colour of the furniture, which is mostly of ash or cedarwood,
the Gothic tracery on the ceiling, all these combine to im-

part to the hall an elegant and picturesque appearance.
This Swan Knight Hall. used as a dining room, is decorated

THE HALL OF THE SWAN KNIGHT (SCHWANENRITTERSAAL)
After an original impression by Franz Hanfstaengel in Munich

by paintings after Rubens; and works by Nehers and Quag-
lio, illustrating the Legend of Lohengrin, the "Swan
Knight". hang on the walls.

Taking the pictures in the order in which they hang, they illustrate the following subjects:

1. "The Swan Knight takes farewell of the Grail Castle."
2. "The Emperor hears the horn of the Swan Knight."
3. "The victory of Lohengrin in the ordeal appointed by God."
4. "The marriage of Lohengrin with the Duchess of Bouillon."

THE "SCHYREN" APARTMENT.
After an original impression by Franz Hanfstaengel in Munich

These pictures all bear the stamp of the middle of the 19 th century art.

The furniture and articles of use are in the Gothic style. The splendid paintings on glass, illustrating sacred and historical events, date mostly from the past century. Two of the same, "St. Sebald and the Emperor Maximilian", and "Albrecht Dürer, holding the ladder", are by Köller.

A beautiful view of the surrounding country is to be had from the balcony of this hall, as well as from the windows of this floor and the floor above.

THE "ORIENTAL" APARTMENT.

After an original impression by Franz Hanfstaengel in Munich.

Adjoining the "Swan Knights' Hall" (on the left) is the apartment consecrated to the 1000 years history of the Schyren. The chief decoration of this consists of the paintings on the walls, the work of Lindenschmitt. These illustrate:

1. "The storming of the Norman camp by Duke Luitpold in the year 892."

2. "Contest between Duke Christoph and the Polish giant Lublin at Landshut in 1495."

3. "Duke Ludwig the Kelheimer saves the Crusaders in the drought by Cairo, 1221."

4. "Duke Ludwig the Kelheimer promises the Countess Ludmilla von Bogen marriage before the painted knights."

5. "Reconciliation of Ludwig of Bavaria with Friedrich the Handsome of Austria."

6. "Repast after the victory at the battle of Ampfing, 1322."

7. "Otto von Wittelsbach protects the Emperor Friedrich Barbarossa (Red-beard) in the revolution in Rome, 1155."

8. "Johann Aventin, Bavarian Historian, 1534."

The most remarkable piece of furniture in this apartment is the large round table. The slab of the same is made of Kelheim marble and is a masterpiece of work in relief. The arms of Bavaria form the centre, and are surrounded by the figures of the twelve Apostles, the arms of various Bavarian towns, the planets, signs of the Zodiac and numerous inscriptions. One of these latter imparts the information "that this slab was made in the year 1591 for William V., Duke of Bavaria."

The windows are ornamented by beautifully painted panes. Work dating from the 17th century. Two of these, most particulary worthy of notice, are in the alcove of the lion tower, showing the arms of Duke Albrecht of Bavaria and his wife Mechtilde with the date 1614.

Oriental apartment.

This forms a striking contrast to the other rooms already inspected. Splendid little Oriental tables, ottomans and portières form the furniture of this apartment.

The decorations are also in the eastern style to correspond with the furniture.

The paintings on the walls (by Scheuchzer and Monten) are scenes taken from the travels of the Crown Prince Maximilian in the east. Amongst others are the following:

1. Smyrna, Troya, Mitylene, the Dardanelles, Constantinople and Bujukdere.

2. "The entry of the Crown Prince into Belger-Beg."
3. "The visit of the Crown Prince to the Sultan Mahmud II."

THE "SCHWANGAUER" APARTMENT.
After an original impression by Franz Hanfstaengel in Munich

4. "The entry of the Crown Prince with King Otto of Greece into Athens."

On the right from the Swan-Knight Hall is

The Schwangau room

in which the eventful history of Schwangau is illustrated in artistic, splendidly conceived paintings by Lindenschmitt: representing the following subjects:

1. "The storming of the monastery Rottenbuch by George of Schwangau, 1280."

2. "Conradin's farewell to his mother in Hohenschwangau, in 1263."

BERTHA ROOM.
United Art Establishments Munich.

3. "The minnesinger Hiltepold of Schwangau."

4. "The dying Emperor Lothar gives over the crown regalia to the Guelph Duke Henry the Proud in Breitenwang, 1137."

5. "Conrad of Schwangau, being wounded, is conveyed to Steingaden, 1310."
6. "Luther's flight with Langenmantel, 1518."
7. "The conference of the Emperor Maximilian I. with Gayler von Kaisersberg at Füssen, 1519."
The clock, dating from the year 1539, is worthy of notice. Now follows

The Bertha room.

This apartment immortalises the saying regarding the birth of the Emperor Charles the Great, and pictures, representing charming love-scenes, are intermingled with those representing the powerful figures of the Carlovingians.

The paintings, as well as the charming ornamentations which surround them, are the work of Glink, after the compositions of Schwind.

Over the door is a picture "The Astrologer and the Legend," allegorically represented, and bearing the inscription "That which the stars reveal, legend faithfully repeats."

The following pictures, as regards richness of imagination and charming formation, may be reckoned as some of the finest in the castle:
1. "Bertha's reception in the Rice Mill."
2. "Pipin finds Bertha in the Rice Mill."
Then follow:
1. "Pipin's hunting suite."
2. "Bertha at the weaving-stool in the Rice Mill."
The large wall picture:
"The entry of Pipin and Bertha in Weihenstephan" is full of poetry and charm.

Above the second door is the picture of "Pipin and Bertha at either side of the throne, in the centre little Charles, who letting go the hand of his father, hurries to his mother, who holds out to him the crown and sword."

Above this is the following inscription:
"On the hidden banks of the Würm,
    flourished the ancient imperial sway."
The decoration of the walls and ceiling is carried out in Gothic tracery work.

The Ladies' or Agnes room.

The cosy alcove in this apartment imparts to it an appearance of homeliness, giving the spectator the impression

Geschichte der Pfalzgräfin Agnes von Wasserburg, Gemahlin Ottos des Grössern von Bayern, von 1159 bis 1190.

THE APARTMENT OF THE LADIES OF THE CASTLE, WITH A GLIMPSE OF THE "BERTHA ROOM".

United Art Establishments in Munich.

Engl. Neuschw.-H.

10

that its inhabitants have only quitted it a few minutes before. The chief ornament of the apartment is the handsome chandelier with its twelve silver swans.

The following inscription stands over the door of the Bertha room:

"History of the Countess (Palatine) Agnes von Wasserburg, wife of Otto the Great of Bavaria."

The paintings, which have above them their description in verse, represent the life of the Lady of the castle in eleven pictures.

"Love-making, Joys of Motherhood,
Sorrows of Motherhood, and Delights of Hunting."

On one of the walls the following words are written:

"Blessed Love, which appears to us on earth, in the sublime form of pure women, heavenly."

A bust of King Otto of Greece in Greek national costume stands on a bracket, and on the table in the centre of the room are several handsome china vases.

The tour of inspection round the first floor is now ended. This was formerly inhabited by Her Majesty the Queen of Bavaria, mother of King Ludwig II. (died 1889), whose life passed away in the Schyren apartment. A life, which at its commencement was so full of happiness and brilliancy, but which ended in such unspeakable sorrow and unhappiness.

The first room on the second floor, formerly inhabited by King Ludwig of Bavaria is

The Heroes' or audience hall.

This is the largest of all the apartments in the castle. The ceiling is supported by huge pillars, and the doors are ornamented by the introduction of old glass paintings. A beautiful view is visible from the alcove adjoining the room.

Sixteen charming pictures, by different artists (after the designs of Schwind) illustrate the principal scenes of the Wilkyna Legend and that of Dietrich von Bern.

The pictures hang on the window wall on the right and represent:

1. "The daughter of Siegfried the Greek goes to visit her lover, the Dane Dietliet, to bring him her father's "Stone of victory" for the battle on the morrow."

2. "Sisielie with her new-born son, Siegfried the Quick."

3. "Herbert, who is intended to woo King Arthur's daughter for Dietrich von Bern, draws the latter on the

wall, presenting him as hideous and grim, in order to make her reject him, and listen to his (Herbert's) protestations of love."

THE HALL OF THE HEROES I.

After an original impression by Franz Hanfstaengl in Munich.

4. "King Osantrix of Wilkinenland decorates his bride, Odo, the king's daughter, with golden shoes."

5. "Dietrich von Bern and Hildebrand von Venedig fight

10*

the giant pair, Grimm and Hilde, and take from them their treasures forcibly."

6. "Dietrich and Wittich's duel and reconciliation."

THE HALL OF THE HEROES II

After an original impression by Franz Hanfstaengl in Munich.

The following pictures hang above the door:

"An Elf surprises the spouse of King Adrian of the Nibelungenlied, asleep in the garden, and becomes the father of the fierce Hagen."

"Rüdiger and Osid abduct the daughters of King Osantrix; Erka for Attila and Bertha for Rüdiger."

"Dietrich and Dietlieb at the fête of King Ermenrich in Rome."

"The sleeping Sintram attacked by a dragon, afterwards rescued by Dietrich."

"Dietrich with his followers retires before the superior forces of King Ermenrich from Bern."

THE "GUABIAN" (HOHENSTAUFEN) APARTMENT.
After an original impression by Franz Hanfstaengl in Munich.

"Bolfriana with the charmed ring, received from Yron, which makes her in love with the donor."

"The king's daughter Herburg throws an apple to her lover Appolonius (containing her declaration of love), the son of King Arthur and the brother of Yron."

"Erka, the Queen of the Huns, equips her sons to go to the war with Dietrich."

"The ingenious Wieland, attired in a robe with wings, fleeing from King Nidung, who commands his (Wieland's) brother to shoot at him, who, however, aimed at a bladder filled with blood, which Wieland had made fast under his breast."

"Dietrich's victory at Gronsport, on the Mosel, which restores to him his kingdom."

Now follows

The Hohenstaufen apartment.

Lindenschmitt has illustrated, in six beautiful paintings, the brilliancy and power of the Hohenstaufen Emperors and the tragic end of their race. They illustrate the great Barbarossa in the following scenes:

1. "Barbarossa as conqueror of the Turkish army at Ikonium in 1100."
2. "The humiliation of Milan in the year 1162 and his (Barbarossa's) death in the river Seleph 1190."
3. "His celebrated successor Friedrich II. receives the key of Jerusalem 1229."

The two following pictures express tragic feeling:

1. "Conradin fleeing, is overtaken by Frangipani 1268."
2. "King Enzio in prison at Bologna 1270."

In the adjoining alcove, which is fitted up as a chapel, two valuable pictures are kept. These were presents from the Czar Alexander I. of Russia to King Ludwig II. and represent respectively "The Madonna of Kasan" and "St. Nicolas."

Now follows ## The Tasso room.

which formerly served as sleeping apartment for the King. The charm which lies in Tasso's poem "Jerusalem delivered" is, here in the pictures of this apartment, fully reproduced. Following the scenes in the order of the poem, they illustrate:

1. "Armida abducts the sleeping Rinaldo."
2. "Armida with Rinaldo, who has been sung into a charmed sleep."
3. "Guelf and Ubald with the Magician."
4. "Guelf and Ubald withstand the enticements of the Naiads on the way to Armida's enchanted garden."
5. "Rinaldo and Armida in the magic garden."
6. "Guelf and Ubald hold the diamond shield before Rinaldo."
7. "Rinaldo's prayer after his return to the Christian camp."

The ceiling is ornamented by the representation of a charming female figure, holding a child on each arm. One of these, its cheeks flushed with the healthy, rosy hue of

THE "TASSO" APARTMENT.

After an original impression by Franz Hanfstaengl in Munich.

refreshing sleep, is leaning against her shoulder; the other, with the gray shade of death upon its little face, crouches like a broken human bud upon her arm. A touching illustration of Death and Sleep as brethren.

On the right of the heroes' hall is

The Guelf apartment,

THE APARTMENT OF THE „GUELPHS" (WELFENZIMMER)
After an original impression by Franz Hanfstaengl in Munich.

formerly the king's library, and decorated with pictures by
Lindenschmitt, illustrating the history of Henry the Lion.

THE APARTMENT OF THE „LONGOBARDS".

After an original impression by Franz Hanfstaengl in Munich

1. "Henry the Lion conquers and converts the Slavs 1170."

2. "Henry the Lion as founder of cities, builds Munich 1172 (corrected 1158)."

3. "The hospitable reception of Henry the Lion by the Sultan of Ikonium, 1175."

4. "Barbarossa on his knee before Henry the Lion, 1177."

5. "The entry of Henry the Lion with his opponent as his prisoner."

6. "Henry the Lion on his death-bed."

The alcove contains shelf after shelf filled with books.

Adjoining this, the Guelf room, is an apartment fitted up as a guest chamber and called

The Longobard room.

The walls of this apartment are hung with splendid pictures by Glink (after the designs of Schwind). The subject of which is the courting of the Bavarian Duke's daughter Theodolinde, by the Longobard King Authari.

1. "Authari as suitor."

2. "Theodolinde and her nurse."

3. "Authari deals blows after this kind."

4. "Authari's battle axe is brought to the Bavarian Duke Garibald."

5. "The expectation of Theodolinde."

The following two glass paintings are remarkable on account of their antiquity; "The arms of Uri, 1586," and "The arms of Benedict Oxenstierna, ambassador of peace for the Crown of Sweden at Nürnberg 1650."

Now follows

The apartment of the knights.

This room served formerly as the study of the king.

The charming paintings on the walls are the work of Glink, Neher and Nilson, and illustrate the following:

"The first instruction in riding; the knight's first armed watch; dubbing the knight; distribution of rewards after the tournament; falcon-hunting; first love; bidding farewell on leaving for the crusades; military feat in the Orient; return."

THE KNIGHTS' ROOM.
United Art Establishments in Munich.

A splendid decoration hangs on the pilaster between the first two pictures; this is the artistic shield which the Bavarian nobility dedicated as a wedding present to the Crown Prince Maximilian of Bavaria. The lofty pedestal is ornamented with battle-axes and clubs, and crowned by a drinking vessel. The marble chimney-piece is ornamented by busts, candalabra, goblets and vases. And the vases and bowls on the centre table, mostly in the form of, or ornamented with swans, are used to contain flowers.

The inspection of the royal apartments is now ended, and the visitor can hardly have failed to observe the innumerable ways in which the swan, that emblem of the castle, has been employed both in the furniture and decoration. This, however, has been carried out in perfect good taste, in no case has the eye been offended either by the oft recurring symbol or by the various ways in which it has been introduced.

The furniture, for modern taste, is far too simple and unpretentious to call forth admiration. But one must not forget that the style in vogue at that period when the castle was erected, was very different to that employed at the present day, and simple as the furniture undoubtedly is, it was at that time imminently suitable and well chosen. In addition to this, the floral decorations, which in former years were employed in such profusion, are also missing, and an atmosphere of sadness and mourning seems to have cast a spell over the whole building.

Down below, in the charming castle garden, vines and ivy encircle the beds filled with gay, sweet-smelling flowers, but no sound is heard save the monotonous murmur of the fountains.

The view from the alcove on the upper storey embraces the wide open plain stretching out as far as the Auerberge. Here one sees, shining and glittering, amid the green meadows, the silver stream of the river Lech, and the waters of the Bannwald Lake, and the picture is completed by the stately building of the Royal Castle of Neuschwanstein.

VIEW OF HOHENSCHWANGAU AND NEUSCHWANSTEIN.

A foot-path (up steps) leads to the village of Hohen-schwangau and at the foot of the castle rocks, half hidden in the shade, the Swan Pond (Schwanenteich) gives back a faithful reflection of the mighty trees which surround it.

A charming path, pleasantly shaded from the sun's hot rays, conducts up to the "Frauenkopf" or "Woman's Head", and if the visitor, after having duly inspected the castle, has still time to spare, he should in no wise omit to climb up to this spot. Here (although at the present day, nothing remains to remind one of the fact, for it dates back to the time of the Romans) a fort (Kastell) stood, which guarded the road coming from Fauces Alpium and leading to Augusta Vindelicorum. From the ruins of this fortress arose later a knight's castle, and the Squires of Schwangaw or Swanegawe (owners of this German castle) appear by ancient charters to have been the feudal tenants or vassals of the Guelphs, and also to have been closely connected with the history of that haughty race.

"On the rocks worn grey by age,
"Cradled in the forest's gloom
"Near two lakes, deep blue reflecting
"The castle, high on guard, it stands."

The domain of Schwangau was encompassed by four fortresses. "Vorder- and Hinterhohenschwangau, Schwanstein and Frauenstein;" and to this also belonged the Simperz-turm, built on the projection of the mountain, where, in the ravine surrounded by dark fir trees, the Halblech immerges from its mountain home.

The name of Hiltebold of Schwangau, the master of German minnesong, has been handed down to us out of the veil of the forgotten past, as the most prominent. The sweet tones of the harp seem to strike the ear at the very mention even of his name.

"Hiltebold of Swanegave,
"Thy music echoes far and near,
"Thy song it treats of noble women
"And could a subject sweeter be?
"Hidden by the leafy branches,
"The harp's pure golden tones resound;
"And Herr Hiltebold sings up yonder,
"Solitude, how beautiful thou art!
"To all the winds I'll breathe aloud,
"To the raw north and balmy south
"To mountain breath and forest stream,
"Solitude, how beautiful thou art!"

Hiltebold accompanied his feudal lord, the active Duke Welf, on many a warlike excursion, and we owe the description of the splendid Whitsun fête on the Gunzenleh, near Augsburg, to him. In the year 1191 the House of Hohenstaufen (or Suabia) celebrated its state entry in the halls of this castle. When the great Staufen or Suabian Emperor Friedrich II. died, far from home, the star of his house began to wane and the glory of Schwangau to decline. Clouds darkened the bright horizon.

Conradin, the golden-haired boy, played by the side of the noble lady, now wearing the weeds of widowhood. With intense grief the Empress sees her beloved son take his departure from Schwangau, the happy play-ground of his youth, to go to Italy, to seek there his fatal heritage. Before leaving, Conradin named as the heirs to his possessions (and with Conrad of Schwangau as witness) his two uncles, the Dukes Ludwig and Heinrich of Bavaria.

One royal house succeeds the other. The flag of the Bavarian Dukes flutters gaily from the pinnacles and towers of the Schwangau Castles.

History relates of many a feat of the warlike knights of Schwangau, innumerable family feuds break up the prosperity of the race.

The frequent visits of the Emperor Ludwig of Bavaria and Maximilian I. are like rays of sunshine in this sad picture. The castles slowly fell into decay.

Documents dating from the year 1523 speak eloquently of their collapse, and according to these accounts, the Castles of Vorder- and Hinter-Hohenschwangau, Schwanstein and Frauenstein were complete ruins. After the family of Schwangau died out, the castles came into the possession of the imperial Councillor Johann Baumgarten. The Castle of Schwanstein was restored in the style of the Renaissance and fitted up in a princely manner. But good luck and splendour had departed from the house, and the family of Baumgarten ended likewise in want and misery. And the storms of the Thirty Years War hastened its fall.

"The beams have fallen,
"The walls have crumbled,
"The bolt rusts, the garden withers;
"And empty are both hall and barn;
"And who ever thought of destroying
"Found there nothing to destroy.

"The war of 30 years has swept away
"Both heritage and heirs.
"And alone, in the fir trees shade
"Stands the castle and its meadows.
"Many a blue eye has closed.
"Only the two lakes still sparkle blue."

The period of its complete decay and subsequent brilliant restoration, is described by Karl Stieler in the following lines:

"Ancient castle amid the pines,
"Thy glory has departed;
"Thy glory sung by Hiltebold,
"And by King Conradin."

"Let them go—both time and things,
"But thou thyself in patience keep.
"The rings of full 200 years,
"The forest trees yet bear for thee."

"For thee again the spring will dawn,
"Thy charms again begin to rise,
"Thy building will mount up again
"And from thy swan will be a phoenix."

"When the Schyren flag shall wave,
"And fore the gate horse hoofs resound,
"And by a king shalt thou be chosen,
"Oh solitude, how beautiful thou art!"

In the autumn of 1832 the noble castle found an important protector in the person of the Crown Prince Maximilian of Bavaria, who caused it to be restored in new and undreamt of splendour, in order to spend here the spring time of his wedded happiness, and once again Hohenschwangau saw an emperor within its walls, namely the victory-crowned descendant of the House of Hohenzollern, King William of Prussia, who, after the war of 1870, came here to greet his young and promising nephew, King Ludwig II.

The affection which Ludwig II. had conceived for the sublime beauty of Schwangau when yet a child, he remained faithful to in later years, and Hohenschwangau, as well as the partially completed Castle Neuschwanstein, were the king's favourite abodes up to the terrible sad days when his life ended.

Within the walls of Hohenschwangau, in which she had spent so many happy hours, the sorely-tried Queen Marie breathed her last sigh, in giving utterance to the wish, "God bless Bavaria, God bless Prussia!"

The names "Hohenschwangau" and "Schwanstein" seem bound up in the happiness and grief of a 1000 years.

A multitude of legends seem interwoven and bound up with the history of the past. The Castle of Schwangau was

THE CASTLE OF HOHENSCHWANGAU IN THE 17th CENTURY.

chosen as the home of Lohengrin and Elsa. And here these two, surrounded by their children, spent many years of happy wedded life. The hero of the Nibelungenlied, Dietrich von Bern, is also said to have lived here. Here it was too, that Authari, the King of the Longobards, celebrated his brilliant marriage with Theodolinde, and lastly, report says that the youth of Charles the Great (Karl der Grosse) was spent within the walls of this celebrated castle.

Not without reason has Hohenschwangau been extolled for centuries past as the most beautiful castle in Germany, for no other possesses in a like degree the charm of a history dating back a 1000 years, united to such indescribable beauty of position and scenery.

After having visited the interior of Hohenschwangau, a pleasant resting place can be found in either of the shady gardens belonging to the inns "Zur Alpenrose" or "Zur Liesl;" both of these afford a beautiful view of the surrounding country.

A pretty little path, called the "Fischersteig" leads down to the shores of the Schwan Lake, and a lovely view can be had from the "Pindarplatz" a "look-out" near the Hotel Alp Lake and on the summit bf a rock jutting out into the lake.

This is a charming spot, and one well suited in which to spend a short time of leisure. The castle, both within and without, has now been duly visited and inspected, and, interesting and beautiful as it undoubtedly is, both mind and eye cannot fail to be refreshed by dwelling awhile on the natural beauties of this lovely neighbourhood before bidding it a last and lingering farewell.

Füssen and environs.

CASTLE LINDERHOF

AND KÖNIGHAUS

ON THE SCHACHEN

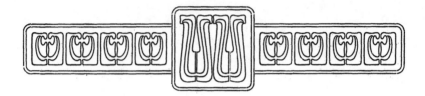

Preface.

The Castle of Linderhof, occupying, by merit of the inventive genius which it displays, a prominent position amongst the other castles erected by King Ludwig II, stands hidden in the grand solitude of the forest and mountain world.

L i n d e r h o f is the only completely finished creation of King Ludwig, and as such, exhibits the highest perfection in the close union of nature and art.

Here, as at Herrenchiemsee, in the charmingly furnished and decorated apartments one sees the true and faithful representation of the French monarchic age—; one room vies with the other in beauty and the splendour of the gardens and park surrounding the Castle forms a fitting framework for this lovely royal jewel.

Here one could spend hours and days enjoying the changes wrought by every passing minute in the beauty of the scenery.

All around, hidden in the heart of the forest, or high up on solitary summits commanding glorious and extensive views, the King has erected lonely seats—, showing thereby his love of nature-; In the Kenzenthal, in the isolated Halbammerthal, then high up on the Herzogstand in the proud Karwendel chain, and finally and most imposing of all, the mountain Castle S c h a c h e n , which, situated amid the wild peaks of the Wetterstein, must well be reckoned as the most isolated and romantic creation of the King.

Here also in this little mountain castle the royal architect again displays his preference for the fashion of pure style building, and here on the summit of this mountain a strange fancy has prompted him to exhibit this taste by the erection and fitting up of a state hall in true oriental style.

From here the road leads away from the mountains through a charming foreground of alpine and lake scenery to Castle B e r g , which was one of His Majesty's favourite abodes when a boy, and which also was destined to be a witness of the sad and terrible end of the beloved and ever-lamented monarch.

Oberau. (Towards the Wetterstein Mts.)   After an original drawing by H. Grabensee.

Routes by which to reach Linderhof.

The visit to the Castle of Linderhof is generally combined with that to the Schwangau Castles, only in the case of visiting the former the traveller is more dependent on the carriages branching off from the nearest stations of Oberammergau (2½ hours distant) and Oberau (3½ hours), or on his own walking powers.

The roads from Oberau and Oberammergau lead through charming country to the royal seat of Linderhof, but the walk from Schwangau to Linderhof is even more beautiful, offering a constant variety of scenery—from the Lech valley surrounded by mountains to the dreamy Plansee and from thence on through the secluded and lonely Ammer valley.

For good walkers there are picturesque routes leading

over mountain passes and through lovely valleys, but for a description of these the tourist must refer to the Guide Books.

The walk to Castle S c h a c h e n leads from Oberau into the heart of the mountains and from thence back to the Walchsee and past the Kochelsee along the shores of the Starnbergersee to Castle B e r g. The nearest route to the Castle of Linderhof is from Munich viâ Starnberg and Tutzing to Murnau. This way presents a view of the wide blue surface of the Staffelsee with its wooded islands, and also of the mountains panorama forming, as it were, a wide screen—, the broad valley of the Loisach with large stretches of brown moorland occupies the foreground, bounded on the east by the summits of the Steingarten, Krottenkopf and Kistenkopf, while on the west are the Ettaler-Mandl, Auf-acker and Hörnle.

Standing far back in the background the Wetterstein-Mts. are dimly visible in the distance.

At Murnau the different lines leading to Linderhof separate.

On the one side, the local line Murnau-Garmisch runs as far as the station of Oberau (in the mountain-surrounded Loisach valley with a charming view of the Zug-spitze); and on the other side, the railway-line Murnau-Oberammergau runs through country which discloses more and more the delightful beauty of the mountain world.

On the route Murnau—Oberau the train passes through the entrance gateway formed by mighty summits into the sanctity of the mountain world, keeping by the side of the wild Loisach in its broad bed of gravel. The view to the left shows the following mountains rising precipitiously out of the valley, the Heimgarten, Krotten-kopf, Bischof, Hirschberg and Fricken, and on descending from the train at Oberau the eye is charmed by the imposing background formed by the rugged massive peaks of the Alp-spitze and Zugspitze.

The new mountain road ascends in zigzag from Oberau to Ettal and affords a charming view of the Loisach valley and of the mountain walls on the east side of the valley. For walkers however, the old road, al-though very steep, is by far the shorter. Here one is sur-rounded by forest and mountain, while on the' left the Giessenbach tosses and rushes down its stony bed to the valley below; no other sound disturbs the stillness of the spot.

The first glance falls upon the rocky mountain peak of the Kofel, which lends its signature to the whole neighbourhood. The alpine valley lies bathed in the warm rays of the sun, the neat little homesteads, over which towers the high steeple of the Ettaler church, all combine to make up a scene of peaceful and picturesque beauty—. "Here in the

Ettal, with glimpse of the Graswang Valley.   After an original drawing by H. Grabensee.

grand solitude of the forest, through which once the threatening footsteps of the Roman hordes wended their way to Augusta (Augsburg), in which too the Guelf Ethika with twelve companions settled and lived a monastic life, was raised by the great Wittelsbach Emperor Ludwig of Bavaria a monastery of a special kind, dedicated to our Lady of Ettal."

The rules for this institution for members of knightly families, modelled after the Benedictine monastery, were drawn up even to the most minute details. — Here in this lovely mountain wilderness a Grail Temple was to be erected, kept watch over and guarded by knights and monks after the fashion of that great Epic Poem of the middle ages "Parsival", the mysterious captivating charm of which had again been awakened by Richard Wagner's wonderful composition.

Information from historical sources respecting this institution is very meagre, all the more therefore has legend interwoven a glorifying halo round about the foundation of this monastery. The Emperor is represented on his way to Rome in a lonely cell praying for a gracious change in his unpleasant situation in the terrible strife and dispute between Pope and Emperor.

An aged monk inspires him with comforting hope and presents him with a "White Madonna" picture, with the injunction to erect at Ampfrang a monastery for the disciples of St. Benedict in honour of the Mother of God.

When the Emperor on his return rode up the old bridle path with his followers, his horse sank three times upon its knees and all efforts to urge it on were unavailing. Here on this spot the church and monastery were erected, richly endowed by the Emperor, and the picture of the Madonna, which had designated the spot in so wonderful a manner, was set up on the High Altar.

The knightly institution fell into decay soon after the great Emperor's death, but the monastery attained to a flourishing condition.

When in 1744 a terrible fire laid the institution of the Emperor Ludwig in dust and ashes, the mighty domed building arose as a splendid example of Bavarian Barok architecture on the original Gothic foundation, making an impression upon our artistic feelings which cannot be surpassed. Even here secularisation intruded itself. For years everything seemed consecrated to decay and ruin and it was only owing to the noble generosity of Baron von Cramer-Klett that the sons of St. Benedict were again enabled to take up their abode there and continue their work, which now already after a few years shows again life and new hopes of success. The grey weather- beaten giant rocks, dark fir forests and fresh green alpine slopes are all visible from the monastery courtyard, and the partially completed Barok-façade of the cathedral unites with the powerful cupola standing high above it in forming an imposing and effective picture. The cloisters with their Norman cross-arch vaults betray their Gothic origin and this makes the appearance

East view of Ettal.

After an original photograph by Ferd Finsterlin, Munch.

of the interior of the church all the more striking by contrast. The centre dome-shaped space is ornamented with charming frescoes and reliefs in the Rococo style, making of the whole a beautiful ensemble of form and colour. To see this cathedral to perfection, it should be visited while Service is being carried on—, the colours lighted up by the rays of the sun, the clouds of incense mounting to the domed roof and the glorious organ sending forth tones of sweet music—. On leaving the church one is greeted by the beauty of the mountains. The buildings all around remind one of the past splendours of the monastery, and above the archway of the gate leading to the inn (where, as well as in the bar-room of the monastery itself, the national drink brewed on the premises is dispensed) are the Arms of the Abbots of Ettal, while high above in a grey rocky mantel stands the „Ettaler-Mandl", the history of whom is likewise included in the legend treating of the convent. The wide road leads from Ettal further into the valley to the old monastery mill and at a short distance from here it forms a junction with the road coming from Oberammergau. The second approach to Linderhof by the local railway from Murnau to Oberammergau offers numerous grand points of view. Just after leaving the station a lovely glimpse may be had of the splendid mountain summits rising up on either side of the Loisach valley, then the Ettalermandl becomes visible, and beyond the broad stretches of moorland stand the Aufacher and Hörnle groups, round which the train wends its way into the Ammer valley.

Above the crests of these last appear the gigantic heads of the Wetterstein mountains. On nearing Altenau the scenery of the Ammergau unfolds itself in all its idyllic beauty and charm. On the left is the Hörnle, while on the right the valley is bounded by the Hochschergen, Pürstlingskopf, Teufelsstätt and Hennenkopf, and the background is occupied by the many jagged points of the Sonnenberg— all forming a beautiful picture. —

The valley, which has taken its name from the river Ammer flowing through it, is bright with fresh green meadows and picturesque groups of trees.

The train now descends rapidly into the valley, passes Unterammergau and in a very short time arrives at the spacious station of Oberammergau.

The profusion of frescoes which ornament the exterior of the old-fashioned houses of the village give it a very pic-

turesque appearance, and lovely glimpses are had of the pretty
houses half hidden in their flowergardens along the banks
of the Ammer.

He to whom it is vouchsafed to see the family life of the
inhabitants (the father, who, in the enormous hall of the
theatre, by his simple natural acting draws tears from the
eyes of thousands, now sitting busily employed at his carving table) may congratulate himself on having gained in
a few scenes a picture of the place and its inhabitants, so
justly celebrated throughout the world.

Beyond from the Osterbichl are visible the gigantic
figures of the Crucifixion. These are the work of Halbig,
and formed the thank-offering of King Ludwig of Bavaria to
the Bavarians, a people so faithful in adhering to the customs
inherited from their forefathers. Not far from this stands
the Marocco Castle of King Ludwig II, transferred hither
from the Graswang Valley and now a private possession.

The road from Oberammergau to Linderhof leads along
the foot of the Brunnberg with beautiful views of the peaceful Passion Village and of the green slopes of the mountains rising up behind, right across to the Graswang Valley, where it joins the road leading from Ettal—. The
view in the background is now bounded by the wooded Laa-
berberg, and on entering the Graswang Valley the whole character of the scenery suddenly changes. The hills which extend along the wooded valley are covered with fresh, luxuriant green. The steep walls of the mountains, covered far
up with beautiful wood, rise up on either side of the valley
and these again are overtopped by grey rocks. These mountains
are stately fellows which, with supreme dignity, keep guard over
the peace and safety of this quiet valley—, on the right stand
the Pürstlingkopf (on which is the Royal Hunting Lodge),
Hennenkopf, Klammspitze and Scheinberg, (this latter in the
background) and on the left the Noth. Enning, Kienjoch and
the long ridge of the Küchelberg. After an hour's walk, the
quiet homely little village of Graswang is reached—. On
leaving here one is surprised by the imposing view presented by the mountain walls, which, on the left, separate to form
the wide valley of Ellmauergries. (The country people call the
stream flowing from the Graswang Valley the "Griessand",
or "Ammergries", over the dried-up stony bed of which the
road crosses by means of a long bridge.)

The beautifully formed Friederspitze and the Griesenberg
rise up out of the valley, and piled up in wild confusion
stands in the distance the rocky summit of the Zugspitze.

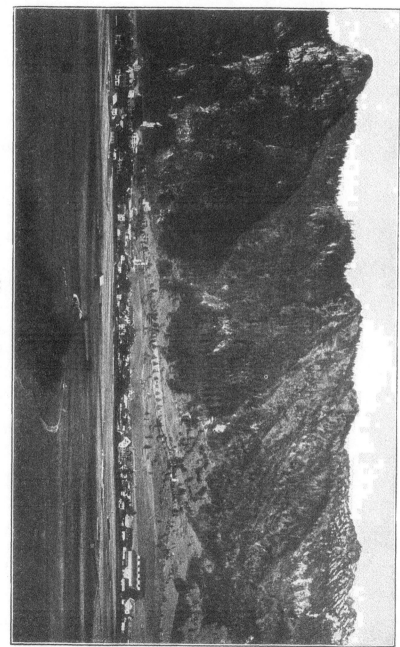

Oberammergau.

After an original photograph by Würthle and Son, Salzburg.

The Ammergries flows along the right hand side of the road which now enters a lovely forest, out of which it emerges only just before Linderhof is reached.

View of the Ammer in Oberammergau.
After an original photograph by the Photographic Society in Zurich.

Beautiful woods surround the green Wiesenau and in the midst stands the neat Forest House of Linderhof.

Oberammergau. The Crucifixion.

After an original photograph by the Photographic Society in Zurich.

The river bed is forced back to the edge of the wooded hill called the "Linderbichl" and no-one would ever suspect the close proximity of the Royal Castle of Linderhof, if he were not made conscious of it by the sign posts on the road.

(The visit to the Castle of Linderhof is almost invariably connected with that to the Castles in Schwangau and therefore the description of the charming tour from these Castles to Linderhof is indispensible.

Between Füssen — Linderhof — Oberau or Oberammergau the carriages of the Official-Carriage-Communication make the route twice a day during the season, and besides this, there is a Post-Carriage communication betwen Füssen-Reutte and Linderhof-Oberammergau.)

Leaving the beautiful scenery of the Schwangau a charming shady walk of one hour along the banks of the Alpsee leads down into the Lech valley to the much frequented Schluxenwirth (inn) and from there, viâ Pinswang, along the highroad to Reutte. The road from Füssen leads along the right bank of the river Lech up past the Lech Gorge to Weisshaus, crosses the river by the Ulrich Bridge and then on, viâ Musau and Rossschlag, to Unterlötzen, where it again crosses the Lech and from thence to Pflach and Reutte.

The view along the whole way, on the right of the precipitious summits of the Tannheimer Group, and on the left of the gigantic cone of the Säuling, which commands the green valley of the stream, is grand and imposing. The pretty market town of Reutte with its stately oldfashioned houses, many of which are ornamented by frescoes, is most charmingly situated in the wide plain.

The following mountains are picturequely grouped round the wide plain of the valley, the Säuling, Zwieselberg, Tauern, Thaneller, then the Schlosskopf with the Ruin Ehrenberg, Gachtspitze, Aschauer Berge, Gern and Köllespitze and Gimpel.

Close to Reutte, the capital of the Lower — (here called Ausserfern —) Lech valley is Breitenwang, where the Emperor Lothar II. on his return from Rome was taken ill and died in a peasant's house.

The imposing Ruins of Ehrenburg are very picturesque; they are the mute, yet nevertheless eloquent, witnesses of a great and glorious past age.

The names of proud Generals, such as Schärtlin von Burtentenbach, the Elector Moritz of Gascony, Bernhard of Weimar, Wrangel and the Elector Max Emanuel of Bavaria are joined together in connection with the hot battles which took place

The Ruin Ehrenburg.　　　　　　After an original drawing by H. Grabensee.

so often round these so much coveted walls, which even now
in their ruinous condition, relate of the former power and
greatness of this important stronghold.

The carriage-road from Reutte to Linderhof leads through
Breitenwang, then up to the Rossrücken, from whence a beautiful view of Reutte and, in the distance, of the Algauer mountains and Hochvogel, meets the eye.

The tourist is surrounded the whole way by the alpine
beauty of the lovely valley. Down below, the river Lech
flows along in its wide bed amid fresh green meadows and little
gravel islands—, the charming mountain-framed picture of Reutte
is before his eyes and on the top of the Kniepass, the green
mountains of the Pfronten valley and the powerful group of
the Falkensteins form a charming picture.

Just beyond Pflach a footpath branches off from the
road and leads to Mühl (where a beautiful view of the ruins
of the Ehrenberg pass is to be had) and continues along the
right bank of the Archen stream. Keeping close by the side
of this wild mountain torrent one mounts up by the Her-

The Stuiben Falls near Reutte.

After an original photograph by Würthle and Son, Salzburg.

2*

mannsteig (Oe. T. C.) on up to the great fall, called the
Stuiben or Staubfall, where the stream descends from an alti-
tude of 30 meters; this is succeeded by another fall of 18
meters in height, which, like the Stuibenfall, is naturally seen at
its best when heavy rains have caused the over-flow from
the Plansee to come rushing wildly down the valley bringing
with it a larger volumn of water than is usual when fine
weather has prevailed.

The footpath joins the road leading up from Reutte and
crosses the Archenbach just before the fall, and now the
little green Plansee becomes visible surrounded by steep wooded mountains, — on the west the Tauern, on the south the
Thaneller, Brandjoch, Zingerstein and Spiesswand and on the
north the Geierköpfe.

The waters of the lake are of an emerald green in which
the mountains are reflected in various shades of grey—, all
around are endless woods full of freshness and perfume—the
charming landscape unfolds new beauties at every step.

At the commencement of the lake, the much frequented
inn „Seespitz" invites the tourist to take rest and refreshment — this inn served formerly as a relay station for King
Ludwig II. The view from here is delightful —, every
hour of the day casting fresh shadows and tints over the
mountains and lake. For those who have time and inclina-
tion an early morning walk along the western shore of the
lake can be strongly recommended. The tourist will be well
repaid by the beauty of the ever-varying scenery. — On the
left hand side of the road is the Kaiserbrunnen, a fountain
erected by King Max II. of Bavaria in memory of the great
Wittelsbach Emperor Ludwig the Bavarian, who formerly
came here for the purpose of hunting. At the east end of
the lake is another well-known and much visited inn "zur
Forelle" (the Sign of the Trout) and from here is another
lovely view of the lake, also of the Thaneller, which latter
seems to send a last greeting from the high mountain region
of Tyrol.

Just before the "Gasthaus zur Forelle" (where the road
branches off leading to Partenkirchen across the Griesenpass)
a simple monument bears witness to the gratitude of the
Tyrolese parishes for the opening up of the whole country by
the building of roads by King Max II. of Bavaria.

One more farewell glance at the lake, then the road
leads up towards the Erzbach into the sylvan beauty of the
lonely Ammerwald valley, which here, before its opening to
the Plansee, is narrowed by the steep rocks of the Torsäule

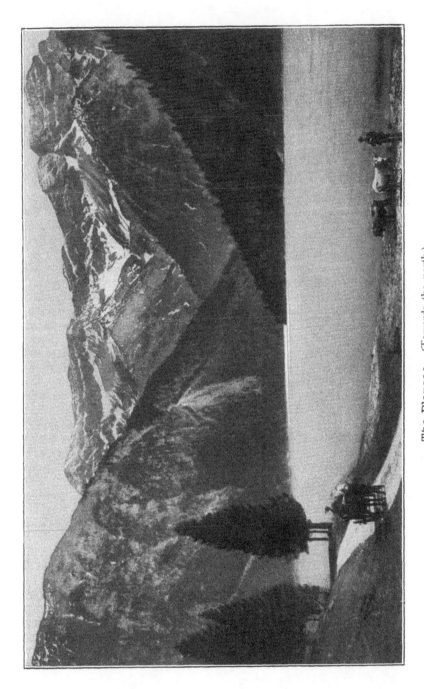

The Plansee. (Towards the north.)

After an original photograph by the Photographic Society in Zurich.

mountains into a charming romantic pass. Just before entering this wooded gorge, a glimpse is seen of the Zugspitze, then the road ascends gently upwards between wooded hills and after an hour's walk the Alpine Hotel "Ammerwald" is reached. From here a read leads across the Jägersteig to the Castle Neuschwanstein and is therefore as a starting point of importance to tourists. This Jägersteig forms the shortest connection between the royal Castles of Neuschwanstein and Linderhof, and, for those who do not care to follow the usual track, possesses great charms and attractions.

Just by the sign-post pointing to the Marienbrücke a footpath branches off from the mainroad leading to Castle Neuschwanstein and joins the road from Blöckenau —, a few steps further on and a wonderful view of the Marienbrücke and Neuschwanstein is obtained — the carriage road continues for an hour in a gentle ascent through splendid woods to the royal shooting Lodge Blöckenau, and from here a pleasant walk of 1½ hours up the Schützensteig leads to the Jägerhütte. (Hunter's Hut.)

The path winds down to the quiet Ammer valley affording a view which is seen in its greatest beauty and grandeur in the early morning hours. — then, in fine weather naturally — one sees the grotesque forms of the Geierköpfe shining in the brilliancy of the dawning day and, beneath, the forests in all their verdant loveliness are still wrapped in shadow. The road leads from Ammerwald on through dense forest— the watershed between the Lech and Isar is passed almost without being observed (the merry little stream which trickles through the meadows is the Ammer) on the left the summits of the Hirschfeng and Hochplatte rise up lofty and solemn, and on the right, out of the wooded valley, the barren rocks of the Geyerköpfe are visible.

At the Bavarian frontier the Ammer flows down in its wide stony bed close to the road, and the Neualpbach, a stream descending from the lonely high alpine valley between the Geierköpfe and the Kreuzspitze, also suddenly appears here in a wide bed, (which in summer-time is generally dry) to join the Ammer.

The scenery of this spot is perhaps the grandest which the valley affords. All round are the wonderful mountains and forests, and even the broad, barren, stony beds of the streams serve to enhance the beauty of this alpine picture and the King could hardly have selected a position more suitable than this on which to erect

The Plansee. (Towards the south.)

After an original photograph by Würthle and Son, Salzburg.

The Hundings Hut and Hermitage. After an original drawing by H. Grabensee.

The Hundings Hut and The Hermitage.

The path to these buildings leads away from the road across the boulders of the Ammer to the right bank where it is shaded by thick wood. After a few steps an enormous Log Hut appears in view. This is built of rough stems of trees and was erected by Jank according to the directions of the great composer Richard Wagner for the first Act of his Drama "The Valkyr" (Die Walküre).

That which on the stage with the assistance of artificial light forms an effective picture, charms here by the faithfulness with which an old German hermitage—corresponding in building and surroundings to the original—is represented.

In front of the Hut is an enormous trough roughly formed out of the stem of a birchtree and into this flow the waters of a mountain spring which issue from the stump of a branch.

On entering the building the visitor sees a dark spacious sort of Hall, the centre of which is taken up by Wotan's Ashtree. The gigantic branches of this tree reach up to the roof of the apartment and, thrust deep into the stem, is "Nothung" the Wälsungen Sword. The Hall is ornamented, with historical accuracy, with battle swords, battle-axes, arrows, shields, spears, enormous antlers of elk and heads of bisons; large carpets made of sail-cloth cover the walls, the window frames are formed of birchrods and the fireplace or hearth with its chimney is of an equally primitive description. Adjoining this apartment are smaller rooms, serving as

The interior of the Hundings Hut.

larder and kitchen,—the sleeping room is furnished with a couch covered with skins and a rough table. The view into the large Hall from this apartment is very interesting; candlesticks formed out of the roots of trees stand on the table and a chandelier of stags' antlers is suspended from a branch of the Ashtree—, the stems of trees serving the purpose of seats are covered with bear and wolf skins.

It is true that the solemn impression which is created in the spectator by the representation on the stage united to the sounds of the "stürmisch bewegten Vorspiels" at the entrance of Siegmund into the Hut cannot here be felt where the Hall is filled by the bright daylight, for that belongs the homely cracking of the fire on the hearth which, with its flickering and uncertain light, makes the room light and dark by turns — the raging of the storm shaking the tops of the enormous trees outside and sweeping round the Hut with wild shrieks, the blue flashes of lightning and the cracking of thunder dying slowly away in the mountain gorges, "then comes like the wail of a stream the feeling of sweet fantasy that here Sieglinde, in the time of winter's frost, had longed to greet the spring, so that the gnawing misery of gnawing love might reawaken in the human breast." Such thoughts form a fitting accompaniment to the inspiring tones of the great Drama of Love's Happiness and Love's Sorrow, which, here in this empty Hall, is especially solemn and impressive.

As in the Hundingshütte a monument has been raised to the great Nibelung Epos, so also does the Einsiedelei (which stands near it), remind one of an episode of Wolfram von Eschenbach's Heroic Poem „Parzival", which describes court and chivalric life in the middle ages.

In the poverty-stricken, with ascetic simplicity furnished, home of his uncle, the Hermit Trevezent, Parzival comes to himself and recovers his belief in God.

The little house, standing on the border of a small meadow and partially surrounded by trees, is built of the stems of trees, bark and branches. It not only derives its character of being a Hermitage from its primitive little belfry, but also from the rigid simplicity of the interior, with its simple bed, table-bench and open hearth. Beneath the little belfry tower in front of the Hut is a humble seat made of the trunk of a tree; from this spot is a lovely view of the Geierköpfe.

This was a favourite seat of the King's and "it was here", so writes Mennel in his "Fantasies of the King", "that his Majesty read "Parzival," (which had been sent to him by his protégé R. Wagner), for the first time, and to see this pomp-loving Monarch here in this lowly spot reading this poem has a wonderful charm for us. Many and great men have come and applauded and admired Wagner's "Swan-Song" but when it is revived in the consecrated Temple at Bayreuth, then flashes across our minds the memory of that lonely King who is reading it in his hermitage". The road leads on from this charming spot through quiet forest along by the side of the broad Ammergries, down whose stony bed the mountain water rushes at times as a powerful destructive stream.

A glance back rewards one by the beauty of the view, the Geierköpfe and the Kreuzspitze being seen here to great advantage.

A wide semi-circle of picturesque groups is formed by the Scheinberg, Klammspitze and Hennenkopf, all of these occupy a position in the foreground, while on the right the steep rocky walls of the Kreuzspitze join the long stretched-out crest of the Küchelberg —; it is this change in the mountain picture, united to the dreamy loneliness of the woods, which makes this ramble through the valley so delightful, although to some perhaps it may be monotonous and uninteresting.

The change from the wide open valley to a narrow dark wooded ravine repeats itself several times-; now the road crosses over the Ammergries, the way is shaded by lovely beechtrees and suddenly above them appears the front of the Castle of Linderhof, the tall fountains are throwing up jets of water, which sparkling and glistening in the rays of the sun add greatly to the beauty of the scene, likewise enhanced and completed by the appearance of the Hennenkopf and Purstlingskopf. This picture lasts but a minute —, a few steps more and the glimpse thus suddenly obtained disappears as suddenly, hidden by the thick foliage and branches of the trees.

Castle Linderhof.

The Hofstrasse branches off from the Reutte—Oberau road and leads across an iron bridge over the Ammergries. The royal Castle with its charming surroundings of meadow and park and wonderful works of art is separated by an iron gate from the free untrammelled works of nature. Carefully kept paths lead past the Royal Gardens up to the Castle Restaurant Linderhof. (Halting place for the official carriage connection, Post and Telegraph.)

In the summertime this spot teems with life—with a continual stream of visitors coming and going. The rooms also belonging to the Restaurant afford a pleasant shelter in bad weather and the cooking and wine are worthy of all praise.

The Restaurant, although near the royal residence, is yet far enough away so as in no-wise to disturb the peacefulness and quiet of the Castle—the hidden royal jewel is, as it were, a kingdom for itself, the property surrounding it consisting of many acres and the length of the paths which have to be kept in order by the Administration amounting to 7 kilometers. Flowering shrubs edge the paths which lead up over undulating ground ornamented by groups of trees and picturesque bushes to the Castle. The simple peasant's cottage which stands on the left of the way is the exact representation of the former Linderhof, which 35 years ago stood on the spot where the Castle now stands. The Linderhof, from the hamlet of Graswang to the Plansee, was the only human habitation in this lovely mountain valley; the peasant's house derived its name from an enormous old lime tree and this name was retained when King Max II of Bavaria came into possession of the estate, which he bought to shoot and hunt over,— nor did the house undergo many

LINDERHOF.

Aus Steinberger's Königsschlösser

Druck von Franz Hanfstaengl, G. m. b. H. in München.

alterations at the hand of its new owner, the modest building with its woodwork, the slate roof weighted down by
stones and the balcony running round it showed after, as
before, the usual style of building adopted in this
mountainous district. Only the interior underwent alterations
and assumed a more elegant appearance; roses bloomed in
the little garden by the house, the beds being divided from
each other by tidily kept paths, and a little fountain played
merrily amid the flowers.

The peaceful repose of this spot remained undisturbed,
nature was still permitted to go her own way and a little
stream, crossed by a primitive and diminutive bridge, flowed
through the meadow hastening onward to join the Ammergries. At the commencement of his reign King Ludwig II
of Bavaria stayed constantly for short periods in this lonely
house, the idyllic situation of which was so much to his
taste and which before long was to see the commencement
of the building of his most charming artistic creation.

"In the midst of a beautiful park, green meadows and
luxuriant flora and not far from the Royal Castle of Versailles, stands the Belvedere Trianon, that favourite seat of
the unhappy Queen Marie Antoinette of France. The charm
of the Trianon had made a great impression on the Bavarian
King and here in the solitude of the forest arose the copy
of that Castle—as a secluded, unapproachable wonder-work
under the intelligent and active co-operation of the King.
The building is not an exact copy of the original, many
deviatious have been made, designs from other small Rococo
castles have been worked into the plan, and the apartments
of this charming Castle are furnished with princely brilliant,
and yet comfortable, splendour."

As the visitor passes from room to room he is filled
with admiration, each one is a mine of interest, a triumph
of united art and industry and an example of perfect beauty
and exquisite taste; the rich embroideries of the furniture
are shown off to perfection by the, sometimes delicately toned
down, sometimes brilliantly coloured, beauty of the ground
tones in the walls and portières, and also by the endless
riches of the designs in the ornamental and figurative decorations. Although the whole ornamentation of the Castle
interior is in the luxuriant Rococo style it must be borne in
mind that the artists were not content merely to copy their
designs, but also in many instances created them themselves
and these, graceful in form and toned down in colour, have
united in forming a most charming whole. The artists also

took part in designing the embroideries. The building and furnishing of the Castle continued almost constantly under the eye of the King, who was assisted by a large staff.

The building was commenced in the year 1869 after the plans and under the direction of Oberbaudirektor von Doll-mann, and it was continued, with various interruptions, until the year 1878.

In May 1885, owing to alterations being made in the sleeping apartment, the Castle was added to after a design made by Architect Drollinger and under the supervision of Oberbaurat von Hofmann: the present pompous decoration of the bedchamber was only completed in the year 1896. Immense artistic taste and activity was shown by Professor Perron in the decoration of the interior of the Castle; to him must be attributed the chief part of the charming sculp-ture, stucco, relief and carved work, the designs of which, and in many cases the carrying out of, were the result of his talented work.

The beautiful pictures on the walls and ceiling of the state apartments are the work of—mostly after designs by Watteau and Boucher—the artists Spiess, Pechmann, Walter Fries, Jank, Zimmermann, Lesker, Benczur, Schwoiser, Heckel, Hauschild and Frank; the pastel portraits in the boudoirs are the work of Gräfle. The following have contributed beautiful works of industrial art to Linderhof; Jörres, (embroideries, after the designs of Oberbaurat von Hofmann); Pössenbacher (joinery); Kölbl (locksmith's work) and Pfister (marble work).

With the commencement of the building of the Castle the laying out of the garden and grounds was also taken in hand—their charming arrangement is due to the genius of Hofgartendirektor von Effner—, the sculptures which orna-ment them being the handiwork of Hautmann, Wagmüller, Walker, Fischer and Perron. The former Shooting Lodge, which had to make room for the Castle, was rebuilt at a short distance by command of the royal architect.

A stronger contrast than is presented by these two buildings—the simple mountain cottage and the royal pomp-ous castle—can hardly be imagined, yet the contrast is con-siderably lessened by the!Castle being surrounded by a garden displaying French art and taste, while the old Linderhof is merely surrounded by a nursery for young fir trees.

Well guarded from every critical eye the idyllic forest treasure was here erected. for in spite of the beauty of the grounds the forest round the Castle remains its most

Castle Linderhof with the Royal Equipage.

United Art Establishments in Munich.

beautiful frame and ornament. A glance down from Monopteros at the hour of noon at the floral beauty of the
terraces and park when the fountains are in full play makes
the Castle appear almost fairy-like in its beauty. As if
owing its existence to a princely freak of the Rococo age, so
it stands—a reflection of that brilliant period, full of
joyous animated beauty, a charming picture, and in contrast
to the enormous buildings of Neuschwanstein and Herrenchiemsee small and graceful, consisting merely of ground-
floor and one storey, the whole building bearing upon it, even
before its interior has been seen, the stamp of the Rococo
period. The principal front of the Castle exhibits in its
profuseness of sculpture and in its artistic construction a
master-work of the Rococo style of architecture; this is most
remarkable in the projecting centre, the frontispiece of which,
picturesquely built up above the cornice of the roof, is of
great beauty of form and finish.

The entrance to the building is formed by three lofty
Norman arches with sandstone pillars and above these is a
balcony supported by four figures of Atlas as Caryatides.
The balcony is completed by a gilded railing of artistic
design. The handsomely constructed columns, with their
richly ornamented capitals, afford space for the two high
balcony windows and a centre niche, which latter contains
the statue of Victoria.

On the balustrade are four charming Amorettes or Cupids
symbolically representing: Music, Poetry, Sculpture and Architecture. Between these are two genii throwing wreaths of
flowers, forming a finish to the principal cornice: in this
latter are three circular "ox eye" windows, while above these,
in the panel of the gable, (a masterpiece of stuccowork) is
the Bavarian Coat of Arms, supported by genii and with
two statues on either side representing respectively: Agriculture, Science, Commerce and Handicraft. The high gable
is effectively completed by a large figure of Atlas carrying
the Globe.

The two sides of the building on the ground-floor have
only one window each to break the simple freestone surface. In
the storey above, these walls are made more elaborate by the
introduction of pilasters, which ornamented by sculpture,
frame in the large Norman windows and niches, these last
containing statues representing the Scholastic and Military
professions, the Civil Service and Working Classes.

The architectural outlines of this Castle front are effectively broken by the sculptural ornamentations and variation

of form. The two long extending side fronts are not less
ornamentally constructed, from these wide outside steps lead
down to the east and west park grounds. The walls are
divided by pilasters into broad panels for the high windows
and niches, the latter containing on the west side statues
representing Poetry and Music and on the east side those of
Peace and Riches.

The straight outline of the long side front is broken by
the oval projection in the centre, and that of the middle-
front, if such an expression can be used, by the statue of
Apollo on the west and on the east of Flora; these stand in
the large niches between the pillars.

The lofty windows in this oval structure are ornamented
with balconies of graceful, gilded iron-work.

Gables with beautiful sculpture crown the principal
cornice of this part of the building.

The north façade of the Castle is considerably simpler.
The niches between the windows hold the statues representing: Strength, Generosity, Constancy and Justice.
The view of the Castle from its side façades is almost even
more charming than when seen from the south side. The
Castle, surrounded by its beautiful grounds, shady paths,
playing fountains and ornamented statues, does not appear
like an erection of modern times, but rather as a real happy
child of the Rococo period, imparting by its graceful beauty
a sense of joyous peacefulness, which transforms the buildings
of that age into charming and incomparably beautiful pictures.

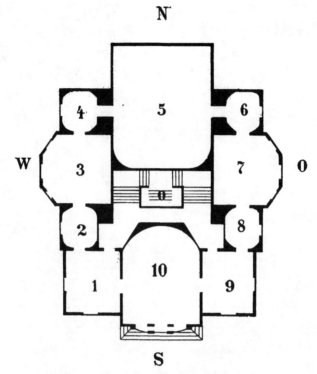

Groundplan of Castle Linderhof.

0. Groundfloor and Staircase.
1. Gobelin Room (west).
2. Yellow Boudoir.
3. Study.
4. Lilac Boudoir.
5. Sleeping Apartment.

6. Pink Boudoir.
7. Dining Room.
8. Blue Boudoir.
9. Gobelin Room (east).
10. Hall of Mirrors.

The Interior of the Castle.

The interior of the Castle is equal in charm and beauty to its graceful exterior.

A glance suffices to convince the visitor that this is the only one of the Royal Castles which was really completed in every detail by the King himself. —

Vestibule.
United Art Establishments in Munich.

Here there is no disturbing element, all is complete, not as in the other Castles, in which some apartments have remained partially, or indeed in some cases, totally unfurnished.

The Vestibule, although otherwise simple, is rendered beautiful by ten large pillars of Untersberger marble, the smooth white surface of which glitters and sparkles in the rays of the sun. The niches in the back wall hold branched candlesticks, richly gilded, and the cornice above the pillars is profusely ornamented.

The chief ornament, however, stands in the centre of the Vestibule and is the equestrian figure of King Louis XIV. of France. This stands on a handsome pedestal of black marble, on which is engraved the following dedication.

F r o n t.

"To Louis XIV the Great, the Christian King of the Franks and of Navarre, the upright Defender of the Faith, and the pious Father of his country

L e f t   S i d e.

this statue is raised by the Prefect and Aedile with the approval of the people in the year 1699.

R i g h t   S i d e.

who, on his part, has decorated the town in the most generous manner by the building of Arcades, Fountains, Streets, by a Stone Bridge and a very large Rampart planted with trees, and otherwise heaped innumerable benefits upon it.
(On either side the Arms of Paris in bronze with the Motto "Fluctuat nec mergitur"

B a c k.

Under his rule we lived in safety and feared none—. He has refused this Statue every time it was offered to him, but at last consented to its erection out of regard for the townspeople.

Erected by general consent."

The perfection of this work of art, which has been executed in so masterly a manner and which presents the King as a Roman Triumphator, reminds one, by the delicacy in which the minutest details have been carried out, of the figure on horseback of the same King, which stands in the "Salle de l'oeil de boeuf" at Herrenchiemsee.

This statue is surmounted by the sun, its rays extending over the entire ceiling.

The sun itself shows the proud motto of the Bourbons "nec pluribus impar" — (And he is greater than many).

Staircase.
United Art Establishments in Munich.

A large and varied selection of books and pictures treating of the buildings erected by King Ludwig II can here be purchased, affording the tourist an opportunity of obtaining suitable souvenirs of his visit to Linderhof.

Leaving the vestibule we now mount two marble steps and enter

The Hall.

The doors on either side lead to the Servants' Apartments. This hall is likewise ornamented by marble pillars and is lighted by the skylight. on the staircase and also by

The Vestibule.

In the centre of the hall on a marble pedestal stands a blue Sèvres vase on which is painted in subdued and charming colours a representation of "Esther before Ahasuerus". This charming centrepiece is undoubtedly the ornament of the entire hall and was a present from Napoleon III. to Ludwig II. of Bavaria.

The Staircase.

Visitors who have seen the enormous building of Herrenchiemsee will probably be disappointed at the comparatively narrow stairs which here in Castle Linderhof lead up to the State Apartments—; yet small as the space here is, everything is in perfect taste and radiant with beauty. The stairs leading up to the first floor are of white Carrara marble and ornamented by a simple gilded bannister. The walls of the first storey are decorated by a profusion of pilasters and pillars by which broad panels are formed, these latter, richly ornamented with gold, serve to relieve the dazzling whiteness of the marble.

The ten state apartments are grouped round the landing; on the south side the two Gobelin rooms with the Hall of Mirrors, on the west the Study, on the north the Sleeping Apartment and on the east the Dining room. — Four oval Boudoirs forming, so to speak, architectural bonbonières, are clustered round the last three mentioned apartments, whereby the largest number of rooms permitted by the laws of the Rococo style is attained.

Each boudoir is a work of art of charming gracefulness and exhibits the perfection of the Rococo style as a mode of decoration.

The doors leading to the state apartments are ornamented by handsome carving. We now enter

The West Gobelin-Room (Music-Room).
(6 meters in he'ght, 8—5 in width.)

The walls are profusely ornamented with pictures, these, painted on strong linen, are an imitation of Gobelin and the work of Heinrich Baron v. Pechmann after designs by Watteau.

West Gobelin Room.
United Art Establishments in Munich

They represent the following subjects:
"Amor's Opfergabe" (The sacrificial gift of Amor),
"Dolce far niente" (The sweet-do-nothing).
"Blaue Traube" (Blue grapes), and
"Der Dudelsackpfeifer" (The bagpipe-player).

A great charm lies in these pictures, a "something" which reminds one of the happy days in the Trianon with their idyllic pastoral plays and pastoral life so celebrated in song. — The corners between these pictures are ornamented by the

West Gobelin Room. Chair and Stools.
United Art Establishments in Munich.

emblems of Agriculture and Pastoral Life. The wing doors are decorated by graceful carvings in wood, richly gilded, and above these are groups of cupids in shells with the emblems of Poetry, Painting and Music. Purple curtains soften the otherwise too dazzling light admitted by the large Norman windows. The ceiling paintings, surrounded by a beautiful frieze, are the next objects worthy of notice—these represent "Evening" and are charmingly executed by the hand of Hauschild after a design by Boucher. "Into the ocean, tinted purple by the dying rays of the setting sun, the Sun-God is descending in his chariot. Glancing back, he stretches out his arms in lingering greeting to the Goddess Venus reclining in her shell-shaped skiff. The Sun-horses are surrounded by Cupids—, and Naiads, engrossed in the appearance of the Sun-God, rock themselves to and fro on the back of a dolphin". The handsome furniture is covered with Gobelins (representing scenes from the Pastoral Poetry of the Rococo period) in delicately tinted beauty and in such unparalleled technique that the needlework resembles artistic genre pictures. A marble mantel supports a group in Carrara marble by Perron, representing the "Canonisation of Louis XIV."—

This is a masterpiece of sculpture as regards technique and perfection of execution, far surpassing the models of the Rococo period. The enormous mirror on the mantel is inclosed in a frame of beautiful carving, garlands of roses stretch, uniting the charming sculpture work of the frame, across the shining surface of the glass, the Bavarian Coat of Arms with the royal crown supported by cupids form the crowning piece to this mirror.

The piano, which is also an Aeolodikon, is richly ornamented with arabesques and cupids.

Above this hangs a second mirror in a broad carved frame and the furniture of this apartment is completed by a brilliantly coloured carpet of great beauty. The door is now reached which leads to the

Yellow or Silver Boudoir.

This apartment has nothing in common with the pomp of the Gobelin room, neverthless it is equally charming.

The plated carvings of the frames and panels of the two doors and the silver embroidery on the walls, which are covered with yellow silk, are resplendent with ornamentation. The ceiling decoration by Perron represents in medallions the four (as then known in the 18th century) continents, the four elements and the signs of the zodiac, symbolically represented.

The surport picture, handsomely framed, is by Leonard Fries after a design by Watteau and represents a pastoral dance in the merry month of May. The Venus statue, surrounded by cupids, will be recognised as the counterpart of that which was erected in Monopteros—Long narrow windows serve as pilasters for the panels on the wall—. these are surrounded by graceful arabesques.—

The Yellow or Silver Boudoir.

United Art Establishments in Munich

The stands of the four handsome china branched-candle-sticks on the walls are ornamented with charming designs after Watteau, and the panels themselves are embellished with floral ornaments. The following pastels in the centre of the panels are by Hofmaler Gräfle and represent
1. "La comtesse d'Egmont Pignatelli",
2. "Louis Charles August Fouquet, duc de Belle-Isle, Marechal de France",
3. "Marquise de Crequi",
4. "Arminius Maurice, comte de Sax".

Graceful glass tables, stools and sofas with gilded carvings (the furniture covered with yellow silk and beautiful garlands of light silver embroidery) complete the furniture of this charming little apartment and the next which we enter is the

Study (Reception Room).

The shape of this room is oblong, the colour of the furniture green and gold.

Architecture, sculpture and painting have united in creating of this apartment a vision of beauty.

The form of the room affords the necessary surface for the round lines of the Rococo style and these have been utilised for sculpture and painting in the most ingenious manner.

The walls, broken here and there by the windows, door and chimney-pieces, are of snow-white, richly ornamented with gold, which represents the symbols of Kingly Rule, Religion, Commerce, Trade and Science.

The archivaults of the ceiling are divided into six circular lunettes, of which two, decorated by sculpture with genii supporting the Coat of Arms and "Bavaria", are over the canopy, while the other four, charmingly framed, represent
1. Above the windows on the left,
"The Castle of Versailles with its surrounding grounds, (Louis XIV's walk) by Jank and Watter.

The Castle, with its world renowned water-works, occupies the background-, the artistic waters of the Latone Fountain are playing in the foreground.

The Sun-King walks majestically past a crowd of court ladies and gentlemen.
2. Above the window on the right,
"The little levëe of Louis XV, in the small apartment at Versailles" by Watter.

A brilliant crowd of court cavaliers surrounds the King, who is about to begin his daily occupations.

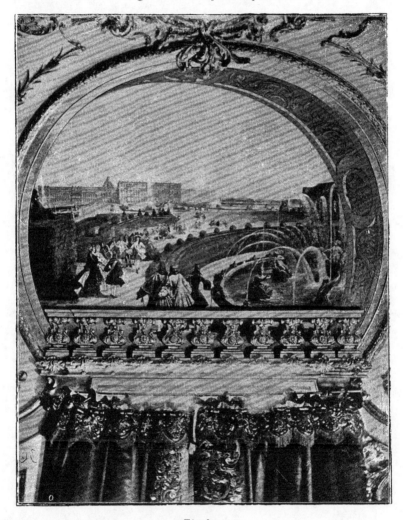

Study.
The Promenade of Louis XIV in the Garden of the Castle at Versailles.
United Art Establishments in Munich.

3. On the left of the canopy is the following picture, "Louis XIV receiving the Turkish Ambassador", by Knab and Watter.

Study.
United Art Establishments in Munich

This scene is represented as taking place in the large Gallery of Mirrors in the Castle at Versailles. The King stands beneath the canopy attired in a gorgeous state robe of embroidered brocade, next to him the Dauphin, equally pompously attired.

The Master of the Ceremonies, in a red robe, conducts the Turkish Ambassador and his suite up to the throne. Ladies brilliantly dressed, stand to the right and left of the balustrades, watching with interest the be-turbaned men bearing the presents of the great man.

Lastly to the right of the canopy "A wedding in the Chapel at Versailles" by Zimmermann.

This represents the interior of the church, the galleries crammed with spectators, the wedding party, with the splendid costumes glittering with jewels of the princely personages and cavaliers, the gorgeous vestments of the ecclesiastical princes, all forming a brilliant picture of Court life at that period.

The pictures above the two windows in carved frames are masterpieces of the Rococo style by Fries from designs by Watteau. "Spring" and "Summer".

Lovely female figures represent the seasons and are surrounded in the idyllic scnery by cupids at play —, a silver streamlet flows down over cascades into a pond below, into which the figure representing "Summer" steps to bathe.

To the right and left of the mirror on the broad oval window-wall hang the charming pictures by Freiherr von Pechmann (after Watteau) representing "Autumn" and "Winter". The first depicts the female figure of "Autumn" in a vineyard crowned with vines, around whom roguish cupids are dancing and playing.

The second picture is a tent opening to the foreground showing a group of cupids restling 'round the fire. "Winter" is presented as a grey-haired old man, warmly clad and bent with age.

Outside the tent one sees a snow-covered frozen landscape enlivened by the figures of wood-carrying cupids. The carved frames containing these pictures are worth noticing, as they display great artistic skill and beauty of form. A handsome crystal chandelier for 80 candles hangs from the ceiling, in the prisms of which the sunlight sparkles and glitters, giving thereby a faint idea of the increased beauty of the apartment when illuminated by the soft light of candles. A throne-canopy, which is necessary to show the character of the apartment as a reception room, is on the backwall, the corners of which are ornamented by tall bunches of ostrich feathers.

The beautifully carved front is surmounted by two genii

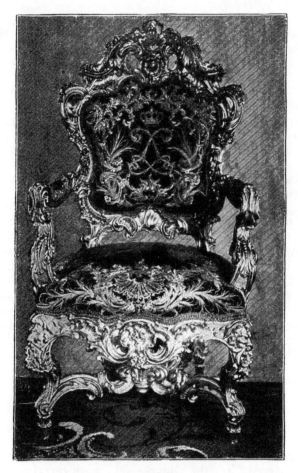

Study. Chair by the Writing-table.
United Art Establishments in Munich.

which support the royal crown high over the Arms of Bavaria.

Green velvet curtains, heavily embroidered in gold and lined with priceless ermine, hang down at either side.

The armchair standing before the writing table is a notable piece of workmanship. The back, the frame of which is of gilded carving, displays the monogram "L" with the royal crown on green velvet surrounded by graceful arabesques worked in gold.

The writing table is an equally handsome work of art. It is covered with green velvet embroidered in gold and is ornamented by branched-candlesticks, a beautiful inkstand with the royal insignia, a handsome blotter and a bronze equestrian statuette of Louis XIV. Two marble mantels with upright mirrors in gilded frames ornament either side of the canopy.

The equestrian statues of the Bourbon Kings Louis XIV. and XV. in bronze on marble pedestals are placed between branched-candlesticks, the pedestals themselves being ornamented with battle scenes and trophies in relief.

The other articles of furniture in this apartment comprise a beautiful table standing opposite the writing table (on which stand branched-candlesticks and a clock in gilded bronze), two little pillar-shaped tables of malachite in the window recesses, two secretaires in rosewood with handsome bronze ornaments and charming miniatures after designs by Watteau and Boucher and a splendid Smyrna carpet.

The Lilac Boudoir.

The soft tones of this room strike the eye pleasantly after the brilliant colours of the other apartments —, the ground colours here employed are lilac and gold. This and the two following boudoirs correspond in the architectural form to the "Yellow Boudoir", but on close inspection however the details will be found to vary in almost every respect, so that really less resemblance exists than appears at first sight.

The charming picture by Fries after Watteau. "The Arbour at Versailles" leads one back again to the careless Rococo period.

This picture, in a beautifully carved frame, represents the "Temple of the Sun" with fountains playing in the background.

The character of this picture is likewise reproduced in the pastels, to which belong the following portraits, "Etienne François, duc de Choiseuil - Steinville, ministre secretaire d'ëtat."

"Jeanne Antoinette Poison, marquis de Pompadour".

"Louis XV., roi de France".

"Maria Anna, marquise de la Tournelle, duchesse de Chateauroux."

The ceiling is ornamented by the following in medallion

Study. Writingtable.
United Art Establishments in Munich.

form; "Zeuss", "Apollo", "Mars" and "Flora", the work of the sculpturer Walker.

Wall brackets for candles in Dresden china decorate this charming boudoir. The narrow mirrors between the panels and above the small pillar-shaped tables were intended

The Lilac Boudoir.
United Art Establishments in Munich.

to reflect the beauty of this charming little room. this real flower of the Rococo period. From here we now pass on to

Sleeping Apartment.

After an original impression by Franz Hanfstaengl in Munich

The Sleeping Apartment

which, unlike the rest of the Castle, is furnished in the Regency style. At the time of the King's death this apart-

4*

ment was undergoing alterations and nothing but the painting on the ceiling remains over from former times. This room,

Sleeping-Apartment. Bed.
After an original impression by Franz Hanfstaengl in Munich.

the colours of which are royal blue and gold, is divided down the centre by a gilded balustrade.

Sleeping-Apartment. Ceiling Picture and Canopy.

United Art Establishments in Munich.

The carving and plastic gold embroidery which cover the surface of the walls were designed by Hofbaurat Drollinger. The back wall is built in a half circle, divided into panels by graceful palmstems, and richly decorated by genii etc. in gold embroidery. The two candelabra are artistic works of great merit, also the smoking tables at either side of the bed, which latter stands on a raised daïs or platform covered with red cloth. Blue velvet curtains hang from the canopy and are held back by cords with blue tassels. The Arms of Bavaria, embroidered in silk, are above the back of the bed, which elaborately carved, represents the Sun. The canopy itself is crowned by delicately carved work and richly gilded, two genii sit at either side and charming little cupids in the centre support the cushion on which rests the royal crown. The prie-dieu is embroidered with the picture of St. George —, while behind the canopy are paintings by Lesker representing "Apollo in the Sun Chariot".

The large painting on the ceiling of the „Canonisation of Louis XIV." is by August Spiess, after an engraving by Le Bruns. A large and beautiful crystal chandelier for 108 candles hangs suspended from the ceiling in the centre of the room. The framework of the pier glasses is charmingly carried out in Dresden china and is a composition of cupids and garlands of roses.

The mantelpieces and graceful pier-tables hold groups in Carrara marble of "Apollo and Diana" and the "Steeds of the Sun Chariot".

The framework round the high doors is likewise of Carrara marble, above which are the following pictures, handsomely framed, "The Morning Toilette of Louis XV."
"The Retiring to Rest of Louis XV."
"A Wedding."

Sleeping-Apartment. Toilet table.
United Art Establishments in Munich.

In the first two the grand ceremonial in vogue at the Palace of Versailles at the commencement and close of the Bourbon King's daily routine is duly represented. The third picture depicts the grand court festivities at a princely marriage taking place in the Gallery of Mirrors in the Palace of Versailles.

The handsome china vases on golden pedestals occupy the niches of the high windows, from which is visible a beautiful view of the Neptune Fountain and cascades.

The Pink Boudoir.

The pale colour of the walls (covered with pink silk) harmonises charmingly with the painting of the ceiling, which represents "Cupids bearing flowers" and also with the surport picture "Cupid crowned with flowers by Genii" The wall panels are decorated by the following pastels,, "Beatrice de Choiseul-Steinville, duchese de Grammont.

"René Nicolas Charles Augustin de Meaupeau, chancelier de France."

"Jeanne Becu, comtesse du Barry".

"Casar Gabriel, duc de Choiseul, Praslain ministere secretaire".

The graceful china wall-candelabra serve to heighten the beauty of this little apartment, also the numberless china knick — knacks on brackets, these, in conjunction with the other charming decorations, fully imparting to it the beauty of the Rococo style. We now enter

The Dining Room

which corresponds in size and architecture to the Study or Reception Room. The furniture of this apartment is covered with purple and gold and reminds one of the dining room at Herrenchiemsee, which is also in the Rococo style, only here is more of homelike comfort than gorgeous splendour and pomp. Windows and doors divide the walls into large panels, which bear symbolical representations of Hunting, Angling, Farming and Gardening, works by Perron.

The frieze in the principal cornice is a beautiful piece of work, representing groups of children, and this serves as a charming border to the lovely painted ceiling, the subjects of which represent

"Amor and Psyche."

The Flower-distributing Flora,

"Venus and Cupid" and "Bacchus and Venus", all carried out in plastic art and painting.

A beautiful china chandelier for 36 candles hangs by a golden chain from the centre of the ceiling —, the middle part represents foliage plants and is surrounded by cherubs at play.

Pink Boudoir.

United Art Establishments in Munich.

Two representations of scenes taken from old Testament History are above the two doors, these are "The dethroned Athalia" and the „Pardon of Esther".

Dining Room.
After an original impression by Franz Hanfstaengl in Munich.

Branched candlesticks and a bronze clock stand on the table by the window-wall—, the massive frame of the mirror is ornamented by charming wall candelabra.

Dining Room. Ceiling Painting

United Art Establishments in Munich

The sideboard or buffet is a masterpiece of art.

The monogram of the King, surrounded by exquisite carving, occupies the panel of the same, while above, let into the back of the buffet, is a mirror, round which are grouped the numerous shelves. Two bronze candlesticks stand on the slab, and above the sideboard on the wall, covered with

Dining Room. Sideboard.
United Art Establishments in Munich.

purple velvet, is a splendid mirror to which are attached branched candlesticks.

The centre of the apartment is occupied by the "Tischlein deck Dich", a table which is so arranged that it may be lowered into the room beneath to admit of its being laid for meals. An artistic piece of work consisting of a bouquet of flowers formed of Dresden china stands in the centre of this table.

The windows are draped with purple velvet curtains richly embroidered with arabesques in gold.

From these windows is a lovely view of the east side of the grounds.

The Blue Boudoir.

The colour employed in this charming little apartment is skyblue. Here also is the ceiling artistically sculptured, serving as a frame to the painting of "Music-discoursing Cupids" the companion picture to the equally charming decoration of the Pink Boudoir. Over the door leading into the Dining Room hangs the representation of "Leda with the Swan". The somewhat coarse subject of this picture has been delicately and guardedly treated by the hand of the artist Julius Frank.

Four pastels, surrounded by beautiful carving, ornament the walls, they are the following

"Germain Louis Chanvelin."
"Julie, comtesse de Molly-Nessle."
"Louis François Armand".
Pauline Felicite, comtesse de Ventimille.

The pierglasses introduced into the panels at either side of the doors have the effect of increasing the length of the room—, to these china branched-candlesticks are attached—. The furniture is covered with skyblue, richly ornamented with gold embroidery and the curtains and portières are likewise of the same colour. The numerous brackets on the walls are laden with beautiful knick-knacks in Dresden and Sèvres china, showing the taste of the 18th. century, and on the table is an equestrian statuette in Dresden china of a German prince, August the Strong.

The light tone of this boudoir is very refreshing to the eye after all the colour and brilliancy of the previously inspected apartments and forms a contrast between what has gone before and what is now to follow in

The East Gobelin Room.

This apartment corresponds in a measure to the West Gobelin Room, although differing in nearly all the details. The eye is instantly attracted by the beautiful wall paintings, (imitation Gobelins) the handiwork of Freiherrn von Pechmann; the subjects of which are taken from classical mythology and represent "The Triumphal Procession of Bacchus". "The Abduction of Europa", "Pygmalion and Venus" and "Cephale abducted by Aurora."

Blue Boudoir.

United Art Establishments in Munich.

East Gobelin Room.
United Art Establishments in Munich

Beautiful portières drape the profusely gilded carvings of the door panels, above which are pictures of cupids in shells, symbolising "Art and Science".

These, as well as the emblems of war and agriculture, (which are between the Gobelin pictures) are the work of the painter Perron, and the ceiling-painting, surrounded by a charming frame of artistic workmanship, is a copy by Hauschild from a design of Boucher entitled "Morning".

"Surrounded by the rosy clouds of morning the chariot of the Sun, drawn by fiery steeds, rises up out of the ocean waves. In this latter are seen Tritons, Naiads and Cupids and, accompanied by the Goddesses of the sea, Apollo, radiant in all his beauty, approaches. Aurora, surrounded by Amorettes, glides before the chariot away into the darkness of eternal night."

An artistic group in Carrara marble, a representation of the "Three Graces" by the sculpturer Bachler, stands on a handsome pier-table between two branched-candlesticks and surmounted by a mirror, the frame of which is likewise ornamented by bracket candlesticks. Between the folding doors, leading respectively to the stairs and the Blue Boudoir, is a handsome marble-mantel on which stand ornaments in bronze.

Here also is the sculptured work of "Apollo and Diana" and a copy of the "Venus of Medici".

The fire screens are here, as in all the other apartments, of beautiful workmanship.

The Hall of Mirrors.
(7½ meters in length, 8 in height.)

This apartment is a miracle of artistic beauty. Like some of the other rooms, it bears a certain resemblance to the Hall of the same name in the Castle of Herrenchiemsee, only that this is naturally on a smaller scale. This fact however, instead of detracting from, rather adds to the charm of its appearance.

Architecture, Painting, Sculpture and Art-Handicraft have vied with each other in the decoration of this apartment, and it is hard almost even for an expert, how much more so therefore for others, to decide to which branch the palm should be awarded. It is just the union of all these branches which has made of the apartment what it is.

The walls are covered by large mirrors in handsome frames in the Rococo style.

Hall of Mirrors.
United Art Establishments in Munich

Hall of Mirrors. (Window recess).

Lindernof

United Art Establishments in Munich.

The colour employed in this room is again royal blue, which here in the glitter of the mirrors and the elaborate gilding of the decorations perhaps hardly seems to show up enough and yet in reality it assists in a great measure in completing the harmony of the apartment.

The charming medallions are the work of Perron and represent the legend of "Amor and Psyche".

The ceiling paintings are by Schwoiser and represent "Venus bathing," after a design by Boucher, and "The birth of Venus".

This pictures, by reason of their artistic perfection, fit into and serve to complete the frame of the whole.

Just in this apartment, which shows the greatest pomp and splendour in its decorations and furniture, ought the ceiling paintings to set forth the object of the Castle as the brilliant after and new form of the Love-Life of the Rococo period on the foundation of Mythological Courtship and Love-Happiness.

All the other rooms show by their decorations the Passion of Love, symbolically represented in the so very original combination of the antique and every-day aspect of the world at the Rococo time, but here in this room, upon which the charming picture of Venus looks down out of the perfect beauty of the Park Grounds, the life of Venus, symbolically represented, should be the most beautiful ornament, thereby imparting to the whole building the character of the Castle of Love at the Rococo period.

Over the doors leading to the Gobelin Apartments (the panels of which, instead of by the usual carving, are ornamented by the introduction of pier-glasses) hang the following two pictures by Benczur,

"A Coursing party in the time of Louis XV." and

"The reception of the ambassadors of Venice by Louis XV".

Two handsome mantels intercept the glass panels of the walls; these are constructed of precious lapis-lazuli and hold the charming marble groups of "The abduction of Helena" and "The Rape of Proserpine". The classical beauty of these sculptured figures (by Walker) are reflected in charming effects of light and shade in the large mirrors standing on the mantelpieces.

Between this is a recess, the walls of which are likewise covered with mirrors, and on the brackets are a number of knick-knacks in Sèvres china—. The ceiling of this recess or alcove was painted by Professor Widmann, a work which represents "The Judgment of Paris."

The space afforded by this little corner is taken up by a sofa, which like all the furniture in this apartment, is of rosewood and covered with light blue, interwoven with silver silk and ornamented further with the Bourbon lilies surrounded by conventional foliage.

Clock in the Hall of Mirrors.
United Art Establishments in Munich.

The table in front of the sofa, which stands upon a snow-white carpet composed of ostrich feathers, holds graceful ornaments of gilded bronze, and the slab of the table (composed of mosaic work) has let into it, in lapis-lazuli, the Arms of Bavaria.

From the ceiling hangs a charming chandelier of ivory for 16 candles—, this is a work of art of the highest perfection, after a design by Hofmann and carried out by Perron. The eight arms, so formed as to represent branches, terminate in calyces into which the candles are fixed. Cupids at play and the royal crown complete this charming piece of carving. The table (above which stands a large mirror) between the windows holds beautiful works by Perron "Apollo in the bath of Thetis", and two groups of "Sunhorses". The writing table, the so—called "Bureau of Louis XV" standing by the east window, is a brilliant accomplishment of industrial art; this is ornamented, in addition to the carving and bronze ornaments, by 12 medallions in china illustrating episodes out of the life of Louis XV. On the centre of the table is a marble statue of the same monarch (by Professor A. Hess) in coronation robes and on either side stand beautiful branched candlesticks of Dresden china.

The inkstand is likewise of the same material and consists of two receptables, the one for ink, the other for sand, so formed as to represent the two globes, the celestial and terrestial. The handbell is in the form of the royal crown. Two large china dishes also standing on this table are ornamented by beautiful paintings by the hand of Karl Grünwedel. The subjects of these paintings are

"The Reception of the Turkish Ambassadors by Louis XV" and

"The entry of Louis XV into Strassburg".

The blotter lying on the writing-table is likewise ornamented by a painting on china from the same hand, and represents

"The marriage of the Dauphin Louis with the Infanta Maria Theresia of Spain".

An étagère opposite the "Bureau" does duty as a bookcase and holds a handsome Paris clock in bronze and two Sèvres vases charmingly painted in the Rococo style.

Two card tables in bronze framework are also adorned by paintings on china by Grünwedel, the subjects of which are "The King playing cards in the large gallery at Versailles" and "The coronation of Louis XV".

The numerous mirrors in this apartment have the effect of greatly adding to its length and impart to it a charming appearance. One can hardly even imagine how magnificent it must appear when seen illuminated by the light of the endless candles in the chandeliers. This, as well as the two adjoining Gobelin rooms, by the extravagant beauty which shows off to the utmost advantage the charm of the Rococo style, form without doubt the pearl of the state apartments of Linderhof.   Unfortunately the time spent in inspecting these apartments is naturally of too short a duration to permit of the visitor taking in all the beauty of the various details.   As in the case of the Island Castle of Herrenchiemsee, it must be visited again and again before the eye is able to do more than merely grasp a general impression of the whole.   One visit can do little beyond leaving in the memory a picture such as is seen in a kaleidoscope

Leaving the Castle we now enter the Park Grounds. A bust of the unhappy Queen Maria Antoinette, erected by the royal architect of the Castle, occupies a prominent position on the terrace.   In the sweet charm of proud youthful beauty the Queen gazes over at the little Castle, which being a counterpart of her own beloved Trianon, awakens in her memories and thoughts of that brilliant epoch of her life.

These memories also serve as an explanation for this building, which, breathing the splendour and beauty of the great French Monarchic Age, is, at first sight, to the German visitor almost inexplicable.

As the Castle of Herrenchiemsee was intended in the majestic form of the Renaissance to represent the proud and stately beauty and power of kingly rule, so Castle Linderhof was to present a picture appealing to the senses, glorified by the poetry of the Rococo period; the whole charm and beauty of the Castle, both in its interior and in its grounds, render this idea undeniably prominent.   The additional buildings, the "Blue Grotto", "Kiosque" etc. which some people regard as disturbing elements in the symmetry of the whole, do not belong, so to say, to the Castle, and putting these aside, the visitor can hardly fail to acknowledge that the charm of the Rococo period has awakened to new life by the perfection of form and colour which here far surpass all previous examples of this style.   The state carriages and sleighs which were formerly used by the King are quite in accordance with the rest of the Castle—all bear the undeniable stamp of the same period.

The Grounds.

These are also in the gay and charming style of the Rococo age.

A broad terrace with a parapet extends along the front of the Castle.   Large stone vases, the bases of which form the royal crown, impart to the same a rich plastic decoration. Three steps lead down from the terrace to the water and

South Garden Grounds.

After an original impression by Franz Hanfstaengl in Munich

flower parterre, which latter is beautifully laid out. The long edges of closely cut grass are bordered by broad bands of flowering plants which surround the oblong basin of the lake.

Carpet-beds and enormous vases (by the sculpturer Fischer), these latter filled with brilliant flowers, intercept with grand effect the bright fresh green of the lawn—, symmetrical rows of trees and high graceful latticework covered with creepers line the long sides of the parterre. The walls on which the Terrace is built and rests are ornamented with two statues representing respectively "Venus" and "Diana" by Hausmann.

A group in gilded zinc, "Flora surrounded by Cupids" occupies the centre of the fountain basin, and two allegorical figures of "Day" and "Night" mark the end of the parterre on the south side.

The two broad carriage roads leading along both sides of the parterre and ascending in a semi-circle unite at the foot of the terrace.

Two enormous lions mount guard over the steps, on the first of these is a statue of Louis II, modelled by Ney and worked out in marble by the sculpturer Ochs. The ideal figure of the immortalised monarch stands on a low simple pedestal, ornamented by a lovely wreath of flowers. The King, wearing the coronation robes of the Grand Master of the Order of the Knights of St. George, is represented as, struck by the view of the Castle which is standing before him, pausing for a moment in order to observe it more closely. The noble head with the high thoughtful brow, the youthful features and the expression are all wonderfully brought out in the marble. All the details, from the characteristically stamped features to the finely modelled folds and embroidery of the pompous attire are executed with the greatest care and accuracy, so that the figure has the appearance of life.—The monument, owing to its pic turesque background, is seen to greatest advantage from the Castle.

The erection of this statue in the year 1896 in the midst of all the splendour designed by the King, speaks eloquently of the esteem in which he was held by Ludwig II. From this spot the three large slopes of the south terrace present a beautiful picture—, the continuation of the long axle of the garden by an alley of trees, a style so much liked at the Rococo period, was here rendered impossible by the steepness of the "Linderbühl". On the summit of this little hill, peeping out amid the rich dark green of the fir trees is the snow-white "Temple of Monopteros".

Steps in the form of a semi-circle mount up from behind the monument of the King to the charming "Watersprite

Fountain" (Wagmüller). Beautiful Naiads gaze down from
the round capitals of the terrace wall at the playing waters.

Monument of King Ludwig II.
After an original impression by Franz Hanfstaengl in Munich.

Handsome vases ornament the broad balustrade of the steps
leading up to the first terrace. This balustrade is continued

along the whole length of the terrace and likewise ornamented. Wide steps lead from here up to the walls supporting

The Water Sprite Fountain.

After an original impression by Franz Hanfstaengl in Munich.

the upper terrace, which is so constructed as to form three large arches—, in the centre of the hall formed by these is a

South Grounds. "Monopteros".

United Art Establishments in Munich.

bust of Marie Antoinette on a high pedestal bearing the motto of the Bourbons "nec pluribus impar". A pretty view is to be had from the steps of the terraces of the parterre and the Castle, behind which are the cascades and archways covered with dense foliage—, far beneath on the west the old "Linderhof" the buildings of the Steward, almost hidden by the groups of trees, and on the east the little church and Kiosque are visible. Steps lead from the upper terrace to the charming little "Temple Monopteros", the circular roof of which is supported by six slender columns. A marble statue of Venus, by the master hand of Hautmann, occupies the centre of this little building. The gardens, which here in Linderhof surround the Castle on all sides, form an integral part of the whole architectural composition.

The ingenious arrangement in front of the Castle of the flower and water-parterres and terraces, at the sides of the same of the trellis-covered walks, and at the back of the pompous finish given by the Cascades, the whole surrounded by meadow and forest, forming thereby an idyllic picture, all this is due to the gardener-artist Effner, who, at his Majesty's command, put forth all his skill and in so doing far surpassed Le Notre, whom he had taken as his model.

The West Grounds.

The west and east gardens are resplendent with beauty and in every detail true to the Rococo style.

These gardens form, so to speak, the continuation and extension of the Castle building—. The cool shady covered walks form the corridors and walls to the space inclosed by them, ornamented with fountains, statues and brilliant flowers.

The entrance is formed by richly ornamented trellis-work covered with creepers of every description, a suitable entrance to this charming boudoir.

Two artificial lakes or ponds; surrounded by large carpet-beds, and bordered with rosetrees, are ornamented, the one by the figure of "Fama" (Walker), and the other by a charming group "Cupids playing with a dolphin", by Professor Wagmüller.

The statues—modelled in sandstone by Hautmann and representing the four seasons "Spring, Summer, Autumn and Winter" also add to the beauty of the garden.

The two long side alleys unite at the end and form a circular space. Enormous sandstone "Ildefonso" vases

serve as ornaments to this creeper-covered boudoir already
spoken of, in the centre of which is a terra cotta bust of

West Grounds.

After an original impression by Franz Hanfstaengl in Munich.

the "Sun-King Louis XIV." on a high pedestal bearing upon
it the usual Bourbon devise "nec pluribus impar".

The North Grounds.

The gardens at the back of the Castle are ornamented with beautiful carpet-beds, in which the "Lily of Bourbon"

North Grounds with the Neptune Fountain.
After an original impression by Franz Hanfstaengl in Munich.

plays a prominent rôle; close adjoining is the "Neptune Fountain", which was constructed after a design by Wagmüller in the zinc foundry of Maffei. "Three wildly rearing horses career madly onward with the chariot of Neptune in which is seated the god of the sea with the trident in his right hand, the left raised with a gesture of command".

East Grounds.
After an original impression by Franz Hanfstaengl in Munich.

Behind this are the steps of the cascades, ornamented on the front side by two groups of Cupids. Large vases with the royal crown and the balustrade of a simple fountain basin act as a finish to the whole.

The steps of the cascades are framed on either side by a high arched covered trellis-way, the terminations of which are ornamented by the statues of the four—(then known in the 18th. century)—continents, Europe, Asia, Africa and America, the work of the sculpturer Hautmann. A spacious pavilion built of wooden trellis-work crowns the whole picture.

From this spot a charming view is to be seen, embracing the cascades, the Castle, the high playing fountains of the South Grounds, the terraces and finally of the glittering little white building of "Monopteros".

A few steps down the east trellis-walk bring one on the way to the Grotto—, this and the Kiosque still remain to be visited.

This same trellis covered walk ends close to the termination of the East Grounds, which resemble those on the western side of the Castle in beauty and charm.

In the centre stands the group in sandstone, by Professor Hautmann, of "Amor and Psyche".

Here in this part of the ground only one fountain is to be seen, out of which rises the charming figure of

"Cupid shooting arrows",

by Wagmüller.

The ctatues of the Four Elements (the work of Professor Hautmann) correspond here to the four statues on the long side of the West Grounds.

Here again the trellis—covered walks terminate in a sort of arbour, in which, on a high pedestal bearing the proud motto of the Bourbons, we see the bust of Louis XVI., that most unfortunate and unhappy monarch that France has ever beheld.

The Grotto.

The way to the Grotto leads across the Grounds on the east side up through the trellis-walk, then out into the open park, gently ascending up to a large rock in which the cleverly concealed entrance is to be found. This Grotto is a copy of the famous one on the island of Capri and a triumph of technical work which, with simple materials, was built by the Landscape Plasticer Dirigl.

Strong wall pillars support the large dome—shaped vault of the principal Grotto, to which the (front and back) lesser Grottos adjoin. The skeleton or frame-work of the interior

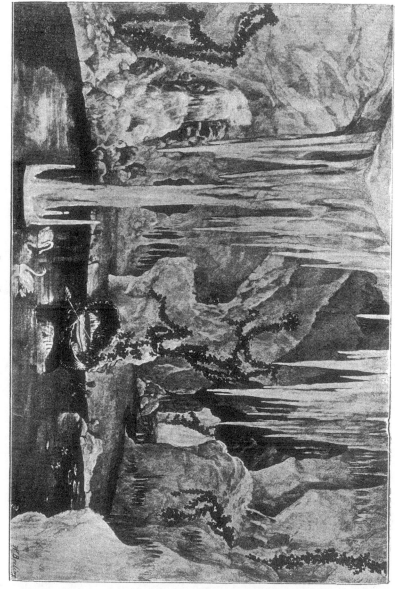

Blue Grotto.

United Art Establishments in München

construction consists of iron girders, to which the trellis
work is fastened with the object of supporting the plastic

Blue Grotto. "Tannhäuser on the Venus Mount."
United Art Establishments in Munich.

work and the beautiful artistic stalactites. The block of
rocks forming the entrance also consists of iron trellis-work

filled in with cement, imparting to it the appearance of a
natural rocky formation.

The front Grotto is illuminated by a dull red light. A
narrow rocky path leads from here into the principal Grotto,
in which is an almost supernatural light—, beautiful stalactites hang down from the roof glistening in the bright red
glow, then as if in the far distance, the murmuring and
rushing of water strikes upon the ear.

The scene that greets the eye on entering the main
Grotto is fairylike. Enormous pillars of stalactites
support the roof, and paths and alcoves are formed by the
same. This hall is illuminated by a blue light which causes
wonderful effects of light and shade on the surface of the
lake occupying the foreground.

The backwall of the Grotto is embellished by the painting by A. von Heckel, a representation of
"Tannhäuser on the Venus Mount",
the scenery of which corresponds exactly with the instructions
given by Wagner for his drama.

This shows by the dancing of the Bacchante a life
overflowing with hot passion— and a maddening abundance
of beauty is seen everywhere. Groups of roguish cupids
carry on their loose play around the shell—throne in which
the Goddess of Love, full of seductive charm, watches over
the slumber of the Minnesinger resting at her feet. Doves
fly round and about the loving pair, and above these are
Amorettes bearing garlands of flowers. Three Graces standing by the side of the throne form a charming addition to
the picture. A beautiful little gilded shell—shaped skiff,
with plastic ornamentations of cupids and doves, rocks gently
to and fro on the edge of the little lake.

Opposite to the picture are placed two seats called
respectively "The King's Seat" and "The Lorelei".

From the former, with its throne of shells, table and
chairs in coral, is seen the best view of the fantastic beauty
of this place.

The Lorelei is constructed of artificial crystals and
coral branches and affords in the almost magical illumination
a charming sight.

The path now leads through the back Grotto, the
bright red light of which dims the charming magic colour of
the main Grotto, and out through an artistic rocky gate
into the pleasant peaceful wooded scenery of the Park. A
few steps now lead the visitor up to the door of

The Kiosque.

This unique graceful structure with its beautifully ornamented surface, resembling a gorgeous carpet with interwoven
borders, combined with the glittering gold of the cupola,
forms a pearl of Islamitic architecture.

The interior presents a most picturesque appearance—
the elegant refinement of its ornamentations, the charming

Kiosque.
United Art Establishments in Munich.

polychrome decoration of the walls in the richest of
colours, the glaced tiles and pavements of bright
marble and the trickling fountain in the centre of the spacious
hall, all tend to impart to it an element of life and animation.

The ornamentations of the windows and arcades are of
a beautiful filigree—like richness and the cluster of slender
columns on high bases are ornamented with ribbon-like lines
and the capitals with conventional foliage. The panels of
the Norman arches are also beautifully decorated with ara-

besques and the horse-shoe arches have the same decoration between the pillars imparting the effect of a scollopped curtain.

The endeavour to create the impression of an oriental state apartment by the fairylike wondrous beauty of the furniture and play of light is at once made apparent. Three bright coloured windows illuminate the dreamy beauty of this hall and form wonderful effects of light and colour on the trickling waters of the fountain, on the tiles of the floor and on the large majolica vases in the corridors, containing blue-white and red-white ostrich feathers.

The Chapel-like apartment on the northside is particularly richly decorated, this recess glitters in the electric light, causing it to stand out sharply from the rest of the room and lights up the three peacocks in enamelled bronze, the wheel-shaped tails of which sparkle with gems and pearls.

There now only remains the chapel to be seen. This is situated in the park just beyond the flower gardens. The principal ornaments of the interior are the four glass paintings in the windows, which are perfect, both as regards technique and execution; in the ornamentation of these also the artist has adhered to the style of Louis XIV. These paintings represent "Jesus as Saviour of the world", "Mary with the Child Jesus", "St. Louis" and "St. Richard".

There is no building erected by the King which presents so much beauty as does Linderhof and its surroundings. The ceaseless stream of visitors which every summer brings to this spot in nowise disturbs or effects the charming peacefulness and beauty which pervades, not only in the Castle itself, but all the surrounding neighbourhood; this latter unfortunately is all too often unnoticed and passed over by tourists, who in their anxiety to "do" the Castle, rush from one object of interest to another and hardly give more than a fleeting glance, sometimes scarcely even that, at the gifts with which nature has so lavishly endowed this beautiful spot. Was it not just for that very reason that the King, that ardent lover of nature, selected this isolated corner of the mountain world in which to erect his home?

Every year in late autumn the blue-white Lozenge Banner may be seen waving from the high flagstaff of the old Linderhof. It announces the presence of Bavaria's Prince Regent Luitpold, who comes here for shooting and hunting.

His simple tastes are satisfied by the modest apartments in the old shooting lodge, and not his tastes alone make

Kiosque-Interior.

United Art Establishments in Munich.

him choose this more simple abode, but because also it goes against him to hinder in any way the visitors who come here in the hopes of seeing the Castle.

Endowed with the same love for nature as was the royal architect himself, he knows that every one who views this royal Castle intelligently wins in his turn new friends for the grandly-sublime forest and mountain solitude of Linderhof.

Königshaus Schachen.

The road from Oberau to the isolated royal seat "Schachen" leads right into the heart of the high Alpine world.

On descending from the train at Garmisch—Parenkirchen a grand view of the Wetterstein Group (with the Zugspitz) becomes visible.

Schachen may be reached by two roads, but whether the one starting from Partenkirchen or the other from Mittenwald be chosen, is merely a matter of taste, as either route takes 6 hours.

The visit to this little mountain castle can only really be recommended to those, who, independent of railway or hired convey ances, are not afraid to face a stiff day's march in order to see this little dwelling buried in the heart of the beautiful mountain scenery. Walkers starting from Partenkirchen should take the path to Vordergraseckmere, here there is an excellent view of the Wetterstein, Dreithorspitz, the Schachen-Plateau and also of the royal residence itself—. Another hour and a half's good climbing brings the visitor to Elmau, where he gains the Königstrasse or Royal Road.

For those who are not good walkers, or who prefer to reach Schachen by less fatiguing means, there are carriages to be had, both at Partenkirchen and at Mittenwald, to convey them as far as Elmau.

From this point the Royal Road winds upwards through lovely forest country, ascending hundreds of meters, a fact

of which the visitor is barely conscious until a sudden
break in the trees discloses to his eyes Parten-

Lake Schachen.
After an original photograph by the Photographic Society Zürich.

kirchen lying far below in the midst of its fresh green
meadows, while high up, beyond the Wetterstein Alp, stands

the King's Shooting Lodge "Schachen", overtopped by the Alpspitz, Hochblassen, Schachen-Plateau and Schneeferner. Below on the right is the pale green Lake Schachen (1670 m.), and also the Schachen Alp—, beyond, towards the plain, a mass of misty clouds and from out of these every now and again a glimpse of the Ettaler Mandl is caught.

An inn "Restaurant Schachen", standing on the left hand side of the Königsweg, invites the tourist to rest awhile and partake of refreshment. — Here also tickets for admittance to the Castle can be obtained. A complete view of the Royal House is visible from this spot. It is built in a graceful style, suitable to its mountainous surroundings. With the exception of the ground-floor it is composed of wood, with balconies and galleries, above which rises the high centre construction.

The lower structure contains sitting, dining, bedroom and study, all of which are extremely simply furnished, one is therefore all the more surprised on entering the large hall on the first floor (which is reached by means of a winding stair-case) to find that it is fitted up in a totally different, and far more elaborate, style. It is typical of the King, here amidst the Majesty of Naturés grandest works, to have designed the exterior of his house in the simplest possible style, allowing nothing which could in any way disturb the eye, and yet, in spite of its outward simplicity, the chief apartment he caused to be decorated and furnished in the attractive fairy-like style of the Orient. The ceiling of this apartment is of deep blue, thickly sown with golden stars and bordered by a broad gold frame ornamented by beautiful arabesques. The decoration of the floor and walls is most cleverly carried out by the employment of ornamental lines in plastic forms, imparting to the same the appearance of embroidered and woven carpets.

The sharp outlines of the stucco reliefs serve to throw up and enhance the colours and brilliant light effects. The pillars on the walls are gracefully and delicately ornamented with conventional foliage and form a connecting link with the sculptures above the wavelike window arches, and the admittance of too much light through the bay and round windows is prevented by the mosaic beauty of colour which illuminates the apartment with charming and harmonious iridescence. The fairy-like, dreamy beauty of the room is increased by the divans or sofas placed along the walls, by the four enormous vases of artistic beauty, filled with ostrich feathers, and the graceful little inlaid tables, (holding

The Royal Residence "Schachen."

After an original photograph by Ferd. Finsterlin, Munich.

the requisites for smoking), and stools, as well as by the
lamps suspended from the ceiling in the corners —, all these
tend to complete the poetical charm of this fairy apartment.

The Moorish Hall.
United Art Establishments Munich.

A handsome balustrade, with upright slender pillars,
(which support the arch) separates the hall from the equally
beautiful anteroom. The long splendidly-embroidered and

Vase.
United Art Establishments Munich.

woven curtains, give a brilliant finish to the state apartment.

All this beauty and grandeur disappear, however, like a fleeting dream, in the face of the Majesty of Nature, before the indescribable glory of the view from the Königshaus, which is surpassed even by that seen from the Pavilion above. On all sides are the wild gigantic rocks of the Wet-

Smoking-table and Sofa.
United Art Establishments Munich.

terstein mountains. The rock which supports the Pavilion descends precipitiously into the giddy depth beneath, where sparkles, (according to the time of day) the blue "Gumpe", a narrow lake, like an emerald or turquoise set in stone—. The Partnach Fall glitters and shines like silver and above this are seen the Platt and Schneeferner, Alpspitz and Waxenstein—, to the left the beautiful Oberrain Valley with the Scharnitzspitz, Oberrainthaler Schrofen, Teufelgrat, Hundstall and Hochwanner —, these proud rocky summits which keep guard over this romantic and isolated high Alpine picture.

The panorama seen from the Königshaus is equally grand. The Ammer Mts., Geierköpfe, Kreuzspitze, Klammspitze, Ettaler Mandl, all these are seen at their full

The Soiern Lake in the Karwendel Mts.

After an original picture in the magazine "Bayerland", by permission of the firm Oldenbourg Munich.

beauty in the bright rays of the sunshine -, the Krotten-
kopf, Heimgarten and Herzogstand stand opposite in picturesque formation and beyond, the eye is attracted by the
glittering blue basins of the lakes, and to the right by the
solitary valley of the Isar.

Above on the Soiern a royal residence is reflected in the
green — black waters of the Soiern Lake, this latter surrounded by the steep walls of the Karwendel Mts. —, high
above this, on the Schöttelkar, stands the Pavilion. The
panorama from this spot is unbounded and yet only completes
that which the Royal Pavilions on the Hochkopf and Herzogstand veil from the eye.

From the Herzogsstand, whoso summit is reflected in
the waters of two mountain lakes, a last glimpse is taken
of the wondrous beauty of the mountain world, — far beyond
in the foreground one sees, sparkling like gold in the brilliant sunshine, the extensive basin of the Starnberger Lake,
the sight of which recalls to the mind of the tourist the
tragic fate which in those waters befell Bavaria's much
beloved and lamented Monarch. It is diffcult to tear ourselves away from this spot, but we must press on to new
sights and new scenes of beauty.

Linderhof und Umgebung.

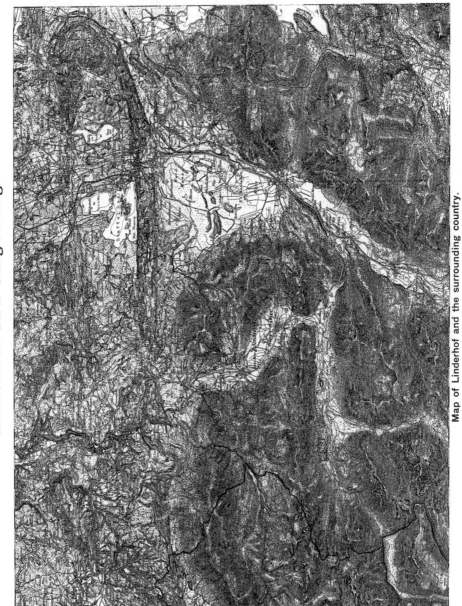

Map of Linderhof and the surrounding country.

THE

ROYAL CASTLE

"BERG"

Preface.

The royal Castle of Berg is situated in the midst of pleasant undulating country, close to the shores of the much frequented Starnberger Lake and within an hour's reach nf Munich.

Dating from an earlier period, it does not belong to those buildings erected by Ludwig II of Bavaria, nevertheless a description of it must be added to the work treating of the King's Castles, as it is closely connected with the life of the King from the days of his earliest childhood up to his tragic end.

Visitors to Castle Berg must not seek for princely pomp or splendour — here the charm lies in the memories which meet one at every step and turn and in the melancholy solitude which envelopes this royal residence.

He, who standing on the terrace of the little Votive Church, gazes down upon the spot where the unhappy Monarch met his death, can hardly help a rush of memories reminding him of the splendour created by that King amid the beauties of the Alpine world.

After an original drawing by H. Grabensee.

Castle Berg. 1886.

A simple, and for the most part, unnoticed, picture hanging in Castle Berg represents the King in the proud beauty of youth when he first visited this mansion.

Through the green of the Park glimmers the House of God, erected to commemorate the tragic death of this beloved Prince. The beginning and end of his Regency are crowded together in this delightfully situated Castle, and the thousands who pass by its gates in the summer season send, pausing for a moment in the fulness of their enjoyment of weather and scenery, a sorrowful greeting to the towers and pinnacles which have borne witness to so many happy and brilliant days, until — meteor-like — the precious life of the beloved monarch met its end in the waters of the lake.

The Halting Station "Castle Berg" is reached by steamer in a few minutes from Starnberg. The full and entire beauty of the landscape unfolds itself during this short trip—. The lake extends in glittering shining blue, its shores surrounded by beautiful forest out of which peep numberless castles and villas — above these on the slopes of the hills are seen the spires of the churches, while at the south end of the lake the eye is caught by a jagged sea of high mountain peaks.

The road which leads up from the landing stage to Castle Berg is pleasantly shaded by lofty trees and brings the tourist in a short time to the entrance gate of the Castle. (Tickets for admission, 50 Pf. per head, are to be obtained at the steward's.)

The Castle has been for over 200 years in the possession of the Royal House of Bavaria. Many a brilliant fête took place within and without its walls in the days when the "Bucentaur", the state ship of the Elector, sailed on the waters of the lake and the horn of the hunter and the cry of the hounds were heard in the forests and the stag was pursued by a brilliant court society—, when the festively illuminated galleys, accompanied by gondolas and skiffs, slowly made the circuit of the lake — the Castle and shores being bathed in a flood of light, colour and brightness. Years come and go — the artistic Renaissance garden ran to waste, solitude took possession of the royal domain and not until the middle of the 19th century did it awake to new life.

Between the years 1849—1851 the Castle was completely rebuilt by King Max of Bavaria — only the ground-plan remained as it had originally been, but four corner towers were added and the walls crowned with pinnacles.

Berg was a favourite residence of the King's and he frequently stayed there with his family, King Ludwig also chose out this peaceful spot as his favourite abode.

KING LOUIS II.

Castle Berg.

After an original photograph by Ferd Finsterlin, Munich.

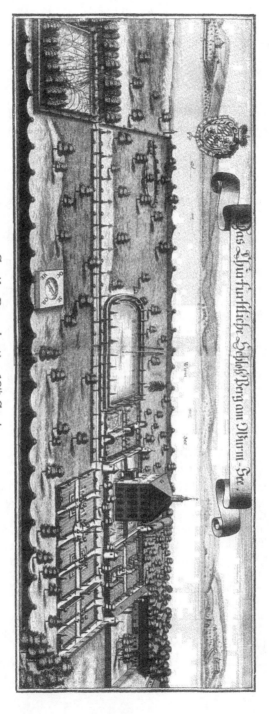

Castle Berg in the 18th Century.

The only notable alteration which the building underwent during the Regency of King Ludwig II. was the erection of
the lofty tower on the north side of the Castle — This
contains on the ground floor the principal entrance, which
lends an imposing appearance to the otherwise simple building. The furniture of the rooms on the 1st and 2nd floors
dates from the time of the King's parents. The most beautiful ornament of the Castle is the Park by which it is surrounded—, on the south side is the garden and immediately
adjoining it the Park—here Nature is permitted to go her own
sweet way—. A shady trellis - covered walk leads from the
Castle down to the shores of the lake and the Bathing House.

The mansion consists of ground-floor and two storeys.
The rooms, to visitors coming from the Royal State
Castles, appear low and small.

A winding staircase leads up to the apartments of the
King. The furniture of these, in comparison with those of
the other Royal Castles, is so simple and modest as to raise
feelings of disappointment in those coming here in the hopes
of seeing princely pomp and splendour.

The walls, however, exhibit pictures of high artistic
value. These, as well as the busts and statues ornamenting
the apartments, were the only addition made by King Ludwig II. in the decoration of the interior of this building.

Two water-colours adorn the corridor, these represent
"The Coronation Carriage" and "The State Saloon Carriage of the Royal Train".

The first of the apartments is

The Flower — room.

(Sitting — room of the Queen.)

This comfortably furnished room shows, by the complete absence of all splendour and pomp, the elegant taste
of the King's parents. The furniture and simple wall papers
may, however, appear to some old fashioned and out of
date. The pictures hanging on the walls represent scenes
taken from the Drama "Don Carlos" by Müller and Jäger,
also a water-colour of "Hohenschwangau" by Neureuther
and an oil painting (copy after Raphael) of "St. Cecilia".
An equestrian statuette of King Ludwig II., in the uniform
of a Lancer, stands on the stove.

In the adjoining cosy little alcove is the painting representing "Father Max surrounded by his family,"— the walls
are further adorned by mountains view and paintings by
Yank.

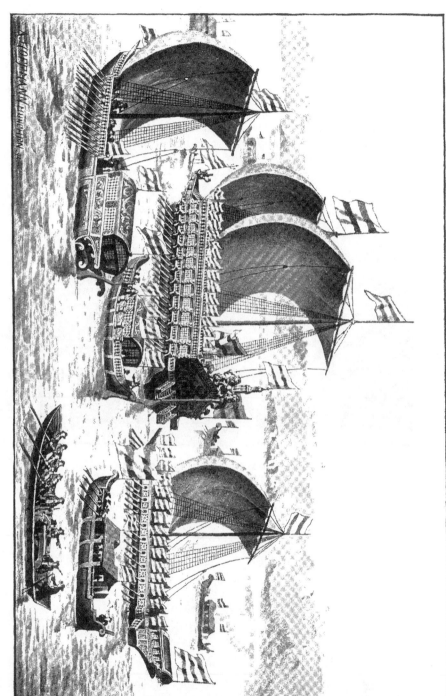

The "Bucentaur" on the Würm Lake.

After an original picture in the Magazine "Bayerland." — by permission of the firm Oldenbourg, Munich.

We now enter

The Drawing — room.

This apartment is somewhat more luxuriously furnished.
The slabs of the tables are of white marble—. A handsome inlaid jewel-box and also a clock standing on a small
side are both worthy of notice.

A beautiful relief of the Lake of Lucerne is a souvenir
of the King's journey to the scenes of the Swiss Legend
of William Tell, and a bust of General von der Tann, one
of the Bavarian leaders, and the following paintings and

The Trellis-walk leading to the Lake.
United Art Establishments in Munich.

water-colours ornament the walls "Munich in the year 1862",
"Rome", "The Lake of Lucerne", "The Himalaya mountains",
also pen and ink drawings by Pixis, representing scenes from
Richard Wagner's Dramas "Tannhäuser", "Lohengrin", "The
Mastersingers of Nürnberg", "Tristan and Isolde", "The
flying Dutchman" and "Rhinegold and the Valkyr".

The next room is

The Sleeping Apartment.

Here it was that the mortal remains of Bavaria's King
were laid out after the terrible catastrophe.

The walls of the room are covered with light blue paper,
strewn with golden lilies—. The simple bedstead is surmounted by a canopy—, the coverings of the bed, like those
of the furniture, are of blue silk.

A statuette of the Empress Elisabeth of Austria on horse back (whose last greeting to the King, an enormous bouquet of white jessamine, lay on the death bed) stands on a side table. On the walls are two water-colours by Seder and Seeberger, representing the interior of the "Residenz Theater" in Munich, an oil-painting "The Rose Island in the Starnberger Lake", two other water colours "A gorgeous apartment in the Residenz in Munich", and "A boudoir in Castle Schlessheim", also pencil drawings from scenes from the Dramas "Maria Stuart", and "Cabal and Love" by Schiller.

This room also contains a bust of the poet Goethe.

The Landing.

Here the only article of furniture is a writing-table. Several pictures ornament the walls, two drawings in charcoal of King Ludwig II, a sepia drawing of Princess Augusta of Bavaria, a print of Richard Wagner, the portraits of the Emperor Alexander II of Russia and his wife, and lastly the representation of a Triumphal Arch built out of huge wine casks and erected by the coopers at Neustadt on the Haardt, in honour of King Ludwig I.

Adjoining is

The Tower — room

entirely without ornament of any description. Here the priedieu of the King (which formerly stood in the royal chapel) is preserved.

The last room on this 1st floor is

The Ministers' Apartment

the arrangement of which is simple to a degree. The chief ornament is a large painting covering the entire side of a wall, by Professor Benczur (after Lecomte), representing "King Charles of France doing homage to Joan of Arc in the Cathedral at Rheims"—. The other walls are decorated with pictures by Jäger—. Scenes from the life of the "Maid of Orleans" by Spiess, scenes from "The Robber", and "Fiesko", an oil-painting by Riedl "A Roman genre picture", a painting by Eibner of "King Ludwig in the procession in the Frauenkirche at Munich", and a print "The Elector Ludwig of Bavaria in the battle of Ulm in the year 1805".

The apartments on this 1st floor are completed by the Tower-room, which contains no furniture—nothing but pictures—these represent a "View of the Winter Garden of King

Ludwig in the Residenz at Munich", an "Oriental Land-scape" and the great Munich actors Rhode and Rüthling as "Don Carlos" and the "Marquis Posa".

2nd Storey.

This floor is decidedly superior to the 1st as regards profuseness of decoration and richness of furniture—.

The Dining-room.
United Art Establishments in Munich

The first room,

The Dining — room,

exhibits much greater comfort.

Between the windows, which are draped with white curtains, are small tables on which stand the busts of Louis and Marie Antoinette before large pier glasses in simple frames. The dining table in the centre of the room is orna-mented by a representation of "Lohengrin in the skiff", and on two little tables near the door are the charming groups, in bronze, of "Faust and Gretchen", "Walther Stolzing" and "Eva von Dernière". The furniture is covered with red plush, the table cloths being likewise of the same material.

The following water-colours are by Echter and are undoubtedly the finest pictures in the whole Castle—.

"Tristan and Isolde" (6 Pictures)
"Lohengrin" (6 Pictures)
"Rheingold" (7 Pictures)
"Walküre" (7 Pictures)
"Siegfried" (8 Pictures)
"Götterdämmerung" (8 Pictures).

These illustrate Wagner's musical dramas, and the explanatory text is attached to each.

The Sitting — room and Study.

The furniture is covered with light blue silk—, the walls papered with blue. A blue glass lamp hangs from the centre of the ceiling, which latter is ornamented in each corner by the Bavarian Coat of Arms. The seven Alabaster statues which stand on high pedestals round the walls are the work of Zumbusch and are very artistic and beautiful. These represent Siegfried, Tannhäuser, Parzival, Lohengrin, Walther von Stolzing, Tristan and the "Flying Dutchman".

A bust of Louis XIV stands on a bracket above the sofa, and over this again hangs a print representing "The body of Siegfried being conveyed to Worms".

A bust of Richard Wagner ornaments the stove. The small table by the window wall holds a clock, representing a reaper with a wreath of corn, and handsome vases. The paintings on the walls, which are the work of Ille, represent scenes from the German Legends and are of high artistic value—, the first of these is the "Niflung Legend". — This consists of 21 pictures.

The second represents scenes from the "Song of the noble Knight Tannhäuser".

Then follows the
"Parzival Legend"
which illustrates in 19 pictures the chief scenes of this legend.

The fourth series sets forth in 11 pictures the
"Legend of Lohengrin"

The centre picture, representing the "Miracle of the Holy Grail", is of particular artistic perfection.

The fifth and last of these series "Hans Sachs and Nüremberg at the zenith of its prosperity".

Beneath these latter are quotatious from the poems of Hans Sachs — in the background of the centre picture is seen the charming representation of the city of "Old-Nürem-berg".

In the alcove adjoining this apartment is the King's writing table and on this is a large porcelain tableau by Dallmeier with portraits of the members of the House of Wittelsbach. A water-colour of "Hohenschwangau", by Breling, ornaments the walls, also seven representations from Wagner's Dramas the "Flying Dutchman", "Tannhäuser", ,Lohengrin" and the "Mastersingers of Nüremberg".

Leaving this apartment we enter the boudoir adjoining. A marble statue of the Elector Max Emanuel of Bavaria ornaments the stove. Three water-colours by Frank and Eibner illustrate "The fête at the knighting of St. George", another water-colour by Correns "The landing of King Ludwig from the steamer "Tristan" at Castle Berg". The last room is

The Sleeping apartment.

The Sitting-room.

United Art Establishments in Munich.

The simple bed with its white silk pillows and blue coverlet is surmounted by a canopy of blue silk.

A valuable crucifix hangs on the wall above the bed—, the furniture and fire screen are likewise covered with blue silk. Polished wardrobes and washing-stand complete the furniture—. On a small side table are a clock and two vases and on another is the "Lohengrin Group with the Swan". The following pictures ornament the walls; an oil — painting of "Ludwig XIV and Molière", "Portrait of the Empress Marie Alexanrowna of Russia", "Views of Hohen-

schwangau and the "Königsee", of the "Bedroom at Hohenschwangau (with artificial light)", of the "Himalaya scenery
in the Winter Garden in the Residenz at Munich", the
"Study of R. Wagner at Munich", "Tell's Chapel", the
"Hermitage near Bayreuth" and the "Starnbergersee".

The King's Bedroom.
United Art Establishments in Munich.

A water-colour represents the arrival of the "Bucentaur"
at the landing place.

The two series of pictures illustrating scenes from
"Tristan and Isolde" and "The Flying Dutchman" are by

2*

Legend of "The Flying Dutchman".
United Art Establishments in Munich.

Spiess. The romantic legend of the "Flying Dutchman" ("Fliegender Holländer") is depicted in five pictures.

The Alcove-room.

The furniture in this apartment is also covered with blue silk. Water colours, illustrating the musical dramas of Tannhäuser and Lohengrin, decorate the walls—.

(The view from the windows of this apartment of the Park and lake is particularly fine.)

The King's Bedroom with a View of the Alcove.
United Art Establishments in Munich.

The visit to the Castle of Berg is accomplished with much greater facility and comfort than to the other royal residences—. Here one has time to observe everything — the guide, no longer being obliged to push onward on account of the never — ceasing stream of visitors behind him, has more leisure and is better able to impart information—, then also the visitors who come here, come for the most part, not out of idle curiosity to see princely pomp and splendour, but attracted by the sadness of the tragic event which took place here, and also to carry away with them memories of that King whom Bavaria so sincerely loved and mourned.

A few steps from the Castle lead up to the Terrace on which the Chapel erected by Ludwig II stands. A small bel-

fry (on either side of which are pinnacles. crowned by graceful finials), and an elegant portico impart variety to the
Façade of the Gothic building—. The Altar is simple, carved

Standing Frame of carved metal, with picture of the King.
United Art Establishments in Munich.

in oak —, the walls are decorated with pictures by Prof.
Hauschild. The following are to be seen in the Presbyter;
    1. "The Baptism of the Frankish King Chlodwig in the
Cathedral at Rheims (496) by Bishop Remigius".
    2. "King Ludwig and St. Louis of France as Crusaders".
In the nave of the Church we see.
    1. "St. George on horseback as the Swan-Knight
slaying the Dragon".

2. "St. Hubert perceives the stag with the Cross on its antlers".

3. "The abundant haul of fish by St. Peter", and

4. "The conversion of St. Paul".

The surface of the Arch above the entrance is filled in with the following pictures, on the left "The Crucifixion", on the right "The Resurrection of Christ" and in the centre above these is" God the Father, surrounded by adoring angels".

Leaving the Church we see, on the left, the land from the shore mounting up, forming a steep hill, and on the right a beautiful view of the lake.

Castle Berg (East View).
United Art Establishments in Munich.

On the western shores stand the princely mansions of Possenhofen and Garatshausen. The Park becomes more open and on the terrace high above the banks of the lake is the "In Memoriam Chapel", erected here by his royal Highness the Prince Regent Luitpold of Bavaria, thus consecrating the scene of the sad and terrible catastrophe, to which the following inscription calls attention "In sorrowful memory of the unhappy and sorely-tried King Ludwig II. Sincerely beloved".

This chapel is built in the Early Norman style and consists of a domed nave with two crescent-shaped side apsis—, a crescent-shaped Altar — apse and entrance porch. The

Votive Church.

By permission of the Firm "Anstalt für christliche Kunst" Munich.

design for this building was made by the late Oberhofbaurat Hofmann.

The large tower structure consists of gigantic brickwork, a double flight of steps lead up to the yellowish-red limestone edifice, the high dome of which, visible from a long distance, makes known the object of the Monument. The architecture of the exterior is rendered imposing by the employment of Norman arches, of columns placed together in pairs and by the frieze surrounding the arches.

The hectagon dome is crowned by a pointed stone roof, which gives to it the form of a tower—: the simply built gable, which contains the entrance porch, is beautified by the introduction of columns. Four of these Norman pillars (employed two and two), with simple bases and beautifully sculptured capitals, support the vaulted ceiling.

The Tympanun above the large oak door is ornamented by a relief in stone, the centre of which represents "Christ as Saviour of the world with the Symbols of the four Evangelists."

On opening the door the visitor finds himself standing before the beautifully gilded iron grating, which, however, does not obstruct his view of the interior of the church, but rather intensifies the solemnity of the scene.

The colouring of the Church is of a soft warm tone. The vaulted roof is painted dark blue, dotted here and there with stars—, The dull green of the wall panels and the yellowish-white (veined with black) marble with which the walls are wainscotted, all combine in imparting to the sacred building an earnest, solemn appearance.

A simple Altar of yellow marble stands in the crescent of the apse opposite the door. On this stand a crucifix and six candlesticks. The front of the Altar contains a representation, inlaid in lapis-lazuli, of the "Lamb" on a white marble ground.

The frescoes are the work of Professor August Spiess. On either side of the apse is the Bavarian Coat of Arms with the inscription "Ludovicus II. Rex Bavariae, Comes Palatinus", this is also introduced into the ornamentation of the centre of the building, surrounded by wreaths of laurel tied with blue ribbons.

The vault of the dome is ornamented by the medallion picture of the patron Saint of Bavaria, surrounded by the Arms of the eight Bavarian bishoprics — (the patrons of these latter, with their legendary attributes, are represented in the frame of the domed roof).

The Interior of the Votive Church.

The "Lamp of Death" before the "In Memoriam" Chapel.

After an original drawing by H. Grabensee.

Beneath the window gallery of the dome are the following, St. Ludwig, St. Hubertus, S.S. Michael and Georg. "The chief object of interest in this building is the beautiful fresco representing" Christ enthroned in the clouds, the open Book in His left hand, the right raised in blessing. Angels kneel at either side of Him in adoration".

The dull gold "secular" screen at the entrance to the Church is a beautiful piece of artistic workmanship. The Latin inscription on the walls of the porch contain the dedication and date of the laying of the foundation stone, as well as of the consecration of this Church. Nothing could have been more appropiately chosen as a Monument to the King than this edifice, which in its entire style reminds one so forcibly of the Prince's own most brilliant creation "Castle Neuschwanstein". Close beneath the "In memoriam" Church stands the simple "Death-Lamp" dedicated to the memory of the King by her Majesty the Queen Mother Marie of Bavaria. On the base of the twisted pillar is written the date "June 13th. 1886" in letters of bronze. On the summit of the column is the little sanctuary to contain the light and above this again a figure of the Crucified.

From this spot the eye wanders across over the shining surface of the Starnbergersee, that silent witness to the drama over which Providence has drawn the impenetrable veil of eternal secrecy.

Castle Berg stands here, ever since the day on which the royal standard was lowered to half mast, in sorrowful and touching silence. Never again will the sounds of fresh young life be heard in its apartments, but forsaken and forgotten it will never be—there are too many true and loyal hearts in Bavaria ever to permit of that, and year by year sees its stream of visitors who come to visit and to mourn for the Monarch, whose end was one so full of sadness and unhappiness.

H. Morin pinx.

A VISION,

By night, when over all
The Moon has shed her light,
Is seen, deep down and phantom-like
Beneath the still waters of the lake
A Royal Picture.

And hovering near, a lovely water-nymph
Whose wringing hands and moan
Bear token to her grief —
The darkness fades and with the break
of early day
Ceases she her cry and glides away.

George Morin.

Published by Caesar Fritsch, Munich.

THE

HÔTEL ᴬᴺᴰ CASTLE RESTAURANT
ᴼᴺ HERREN-CHIEMSEE

IS TO BE WARMLY RECOMMENDED
TO THE VISITORS TO THE CASTLE.

🌷 🌷 🌷

Excellent meals can be had at all times of the day.

🌷 🌷 🌷

Pure wine from the cask and in bottles.

———

LAGER-BEER FROM THE ROYAL CASTLE BREWERY OF HERREN-CHIEMSEE.

———

Glass-Veranda and Dining-Rooms.

Large shady garden with splendid view of the lake and mountains.

Spacious Apartments with excellent beds.

Post and Telegraph.

CPSIA information can be obtained
at www.ICGtesting.com
Printed in the USA
LVHW090155230419
615182LV00001B/31/P